ICNC **MONOGRAPH** SERIES

# All Rise

## Judicial Resistance in Poland

**Marcin Mrowicki**

**ICNC**
**PRESS**

# Contents

## Tables, Figures, and Boxes

# Glossary of Acronyms

| | |
|---|---|
| **AD** | **Action Democracy** *(Akcja Demokracja)* |
| CJEU | The Court of Justice of the European Union |
| **CT** | **Constitutional Tribunal** |
| DC | Disciplinary Chamber of the Supreme Court |
| **ECHR** | **European Court of Human Rights** |
| ERPA | Extraordinary Review and Public Affairs Chamber of the Supreme Court |
| **EU** | **European Union** |
| HFHR | Helsinki Foundation for Human Rights |
| **HRC** | **Human Rights Commission of the Polish Bar Association** |
| KOD | Committee for the Defense of Democracy *(Komitet Obrony Demokracji)* |
| **KOR** | **Committee in Defense of Workers** *(Komitet Obrony Robotników)* |
| KOS | Justice Defense Committee *(Komitet Obrony Sprawiedliwości)* |
| **NCJ** | **National Council of the Judiciary** *(Krajowa Rada Sądownictwa)* |
| OA | The Osiatyński Archive |
| **ODIHR** | **OSCE Office for Democratic Institutions and Human Rights** |
| ORP | Citizen of Republik of Poland *(Obywatele RP)* |
| **OSCE** | **Organization for Security and Co-operation in Europe** |
| PiS | Law and Justice Party *(Prawo i Sprawiedliwość)* |
| **SAC** | **Supreme Administrative Court** |

# Glossary of Terms

| | |
|---|---|
| **Neo-NCJ** | **New NCJ appointed in place of the unconstitutionally dissolved NCJ during its term of office. It does not have representatives of all courts. Its members (judges) are elected by MPs, although Parliament according to the Constitution can elect only four of its own representatives to the NCJ. Its current members are considered to be connected to politicians.** |
| Neo-Judge | Someone nominated by the Neo-NCJ to any judgeship on any court level. In 2020 there were about 1000 Neo-Judges and in 2023, about 2600. |
| **Quasi-Judge** | **A judge of the Constitutional Tribunal whose nomination replaced a seat that had already been filled.** |
| Muzzle Law | The law introduced further limitations on judicial independence by giving the new Disciplinary Chamber of the Supreme Court, controlled by the government appointees, new types of disciplinary torts, including power to dismiss from office or transfer to another court. |
| **Iustitia** | **The biggest judges' association in Poland.** |
| Themis | The second biggest judges' association in Poland. |

# EXECUTIVE SUMMARY

This monograph investigates the strategic and organized resistance of Polish judges against the authoritarian encroachments on judicial independence by the ruling Law and Justice (PiS) party from 2015 to 2023. Under the leadership of Jarosław Kaczyński, PiS systematically targeted key judicial institutions like the Constitutional Tribunal and the Supreme Court, implementing reforms to undermine judicial autonomy. This assault sparked an unprecedented resistance movement among Polish judges, who employed legal and extralegal tactics to defend the rule of law.

The study traces the roots of this judicial resistance to the Solidarity movement of the 1980s and examines the evolution of judicial activism in response to PiS's authoritarian measures. It highlights the creative and sustained efforts of the judiciary, including public demonstrations, social media campaigns, legal challenges, and noncooperation with government-appointed "neo-judges." The judges strategically used the constitution and EU law to counter unconstitutional provisions, effectively resisting the systemic changes imposed by the ruling party.

The resistance movement led to significant national and international outcomes, including presidential vetoes of controversial judicial reform bills, the reinstatement of judges, and actions by the Court of Justice of the European Union (CJEU) and the European Court of Human Rights (ECHR) against Poland. These efforts not only emphasized the importance of judicial independence as a cornerstone of democracy but also provided a powerful example for other nations facing similar authoritarian threats. Ultimately, the PiS party lost control of the government in the 2023 elections.

Through interviews with key judicial and legal figures, the monograph offers a comprehensive account of the motivations, actions, and consequences of judicial resistance in Poland. Furthermore, it catalogs the judges' many actions according to Michael Beer's framework of tactics from *Civil Resistance Tactics in the 21ˢᵗ Century*. Herein are valuable insights into the role of the judiciary in defending democracy, with broader implications for pro-democracy movements worldwide.

**Key Takeaways for Stakeholders:**

For Judges:

- Engage with the public to restore confidence in the judiciary.

- Uphold judicial oaths and practice judicial disobedience when necessary.

- Use social media and communication platforms to organize and spread awareness.
- Resist from within the system rather than resigning, to maintain influence.

For Lawyers:

- Collaborate across borders with other legal professionals.
- Provide pro bono support to judges and prosecutors facing repression.
- Engage in immediate resistance actions against threats to judicial independence.

For Civil Society and Activists:

- Support judicial resistance by attending hearings, offering legal aid, and organizing protests.
- Use mainstream and social media to raise awareness and counteract government propaganda.
- Foster solidarity among various sectors to create a unified front.

For International Allies:

- Raise awareness of the situation abroad, particularly in English-language media.
- Apply political pressure through EU bodies and other international organizations.
- Collaborate with foreign judges and legal professionals to support the defense of the rule of law.

For Scholars:

- Research the common characteristics of judicial resistance globally.
- Explore the role of prosecutors in resistance movements.
- Investigate the reasons why Polish judges refrain from striking, compared to their counterparts in other countries.

# Introduction

Jarosław Kaczyński, the leader of Poland's nationalist party, Law and Justice (PiS), is arguably the most influential politician in the country. Together with his deputies, he orchestrated an unprecedented assault on the independent judiciary, a significant event in modern Polish history. This assault was disguised as an initiative correcting historical inaccuracies, addressing economic grievances, fostering future progress, and improving quality of life. According to Kaczynski, "courts are not the last bastion, because there are, unfortunately, many more of these bastions like the media, but they are the most important bastion of the old system.... A change in this situation... is a condition for Poland to be able to solve other problems, develop well and, above all, be fair" (TVP 2020).

Between 2015 and 2023, PiS assumed control over various key institutions in Poland, including the Constitutional Tribunal, the media, the prosecutor's office, and the Supreme Court. Simultaneously, they undermined the independence of the judiciary by seizing control of bodies responsible for upholding the Constitution. This involved taking charge of the National Council of the Judiciary, enabling them to influence judicial appointments and promotions. They also replaced presidents of lower courts with individuals aligned with the ruling party. Additionally, PiS implemented a disciplinary system overseen by those in power, targeting dissenting judges who opposed their agenda. Furthermore, they launched a smear campaign against judges, seeking to erode public trust in the judiciary and targeting those who resisted their efforts most vehemently (see Chapter 2).

Authoritarian assaults on judicial independence align with a predictable and familiar pattern of undemocratic conduct. However, the responses of the judiciary and the legal profession to these attacks are seldom explored and comprehended. Surprisingly, there is a lack of in-depth study regarding how the judiciary counteracts threats to its independence. Yet, actions taken by the judiciary hold the key to effectively safeguarding democratic rule of law and resisting authoritarian rulers who seek to exert control over vital state institutions for their own agenda.

The responses from those inside the judicial profession to authoritarian assaults on its independence vary. Some exhibit ignorance or a lack of awareness regarding the attacks, while others choose to turn a blind eye or act subserviently. Others participate in hidden yet deliberate acts of defiance, courageously standing up against the encroachments. Others, taking it further, partake in collective organizing, mobilization, and open resistance, coming together to defend their independence against authoritarian encroachment.

Judicial resistance spearheaded by judges is a complex phenomenon. Judges are obligated to uphold the law, which necessitates maintaining their independence and staying above the political fray. However, there come times when they are compelled to step out of their courtrooms, leave behind their perceived detachment, and engage directly in the public arena. This can involve actively participating in political conflicts and, in some cases, even deviating from or disregarding existing laws in order to safeguard higher values such as constitutional principles, democratic rule of law, or the independence of the judiciary from political interference.

Resistance, by its nature, is a political act. As a result, judges who resist external pressures become, by necessity, agents of political change. To prevent their ranks from being manipulated by partisan politicization driven by politicians and policymakers, judges must become agenda-driven activists and political fighters. This shift may require them to operate beyond the confines of their courtrooms, taking to the streets to advance their agendas and protect the integrity of the judiciary. By engaging in these actions, judges strive to ensure the preservation of their independence and demonstrate the vital role of the judiciary in upholding democracy.

Journalist and writer Klaus Bachmann (2021, 23) captured the phenomenon of politicization among resisting judges in Poland, writing, "When [the ruling party] PiS claims that judges are political or 'politicized,' this is correct. The judges became [so because of] the government's so-called reform of the administration of justice. The most neutral profession is attacked, and its representatives defend themselves. Consequently, they lose the attribute of neutrality in the eyes of citizens."

The judges' resistance—whether defending their autonomy and independence or upholding democratic rule of law against encroaching authoritarianism—isn't novel. While observed globally, it's relatively rare and lacks widespread understanding in terms of effective civil resistance strategies. Additionally, it's often not widely shared among pro-democracy activists as practical lessons for effectively countering significant democratic backsliding.

## The Turning Point

The struggle for an independent judiciary in Poland reached its apex on September 7, 2021, when the European Commission made a request to the Court of Justice of the European Union (CJEU) to impose daily financial penalties on the Polish state for violating judicial independence. In response, on October 27, 2021, the Vice-President of the CJEU ordered Poland to pay the Commission €1 million per day, from the notification date until Poland ensures the independence of its judiciary, or, if it fails to do so, until the date the CJEU delivers its final judgment (Order of the Vice-President of the Court 2021).

The key reason for the imposition of penalties on Poland was the government's failure to suspend national legislation related to the Disciplinary Chamber, which was established by the Polish government as part of the High Court. This Chamber, staffed by government loyalists, had been conducting disciplinary proceedings against judges considered too independent by the ruling party. As it only ceased these proceedings on July 15, 2022—and was "replaced" by the Professional Liability Chamber, essentially the same institution under a new name—the total financial penalties imposed on Poland reached an astounding amount of more than €996 million as of 28 May 2024. Consequently, the European Commission froze the EU recovery funds intended to support Poland in its post-pandemic economic recovery and, from there, deducted the debt.

This order came juncture, as Polish judges had been engaged in a prolonged resistance against the government's actions and the portion of the judiciary captured by the regime. The resistance was steadily growing, with new faces of defiance emerging—judges who might have stayed on the fence before the actions of the European Commission and the Court of Justice of the European Union (CJEU).

On June 5, 2023, the Court of Justice of the European Union issued its fourth infringement judgment regarding the "Muzzle law." This law aimed to deter judges from applying EU law when assessing the status of the "neo-judges"—the commonly used term for those judges nominated by the government-controlled National Council of the Judiciary. In 2021, the CJEU halted the exercise of new powers by the Disciplinary Chamber of the Supreme Court (Order of the Court of Justice, July 14, 2021). Furthermore, the CJEU deemed a central aspect of Poland's judicial reform incompatible with EU law and expressed concerns about the independence of the Polish judiciary (Judgment of the Court of Justice, July 15, 2021).

Subsequently, an increasing number of Polish judges have engaged in open judicial rebellion by issuing rulings that directly challenge the legitimacy and actions of the Disciplinary Chamber. One notable example is Judge Marta Pilśnik from the Warsaw-Śródmieście District Court, who determined that the Disciplinary Chamber lacks the legal authority to provide valid consent for the prosecution of a prosecutor (Jałoszewski 2021c). This court also ruled that the Disciplinary Chamber was unlawful.

Additional judges, such as Judge Adam Synakiewicz from the Częstochowa Regional Court, quashed the rulings issued by neo-judges. Similarly, Judge Jacek Tyszka and Judge Piotr Gąciarek from the Regional Court in Warsaw issued a declaration of their refusal to sit on the bench and rule alongside neo-judges (Jałoszewski). In another defiant stance, the Criminal Chamber of the Supreme Court quashed a Supreme Court decision because of the presence of a neo-judge in the judicial panel and during court deliberations (Sitnicka 2021).

Judge Synakiewicz's reflective words epitomize the motivations behind the stance of many resistance judges in Poland: "I am not afraid of lawlessness. I will not be scared.... I shall continue to be faithful to the oath I took and the principles that all judges should observe. I shall continue to be independent" (Jałoszewski 2021d).

The response of the European actors, such as the CJEU[1] and the European Court of Human Rights (ECHR),[2] and the expression of European solidarity only came after significant domestic mobilization by various groups, including the judges. These judges demonstrated extraordinary resistance by publicly dissenting, participating in protests, and employing creative legal and inventing extralegal measures to prevent the regime from fully capturing the judiciary. Their actions not only safeguarded judicial independence but also provided a legal avenue for EU allies to intervene in the Polish judiciary crisis. Finally, in Poland's parliamentary elections in autumn 2023, PiS suffered defeat, leading to the formation of a new government on December 13, 2023, comprised of former "democratic opposition" members. One of its primary objectives is to restore the rule of law and judiciary independence in Poland.

This is the story of judges who have emerged as leaders in defending democratic rule of law in the face of significant authoritarian challenges within their country. Their actions have been unparalleled, strategically planned, organized, and executed by a dedicated group of judges, with the support of civil society allies, prosecutors, and lawyers. Poland's situation stands out amidst rule of law crises in other nations (Safjan 2020). Their resistance inspires many and offers important lessons for those in the judicial robes in other countries, demonstrating how they themselves can take a public stand against aspiring populist rulers. Their resistance was also one of the important factors that led to the fall of the PiS government and the victory of the democratic opposition.

There is a general lack of systemic analysis of the strategic nature of judges' resistance, the dynamics of their creative, constructive, and disruptive tactics, and the immediate and long-term impact of their defiance on the direction, progress, and outcome of the overall resistance against the authoritarian grab on political power. This study attempts to redress

---

1    Order of the Court of Justice of 14 July 2021, Case C-204/21 R, *Commission v Poland*, EU:C:2021:593; Judgment of the Court of Justice of 15 July 2021, Case C-791/19, *Commission v Poland*, EU:C:2021:596; Judgment of the Court of Justice of 6 October 2021, Case C-487/19, W.Ż., EU:C:2021:798; Order of the Court of Justice of 6 October 2021, Case C-204/21 R-RAP, *Commission v Poland*, EU:C:2021:834; Judgment of the Court of Justice of 5 June 2023, Case C-204/21, EU:C:2023:442

2    Judgments in cases: *Xero Flor w Polsce sp. z o.o. v. Poland* (no. 4907/18); *Broda and Bojara v. Poland* (nos. 26691/18 and 27367/18) and *Reczkowicz and Others v. Poland* (nos. 43447/19, 49868/19 and 57511/19), *Dolińska—Ficek and Ozimek v. Poland* (nos. 49868/19 and 57511/19), *Advance Pharma sp. z o.o. v Poland* (no. 1469/20), *Grzęda v Poland* (Grand Chamber, no. 43572/18), *Żurek v Poland* (no. 39650/18), *Juszczyszyn v. Poland* (no. 35599/20), *Tuleya v. Poland* (nos. 21181/19 and 51751/20), *Pająk and Others v. Poland* (no. 25226/18), *Wałęsa v. Poland* (no. 50849/21).

this significant gap in our understanding of the role of judicial resistance in sustaining and defending democracy.

## Key Research Questions and Analytical Framework

This monograph explores the initiation and impact of judicial resistance in Poland's rule of law crisis. It examines the motivations for joining the resistance, who joined, their actions taken, and their consequential influence. By doing so, it provides a thorough understanding of how judicial resistance has played a pivotal role in confronting the crisis. This monograph asks the questions:

- How did the judges' journey toward resistance begin, and did the broader movement to protect democracy influence their decision?

- Do judges consider themselves part of a resistance against unconstitutional changes in the administration of justice and the rule of law?

- What were the specific changes that they opposed and how did their professional stance change in response?

- What legal instruments, related and unrelated to judicial activity, did they use to oppose the unconstitutional reform of the administration of justice?

- Did they engage with colleagues in the judicial system, informally or methodically, to discuss the changes, seek support, or convince them to join in opposing the unconstitutional changes?

- Did they organize formal or informal meetings or groups within the judiciary to plan and implement actions against the changes?

- How did they support other justices facing administrative repression for opposing unconstitutional changes?

- How did they use digital technology and media platforms in their resistance, and what role did the media play in the dynamics of the resistance?

- What other resistance actions did they take?

- What were the consequences of their resistance, including repressive measures, and how did they react to that pressure?

- What was the impact of their resistance on political developments in Poland, the broader movement to protect democracy, the EU, and bodies within the EU?

In this monograph, I employed a mixed methodology (Creswell, 2017), which combined 54 semi-structured interviews conducted via Zoom with 43 participants, including judges, prosecutors, lawyers, and activists, along with a comprehensive review of nearly 50 legal documents, ECHR and CJEU judgments, 12 video and audio materials, and over 250 articles from press and scientific literature related to rule of law backsliding and judicial resistance.

Regarding the interviews, participants were selected from both the forefront of the resistance and those with varying degrees of involvement. This included individuals who took significant professional risks as well as those who were less actively engaged. Judges from different regions of Poland and various types of courts, with varying levels of experience and genders, were included in the sample. Additionally, the interviews encompassed perspectives from prosecutors, lawyers, and activists critical of judges but supportive of the need for action. Due to the pandemic, all interviews were conducted online via Zoom.

The 'expert' interviews, particularly those with lawyers, provided valuable insights and helped to delve into the intricacies of the issues surrounding judicial resistance. These interviews facilitated a deeper understanding of the motives behind judicial resistance, shifts in stance, choice of tactics, and other pertinent factors. Prior to conducting interviews in 2021, an extensive review of existing literature on judicial resistance in Poland and the rule of law crisis, as well as media coverage of the crisis, was conducted.

Anonymity was guaranteed to all interviewees, ensuring they could freely express their views, although many were willing to have their names published (see **Appendix III**).

Quantitative data was sourced from the Eurobarometer survey regarding the perception of judicial independence in Poland.

## Monograph Structure

This monograph consists of six chapters following the introduction, which establishes definitions and provides examples of key terms.

Chapter 1 delves into the historical tradition of judicial resistance in Poland, examining how past instances of resistance have shaped present-day actions. It is divided into two subchapters: one exploring the judicial Solidarity Movement in the 1980s and protests by Polish judges in democratic Poland from 2008 to 2014.

Chapter 2 offers a detailed analysis of the PiS party's takeover of the independent judiciary from 2015 to 2019, laying the groundwork for understanding the genesis of judicial resistance against democratic backsliding.

Chapter 3 analyzes the phenomenon of judicial activism, disobedience, and resistance, focusing on constructive and disruptive activism. It also explores the emergence of the "people's judge" role and the limits of judges' freedom of expression. This chapter traces the evolution of resistance from 2015 to the present, highlighting changes in judges' perceptions of their role and the role of judges' associations.

Chapter 4 outlines professional groups supporting judicial independence, such as AD, KOD, Free Court Initiative, ORP, OA, HRC, Lex Super Omnia, and resisting prosecutors, as well as the coordinating body (KOS).

Chapter 5 examines the impact of judicial resistance, both at the European level and among ordinary citizens, politicians, and legal professionals. It emphasizes the importance of coalition-building among these actors.

Chapter 6 maps the catalog of judicial resistance actions based on Michael A. Beer's framework of civil resistance actions. It analyzes acts of expression, omission, and commission, providing insights into various strategies employed by judges.

The conclusion summarizes key findings and takeaways for stakeholders, drawing on empirical analysis and offering insights useful to academics, judges, lawyers, activists, and organizers.

Appendix I presents examples of judicial resistance from other countries, illustrating the global nature of the phenomenon.

Appendix II describes the structure of the Polish judiciary, providing essential information about court bodies and judicial self-government, and analyzes the conflict between the Supreme Court and the Constitutional Tribunal.

Appendix III explains the methodology used for conducting interviews.

# Chapter 1. The Tradition of Judicial Resistance in Poland

Contemporary judicial resistance in Poland is philosophically and strategically rooted in the Solidarity movement, a broad, anti-authoritarian, Polish social movement that used civil resistance methods to advance workers' rights in the 1980s. Interviewed judges noted taking inspiration from the 1980s movement against authoritarian rule, specifically in how their resistance originated from and was organized around the Committee in Defense of Workers (KOR). KOR, founded by intellectuals in 1976, provided legal aid and financial support to workers arrested during demonstrations and protests. They also offered psychological assistance and medical evaluations to those arrested to shed light on regime repression (Lipski 1985).

According to interviewed Judge 17, the resisting judges formed a community of shared values despite their differences. Just like KOR, which united individuals with diverse personal and professional backgrounds, they collaborate based on their common principles and goals.

> *Each meeting gives us an incentive to help others. [Using technologies of the day] we are able to reach every judge in Poland with a question for help, whether financial, material, or emotional help. We sign appeals collectively. Send supporting emails. We travel several hundred kilometers to attend trials so that [prosecuted] judges do not stand alone in the courtrooms. I saw how these people were grateful [for that solidarity]. All this is the KOR behavior even if we do not necessarily do it consciously, but we are walking in its footsteps.*

The judge, who had regular conversations with people from the Solidarity and pre-Solidarity movements like KOR observed that acting against wickedness and fostering "systemic solidarity" in the absence of hope has become a matter of good taste. "Strangers meet and immediately get onto first-name terms, they get infected with their own enthusiasm and they trust each other completely because we are all united by common values. So we are reviving the ethos and practice of the movements from the 1970s and 1980s while we are united by the values of human dignity, civil rights, and honesty."[1]

---

1    This corresponds with the way Adam Strzembosz (2005, 55) described "the extraordinary atmosphere of solidarity, and in many cases even brotherhood, that prevailed between its members. All divisions resulting from the positions held, the level of education and other determinants of social position have disappeared. Everyone was kind to each other. Undoubtedly, such relations also resulted from a common sense of threat and uncertainty as to the further fate of each of us and the need for mutual support. This atmosphere of true equality in humanity was also born of a sense of self-dignity, for which we fought, after all, and an understanding of the role of workers in restoring basic human rights and civil liberties."

## Judicial Solidarity Movement in the 1980s

Judicial resistance in Poland has not only philosophical roots in shared values but also has a historical practice. It began in the summer of 1979 when disciplinary proceedings were initiated by the communist regime against Judge Jacek Ambroziak for bringing prohibited books into the country. Despite being eventually acquitted, this case sparked opposition within the judicial community. Other judges showed their support by attending the disciplinary hearings. Trust and friendship among these judges led to the formation of Solidarity in the Warsaw common courts (Strzembosz 2005, 50–1).

This movement started with young judges in the Warsaw—Praga District Court, who established an independent body called the Representation of the Praga Court. Other independent judiciary organizations followed, including the Solidarity committee in the Supreme Court by the fall of 1980 (Rudnicki 2002, 293–300). In Cracow, where the Solidarity movement in the courts counted 600 participants, the local branch organized national legal forums and legislative initiatives. The First National Justice Staff Forum was held in the Cracow Regional Court on 17 January 1981 and attracted 250 judges from 65 courts, resulting in the establishment of the Center for Civic Legislative Initiatives (Olszewski 2001, 546–7). The Second National Legal Forum on 13 June 1981 established the Social Legislative Council. These bodies played a significant role in providing opinions on dozens of proposed statutory amendments, all on a pro bono basis (Strzembosz 2005, 42–66).

Judges wore national white-and-red armbands or hung Polish flags on the court buildings despite management's objections. They held discussions on judicial independence and sovereignty. They organized free elections for the president of the Warsaw Regional Court and hosted nationwide legal forums, not forgetting to address legislative initiatives concerning the administration of justice (Strzembosz).

During and after martial law (December 1981–July 1983), judges resisted through their judgments in political cases. When possible, they acquitted suspects due to lack of evidence for guilt, or they imposed non-custodial and milder penalties considering mitigating factors. If they ruled in "bad panels" dominated by pro-regime judges, they wrote dissenting opinions. They also resisted by refusing to sign loyalty declarations, refusing to withdraw from Solidarity, resigning from posts, and quitting their jobs. Furthermore, they challenged the legality of the dismissal of judges, declined to answer provocative questions regarding martial law, and protested delegations to different divisions. Judges openly supported dismissed colleagues by signing applications for support and defending them in disciplinary courts (Strzembosz 2005, 50–69). Eventually, the Solidarity trade union in the courts consisted of 9,000 members, including 1,000 judges. These stances became a source of inspiration for judges in the rule of law crisis in Poland after 2015.

## Protests of Polish Judges in Democratic Poland (2008–2014)

Prior to the broader resistance that grew in 2016 and 2017, some Polish judges had already been involved in organizing efforts within the judiciary. On November 26, 2008, the Association of Polish Judges, Iustitia, began a three-day protest called "Days Without Hearing" ("DNI BEZ WOKANDY") in which judges refrained from conducting hearings. The hearings were either not appointed or their dates were changed and the parties notified in advance. Judges protested the lack of effective measures to reform the common judiciary system, unclear and biased criteria for promotions and the liquidation of the judiciary's self-governance, the government's lack of genuine will to make the judge's position "the crown of the legal profession," reducing judges to the role of officials by the legislative and executive power, low salaries compared to all other legal professions, subordinating judges to the administrative supervision of the minister of justice, which violated the principle of the constitutional balance of the authorities (Iustitia 2008). Judges demanded systemic changes.

In 2010, Polish judges protested the amendment of the Act of the Common Courts Organization concerning obligatory periodic reviews of their work. In an open letter, the judges appealed to the parliament and the government to suspend work on amendments to the act on the courts, which, they argued, violated the separation of powers. They considered them to be another administrative supervision by the minister of justice. In an appeal organized by Iustitia and signed by nearly 5,000 judges, they argued, "The judiciary requires reforms, but we do not approve of solutions that risk leading judges to the role of officials subject to the executive power.... It is unacceptable for the executive to influence the judiciary by setting standards for judging judges and exercising supervision over this process.... Paradoxically, recent changes in the prosecution system, strengthening its independence from the executive, place this body in a more favorable position in relation to the common judiciary" (Sędziowie 2010). Copies of the letter were submitted to the chancelleries of the president, the sejm, the senate, and prime minister.

In 2012, Iustitia-affiliated judges resisted the closure of one-third of the courts in small towns and cities.[2] In protest, 74 judges from the smallest district courts, which were scheduled

---

2     Pursuant to the Ordinance of the Minister of Justice, Jarosław Gowin of 5 October 2012, 79 district courts were abolished. Never before has any minister terminated the activity of so many common courts as independent units with a single legal act, in fact with one signature. In 2013 the Constitutional Tribunal declared that it was in accordance with the Constitution (K 27/12). Nevertheless, the small courts were reinstated in January 2015 by the same government. The presidential amendment to the Law on the System of Common Courts in 2014 introduced objective criteria for the establishment and abolition of district courts, and also—as indicated—met the needs of local communities and the judiciary. The president explained that, when preparing the proposal, he was guided by the will to end the instability in the judiciary, which had an impact on the work and the climate in the courts.

    According to this act, a district court is to be appointed for the area of one or more communes inhabited by 50,000 people, where at least 5,000 make it happen. The court may also be optionally established for an area inhabited by a smaller population, if the number of cases filed annually would be at least 5,000.

    At the beginning of October 2014, new Minister of Justice Cezary Grabarczyk signed the first ordinance

to close on January 1, 2013, applied for retirement. However, their request was denied by the minister of justice. The judges refused the minister's decision and criticized him for disregarding their arguments and the opinions of the judiciary and the NCJ (Łukaszewicz 2012). They subsequently appealed to the Supreme Court, which ruled in a seven-judge panel that the authority to transfer judges to another place of service rested solely with the Minister of Justice and could not be delegated to other individuals, including secretaries or undersecretaries of state (Resolution of the Supreme Court of July 17, 2013). As a result, judges who had been transferred based on the decision of an undersecretary of state refrained from adjudicating for nearly 100 days. It was only in a January 28, 2014, resolution by the full body of the Supreme Court that it was clarified that the Minister of Justice alone had the authority to issue decisions regarding the transfer of judges to another place of service, excluding secretaries or undersecretaries of state (Resolution of the Full Composition of the Supreme Court January 28, 2014). Thus, all the delegations of judges from the lesser court were invalid.

Some judges during the mid-2010s began attending their training in Europe. Judge 8 acknowledged that during these training sessions with European colleagues, "it occurred to me that judges can get involved in public life, like in the Scandinavian countries. It is not impossible for a judge to meet the citizens [outside the courtroom]."

---

implementing this act, under which, as of January 1, 2015, 41 district courts would return. On the other hand, in the second stage, from 1 July 2015—under the regulation signed in mid-November—another 34 courts will be restored. In total, 75 district courts will be re-established in two stages.

# Chapter 2. The Law and Justice Party's Grab on the Independent Judiciary

The constitutional crisis in Poland began soon after the Law and Justice party (PiS) won the parliamentary elections and formed the government in the second half of 2015. It was essentially a hostile takeover of the constitutional order by the parliamentary majority through ordinary legislation without the need to amend the Constitution of the Republic of Poland (Wyrzykowski 2019, 417–22).

The ruling PiS passed systemic amendments to Polish law that led to the continuous infringements of the rule of law in the country. These amendments have been described as the "rule of law backsliding," "legal despotism," "autocratic legalism," "anti-constitutional populist backsliding," and "competitive authoritarianism" (Pech and Scheppele 2017; Sajó 2019; Scheppele 2018; Sadurski 2019; Levitsky and Way 2010). The ruling majority undermined the rule of law through salami tactics by gradually eliminating the democratic and constitutional safeguards (Von Notz 2018).

Soon after they returned to power in December 2015, the ruling party focused its efforts on the judiciary, which it saw as one of the obstacles undisturbed power. It began by attacking the judges as an "unprecedented caste" that was unaccountable to the people and living in a hermetic bubble (Bachmann 2021, 23). In subsequent months, PiS succeeded in taking over the Constitutional Tribunal by replacing three judges already duly elected by the former parliament with loyalists to the regime (Radziewicz and Tuleja 2017). This could not happen without the support of the President of Poland, Andrzej Duda, who came originally from the same political group as the ruling party. He first refused to swear in the elected judges and then swore those appointed by PiS. The Constitutional Tribunal declared those appointments contrary to the constitution, but the prime minister from PiS refused to publish the judgment in order to prevent it from coming into force (Sadurski 2018). Further PiS appointments of judges to the Constitutional Tribunal led to its total subordination to the ruling party.[1] According to Agnieszka Bień-Kacała, "the CT acts as an agent of a certain political party without forcing a certain ideology" and "employs the partisan agenda of the ruling party and justifies its political actions," becoming a "façade body" (Bień-Kacała 2016).

The newly constituted loyalist majority in the tribunal considered and maintained in force various laws passed by the new parliament that essentially recused PiS from political responsibility and settled highly charged political disputes in their favor (Sitnicka 2020). First, the

---

[1]     Lech Morawski stated at the University of Oxford that the CT judges represented the government (Oxford 2017).

Constitutional Tribunal issued "a highly publicised ruling declaring the provision of the so-called 1993 Anti-Abortion Act allowing abortion in the case of a severe and irreversible impairment of the foetus or an incurable disease threatening its life to be unconstitutional" (Gajcy 2019). It ruled on the case, although the parliament could amend the law with a simple majority. Second, in June 2019 it decided that the article of the Code of Administrative Offenses assuming punishment for premeditated and unjustified refusal of service was unconstitutional. In 2017, a printer from Łódź had refused to make posters for an LGBT foundation because of his religious beliefs. He was fined by a court of first instance for his administrative offense. In 2018, the Supreme Court upheld the ruling by the local court and rejected Minister of Justice and Prosecutor General Zbigniew Ziobro's appeal against the decision. The minister then decided to turn to the Constitutional Tribunal. On the basis of the judgment of the Constitutional Tribunal the case was reopened and the printer acquitted. Third, the Constitutional Tribunal attempted to release the Polish government from the obligation to execute judgments of the ECHR and the CJEU. It ruled that parts of the EU's treaties are incompatible with the Polish constitution and that the ECHR had no power to question Poland's appointment of judges, to reject their ruling in the case of the quasi-judge in the Constitutional Tribunal, or to question the status of newly appointed judges in the Supreme Court (Judgments of July 14, 2021, October 7, 2021, November 24, 2021, and March 10, 2022).

Subsequently the prosecutor's office was subordinated to the executive power by the merger of the office of the Minister of Justice with that of the Public Prosecutor General. This change was accompanied by "an important increase in the powers of the Public Prosecutor General in the management of the prosecutorial system, including new competences enabling the Minister of Justice to directly intervene in individual cases" (Opinion of the Act on the Public Prosecutor's Office 2017). Then the government took control over the public media (Klimkiewicz 2016). Those actions were possible due to lack of constitutional control earlier exercised by the Constitutional Tribunal.

Consequently, the ground was prepared for a complete takeover of the courts. The series of laws had been enacted in 2017 with only the simple parliamentary majority held by the ruling party. They were unconstitutional and aimed to abolish judicial independence. Since the Constitutional Tribunal was gutted, the ruling party had no independent arbiter to stop its onslaught. They first went after the NCJ, which was designed to ensure the independence of the courts and impartiality of judges. According to the constitution, it was parliament that held powers to elect judges to the NCJ. Once in the majority, PiS used these powers to pass the legislative amendment stopping the constitutional tenure of the whole NCJ, prematurely terminating the terms in office of 15 member judges. On March 6, 2018, the Sejm with a majority of a ruling party appointed new members to the NCJ under shortened four-year terms (Final Opinion of the ODIHR 2017). That the member of parliament recently became the vice-president of the NCJ—a post held only by judges—shows the extent to which this institution has been politicized by the ruling party. Since the takeover of NCJ, independent judges and other civic actors have referred colloquially—and with a degree of contempt and ostracism—to the institution as the "neo-NCJ" and its newly appointed members as "pseudo-judges." The terms "pseudo-judges" and "neo-judges" have also been used by the resistance to describe any judge appointed to any court by the neo-NCJ.

This erosion of the rule of law in Poland has been referred to as "undermining the independence of the courts and sovereignty of judges until they lose their essence" (Wyrzykowski 2019, 11:421). The so-called reform of the judiciary involved the replacement of 158 presidents and vice presidents of the domestic courts with regime loyalists, curbing the self-governance and political oversight of the judiciary (Gajda-Roszczynialska and Markiewicz 2020). The problem was exacerbated by the work of the Department of Internal Affairs in the National Prosecutor's Office, which had been created in March 2016. With ten prosecutors, the office was tasked with supervising criminal proceedings against independent judges and prosecutors that did not fall in line with the ruling party (Łukaszewicz 2018).

*Since the Constitutional Tribunal was gutted, the ruling party had no independent arbiter to stop its onslaught.*

PiS also passed amendments concerning the Supreme Court. They established two new chambers: the now-infamous Disciplinary Chamber (DC) and the Chamber of Extraordinary Claims and Public Affairs, which introduced a new method for the allocation of cases among judges of the Supreme Court and changed the rules for the appointment of the new President of the Supreme Court so that the neo-judges could be indicated as candidates and the president of Poland could assign the role (Wróbel 2019; Krajewski and Ziółkowski 2020). The ruling party also attempted to lower the retirement age in the judiciary and use it to remove the Supreme Court judges (Filipek 2019). Although the European Commission forced the Polish government to stay the action and the interim measure forced by the Court of Justice of the European Union led to the reinstatement of the Polish Supreme Court judges, the Supreme Court was ultimately silenced with the nomination of a PiS loyalist as the new President of the Supreme Court in May 2020 (Order of the CJEU of December 17, 2018; Gersdork and Pilich 2020).

The PiS government continued its so-called reform of the judiciary. Consequently, the disciplinary proceedings against independent judges became more inquisitorial and heavily handed by a Minister of Justice bent on destroying any semblance of judiciary independence.

The judicial self-governing organizations were stripped of their significance, losing the right to provide opinions on candidates for judicial positions and resolutions crucial for the administration of justice. The judges became obliged to disclose their associational affiliations

(Gajda-Roszczynialska and Markiewicz). Moreover, beginning in June 2018, judges and prosecutors were subject to harassment and psychological pressure through a smear campaign organized by a secret troll farm set up within the Ministry of Justice (Gałczyńska 2019).

A group associated with the Deputy Minister of Justice planned to slander judges not only in the mainstream media but also on social media platforms. Everything was supposed to be kept in absolute secrecy (Pankowska 2019). The campaign used billboards and television spots with sinister black-and-white photographs accompanied by stories and slogans that distorted the image of the judiciary. It presented a biased representation of disciplinary proceedings against judges, highlighting their errors (e.g., cases of stealing a sausage or trousers) without mentioning that the judge involved was no longer adjudicating and had mental health issues (Applebaum 2020). There was also the television series *The Cast*—a derogatory term that the PiS used to depict independent judges—which was produced by public television to defame judges (Sukiennik 2020).

Starting in the fall of 2017, the Polish National Foundation, established by the ruling party the previous year, launched a smear campaign titled "Just Courts." This slick $2 million ad campaign was executed through various channels, including the internet, large street billboards, and television, with financial support from 17 state-owned companies. Officially, the campaign aimed to promote necessary judiciary reforms, but its true purpose was to undermine the legitimacy of independent courts in the eyes of the public and pave the way to bring in judges and establish courts' loyalty to and dependence on the ruling party (Sanders and von Danwitz 2017).

The campaign portrayed the current judiciary and judges in an extremely negative light. The billboards were designed in black and white, displaying the "real situation" on the black side and the "expected situation" on the white side. For instance, one billboard featured the statement, "How it is: Judges about themselves: An extraordinary caste" in the black half. Below it read, "It is time that this changes." In white half, it read, "How it should be: Judges are responsible like other citizens when they break the law."

In late December 2019, the ruling party enacted what became known as the Muzzle law, a term coined by the judges to highlight its intent to silence their dissent. The law introduced further limitations on judicial independence by giving the new Disciplinary Chamber, controlled by the government appointees, new types of disciplinary torts, including power to dismiss from office or transfer to another court.

The Muzzle law introduced several prohibitions and disciplinary offenses for judges, including:

1. Prohibition on refusing to recognize judges appointed by the ruling party to the neo-National Judiciary Council (neo-NCJ).

2. Prohibition on questioning the legal validity of appointments made by the neo-NCJ and seeking preliminary rulings from the Court of Justice of the European Union (CJEU) on controversial laws passed by the ruling majority.

3. Restriction on judges' engagement in public activities, effectively discouraging them from speaking to the media and voicing their criticism of government actions.

4. Prohibition on questioning the authority of the Constitutional Tribunal, preventing judges from challenging its rulings.

5. Seized the courts' self-governance through the board of judges of a court[2] (kolegium) and general assemblies (protested through resolutions) after the regime castrated them. The Muzzle law reduced the participation of judges, judicial self-government, and judicial collegiate bodies in sharing decisions on the functioning of the judiciary. It transferred further competences to court presidents, thus increasing the scope of influence of the Minister of Justice on the Polish judiciary.

The goal of the Muzzle law was clear: to subordinate judges to the executive branch and prevent them from questioning the independence of the courts and judges according to the criteria listed in the judgment of the CJEU in Joined Cases C-585/18, C-624/18, and C-625/18. The criteria were:

1. Assessment of the degree of independence enjoyed by the NCJ in respect of the legislature and the executive in exercising the responsibilities attributed to it under national legislation, as the body empowered to ensure the independence of the courts and of the judiciary, may become relevant when ascertaining whether the judges which it selects will be capable of meeting the requirements of independence and impartiality;

2. All of the relevant points of law and fact relating both to the circumstances in which the members of the NCJ are appointed and the way in which that body actually exercises its role.

3. The way in which the NCJ exercises its constitutional responsibilities of ensuring the independence of the courts and of the judiciary and its various powers, in particular if it does so in a way which is capable of calling into question its independence in relation to the legislature and the executive.

---

2    The board of the court of appeal performs the tasks enlisted in the bill, and *inter alia* expresses an opinion on the appointment to perform the function of a press spokesman or entrusts the duties of a press spokesman in a court of appeal, and expresses an opinion on dismissal from performing this function or performing these duties; gives opinions on candidates for the positions of judges of the court of appeal; considers applications resulting from court visits and vetting; expresses an opinion on judges' personal matters; expresses an opinion in cases of judges' conduct violating the principles of ethics; expresses an opinion on other matters presented by the president of the court of appeal, the National Council of the Judiciary and the Minister of Justice.

Such an approach by the judges would completely erase the so-called reform of the judiciary. It would question the judges' nominations and the ability to adjudicate of two new chambers of the Supreme Court.

As a consequence of this law, as observed by Professors Małgorzata Gersdorf and Mateusz Pilich (2020), "Courts in the Republic of Poland cease to be an equal partner in the constant dialogue with the legislator and the Constitutional Tribunal; moreover, as it turns out, their legitimacy for exercising public authority is being undermined."[3]

The Venice Commission[4] argued that the Muzzle law would "put Polish judges into the impossible situation of having to face disciplinary proceedings for decisions [they make as] required by the ECHR, the law of the European Union, and other international instruments" (Opinion no. 977/2020 of the Venice Commission).

Interestingly, the provisions of the Muzzle law betrayed the ruling party's fears that the resistance actions by the judges—including boycotting judicial appointments and questioning legitimacy of the rulings by the neo-judges—were effectively undermining the government's attempts to capture the judiciary.

## A Loss of Public Confidence in Judges

The ruling party's attacks on the judiciary beginning in Fall 2015 had a negative impact on the social perception of judges and the judiciary. According to a survey from 2018, public trust in judges declined by 8 percentage points in comparison with 2016 (from 54% to 46%). Judges were only 28th in the ranking of the most trusted professions. This situation was likely caused by government's concerted attacks on the judiciary (Trust 2018).

However, over the next two years, trust in the judiciary increased. In 2020, after previous declines, the trust in courts grew 9 points since 2018 (from 33% to 42%). Trust also increased in the Constitutional Tribunal (from 24% to 40%) and the Ombudsman (from 54% up to 64%) over the same period. The level of trust in these institutions approached the level recorded in 2016 before the anti-judiciary campaign led by PiS (CBOS 2020). This change was arguably

---

3    Gersdorf was the Full Professor Labor Law at the Faculty of Law and Administration, University of Warsaw and, from 2014 to 2020, the Chief Justice of the Supreme Court of the Republic of Poland. Pilich was the Professor Associate of Private International Law at the Faculty of Law and Administration, University of Warsaw and a member of the Research and Analyses Office of the Polish Supreme Court.

4    The European Commission for Democracy through Law—better known as the Venice Commission as it meets in Venice—is the Council of Europe's advisory body on constitutional matters. The role of the Venice Commission is to provide legal advice to its member states and, in particular, to help states wishing to bring their legal and institutional structures into line with European standards and international experience in the fields of democracy, human rights and the rule of law. It also helps to ensure the dissemination and consolidation of a common constitutional heritage, playing a unique role in conflict management, and provides "emergency constitutional aid" to states in transition.

a result of the judges' resistance which brought them closer to the citizens, public education led by the resistance judges about the necessity and importance of maintaining independent courts, and their visible courage taking a public stance.

According to a 2019 survey by Court Watch Foundation, the subjective assessments of the independence of the judiciary and, to a lesser extent, the fairness of trials and the independence and impartiality of judges decreased significantly. Trust in the courts is still slightly higher than a few years ago, but not as high as in 2016 (Plitikowski and Kociołowicz-Wiśniewska 2021). In April 2022, the work of the courts was positively assessed by less than one-third of the respondents (30%), and negatively by almost half (46%) (CBOS 2022).

Among EU countries, only Croats have a worse opinion than Poles about the independence of their respective judges. According to the 2021 Eurobarometer survey, as much as 64% of surveyed Poles, asked the question, "How would you rate the justice system in Poland in terms of the independence of courts and judges?" replied "fairly bad" or "very bad." Only 24% responded "fairly good" or "very good." For comparison, in 2016, optimists (45%) outnumbered pessimists (44%).

The *2023 Rule of Law Report on Poland*, compiled by the European Commission, revealed a persistently low level of perceived judicial independence in the country, as indicated by both the general public and companies. In 2023, only 23% of the general population and 17% of companies considered the level of independence of courts and judges to be "fairly or very good." Data from the 2023 EU Justice Scoreboard further illustrates this trend, showing a continuous decline in perceived judicial independence among both the general public and companies since 2016 (from 45% to 24% for the general public and from 35% to 19% for companies). The primary reason cited by both groups for the perceived lack of independence of courts and judges is the perception of interference or pressure from the government and politicians.

However, as stated by journalist Stefan Sękowski (2022, 9), "To a large extent, this is also their [judges'] own fault, as evidenced by the fact that even before Jarosław Kaczyński's party came to power, Polish judges enjoyed much less trust than those from other EU countries. This is the effect of elevating himself over the ordinary Kowalski (the term "extraordinary caste" did not come out of nowhere) or prolonging the proceedings, often for trivial reasons. However, this does not change the fact that in 2016–2022, according to CBOS, trust in the courts dropped from 45 to 33 percent, and the percentage of distrust rose from 42 to 53 percent. It was bad, and it is even worse—no longer the fault of the judges."

# Chapter 3. Judicial Activism, Disobedience, and Resistance

The positivist, or formalist, approach to law has dominated legal education and professional growth of Polish judges. It assumes that the law is sacred and that judges' actions are limited by its provisions (Judge 8). Thus, the formal compliance of one's actions with the letter of the law is a sufficient basis for their legality. Judges learn that it is judgments, and not the judge, that should speak.

This formalist judiciary culture has often discouraged most judges from engaging in resistance or defiance against laws enacted by an arguably democratically elected parliament (Matczak 2020). However, in the face of authoritarian encroachment, judges have recognized that a strict reading of the law under positivism has in fact led to terrible tragedies in the twentieth century. It is a necessity for resisting judges to "talk about [the authoritarian assault on judiciary] like doctors about the diseases. We have a duty to say that the law that is passed is inconsistent with the Constitution" (Judge 8).

In taking this stance, a judge abandons formalism to prioritize his conscience. This requires virtues like justice and personal courage to resist the pressure of formalism and the powerful political forces that often support it (Górski 2010). According to Professor Jerzy Zajadło at the University of Gdańsk, instead of following an immoral law, a judge can either resign or ignore such a law to embark on judicial activism.[1] The constitutional crisis[2] in Poland brought about by the ruling party to subordinate the judiciary made judges remember the importance of judicial activism (Campbell 2004; Allan 2015).

## Constructive and Disruptive Activism

Judicial activism can manifest in two ways: constructive (or legal) and disruptive (or political/civic). Constructive judicial activism is the dynamic and creative interpretation of existing laws outside a judge's formal scope but within the boundaries of constitutional or international law. Such activism complements instead of defies any law or authority, particularly in a legal or legislative vacuum would otherwise lead to systemic violations of basic rights.

---

1   See more about judicial activism: Skuczyński 2019; Gomułowicz 2019; Pilich 2021. Compare Morawski 2016.

2   See Taborowski 2019; Barcik 2019; Bojarski, et al 2019; Barcz, Zawidzka-Łojek 2018; the 2020 Rule of Law Report.

Constructive judicial activism involves judges going beyond their traditional role of applying existing laws and taking creative approaches to interpretation. Judges act to reconstruct norms in ways unsanctioned by the government although still within constitutional and international legal boundaries. This is professionally risky when facing opposition from the legislative or executive branches.

Such predispositions pave the way to disruptive actions. Disruptive judicial activism, such as a judicial disobedience (Bojarski 2020),[3] goes beyond constructive activism and involves defending democratic values through civil courage. It transcends legal boundaries and takes on a political and civic nature (Skuczyński 2016). This approach recognizes that protecting judicial independence requires more than legal arguments and regulations. Judges must reject isolation and anonymity, instead engaging in public presence, communication, and civic and political engagement with the goal of demonstrating "the superiority of the application of law by independent judges... and superiority of an idea of a democratic state and rule of law over other types of governance" (155–7).

*Judges must reject isolation and anonymity, instead engaging in public presence, communication, and civic and political engagement.*

Disruptive judicial activism in the form of judicial disobedience is rooted not in the law that oftentimes needs to be disobeyed but in the judge's conscience or moral virtue, allowing them to bend the rules (Laurence Ross and Foley 1987). The legal philosophy literature acknowledges this tension. The Radbruch formula recognizes the potential conflict between judicial conscience and legal obedience (Radbruch 1946).

This framing says that judges who encounter a conflict between a statute and what they perceive as just must decide against applying the statute if the legal premise seems either "unbearably unjust" or in "deliberate disregard" of human equality before the law (Müller 1989). In the 1958 Hart–Fuller debate on morality and law that demonstrated the division between the positivist and natural law philosophies. Hart took the positivist view by arguing that morality and law were separate. Fuller in turn argued for morality as the source of law's binding power (Zajadło 2001).

Juxtaposing these debates with the reality faced by resisting judges in Poland, it is helpful to quote at length the public statement of the First President of the Supreme Court Małgorzata

---

3    Judicial resistance against the authoritarian drift of the state should be distinguished from judicial resistance against legal change. See Tokson 2015; Zajadło 2016 and 2017. By "judge's conscience" is meant mental quality, the ability to adequately assess one's own behavior as compliant or inconsistent with accepted ethical standards, and the awareness of moral responsibility for one's actions.

Gersdorf who, in April 2016, addressed the General Assembly of Constitutional Tribunal's Judges:

> *I would like to ask all Polish judges to have courage. Today they are not only "mouths of the law", but... depositories of the values of Polish democracy, and at the same time-keepers of public authority. It depends only on them whether Polish citizens will appreciate the importance of the separation of powers and the validity and compliance with the law. Judges must patiently explain the intricacies of the law and bring the Constitution closer to the citizens by better and better justification of judgments. Therefore, let the courts raise legal questions when they see a bad law and let them not apply this law if a Constitutional Tribunal rules it unconstitutional, even if the ruling is not promulgated in the Journal of Laws!*

Here Gersdorf evokes here a higher, moral, calling that the Polish judges must embrace to defend democracy and uphold the separation of powers, particularly the independence of the judiciary. She advocates for a radical proposition, urging judges from all courts to demonstrate courage by disobeying laws that undermine the constitution and by refusing to legitimize government actions aimed at obstructing laws that the ruling party seeks to invalidate. As Judge 2 explained in their second interview:

> *Judicial disobedience means obligation to carry out a judicial mission regardless of what legal acts are enacted and denying such actions that violate basic human and civil rights. This must be done even if it means being subject to disciplinary proceedings.*

Judicial disobedience involves the refusal to apply laws that are seen as violating the Polish Constitution or European law, instead prioritizing domestic laws that the government seeks to undermine in its populist agenda. A vivid example is the dispersed judicial review conducted by resisting judges of the common courts. Through this approach, judges independently assess the constitutionality of provisions enacted by the ruling regime, bypassing the role of the government-controlled Constitutional Tribunal. This demonstrates a creative reinvention of judicial prerogatives aimed at resisting creeping authoritarianism by slowing down and halting its progress.

Judicial disobedience, as described by interviewees, differs from civil disobedience as it requires judges to seek solutions that defend core values within the framework of applicable law (Zajadło 2016, 37). This may involve interpreting legal norms appropriately or directly applying constitutional principles. At the same time, judges in Poland showed that they are ready to engage in more than just judicial disobedience. Their resistance encompasses various tactics both within and outside the judicial system, such as street protests, marches, demonstrations, boycotts, and engaging with ordinary citizens to educate them about regime actions and judicial disobedience. However, judges perceive judicial resistance as an exceptional response, reserved for situations of extreme crisis concerning the rule of law (Gersdorf and Pilich 2020). According to Judge 1, the boundaries of all resistance are defined by the Polish constitution and the principles of the European rule of law.

## Becoming a People's Judge

The strategic approach adopted by resisting judges in Poland involved a shift from being solely courtroom judges to becoming "people's judges." This transformation was necessary to effectively engage with ordinary citizens and gain their support. By becoming people's judges, they aimed to reach a wider audience, establish channels of communication, and persuade the populace. "When it comes to the strategy, the most important thing is to get the audience, the channel of reaching support, and convincing the unconvinced," noted Judge 9.

The positivist stance emphasized that judges are not allowed to speak out in public debate for fear of politicizing the judiciary or because it was inappropriate. As Judge 20 noted, "I wouldn't have thought before of taking part in public events, being on the radio, or going on social media. During the judge's professional training we were told it was not appropriate for a judge to do those things." Judge 4 added: "I spoke up. For a judge, it is a taboo broken. Before 2017, this speaking out was a contradiction to the ethos of the profession."

Such a model of judicial behavior demanded the avoidance of any political activity and expected the judiciary to be completely withdrawn into their ivory tower where they express their attitude to the law only through their rulings. In normal times, this judicial culture protects judges. However, at a time of unprecedented attack on the independence of courts and the constitution such a positivistic behavior was willfully insufficient, and judges recognized it.

During a time of unprecedented attacks on the independence of courts and the constitution, the traditional positivist model of judicial behavior, which emphasized withdrawal and refraining from political activity, proved to be inadequate. Though this model is designed to protect judges in normal times, the positivist approach had become insufficient, and judges realized the need to go beyond it.

"Freedom of Choices," one of the video shorts produced and launched by Iustitia (2021), highlighted this challenge by noting the key characteristics of the traditional role of a judge and its shortcomings in the current crisis: "We have been taught for years that we are supposed to be seen-through-transparent, invisible to citizens, unknown to society. We were supposed to speak only through rulings. A mute judge, a phantom judge, a judge no one knows. That's convenient for the rulers but in time of trial you can't stand aside."

> **Box 1. The 10 Principles of a Good Judge**
>
> 1. Hold your independence!
> 2. Remember that they may bill you someday!
> 3. Do not listen to the murmurs of the street and newspapers!
> 4. Stay away from politics!
> 5. Don't let your head jump!
> 6. Don't get pulled out of court!
> 7. Don't be the executive's nanny
> 8. Hold on until the state gets wise!
> 9. Be independent from yourself!
> 10. Be great!

According to Judge 19, the regime influences society through captured public media. If judges remained completely withdrawn, continuing to express their attitude to the law only through rulings, their views would never be communicated to the public. Consequently, "we cannot assume that the judge is to be completely invisible in the public sphere... [and] we cannot limit ourselves to jurisprudence and be completely absent from the public debate."

The relentless political assault on the judiciary compelled judges to adapt and redefine their principles of being a good judge, breaking free from the confines of their secure ivory tower and engaging with ordinary people (Łętowska 1993 and 2019). Judges had to cross the Rubicon as their disobedience contradicted entrenched conservative ethics that previously guided them, while exposing themselves to harsh disciplinary measures for their new courageous stance (Wróblewski 2017).

Faced with an extraordinary challenge, resisting judges embraced "the model of a people's judge that leaves the court and goes out to the people," in the words of their leading representative, Judge Igor Tuleya (Rigamonti 2020). Anonymity expected from a judge in their traditional role is reconsidered in the idea and practice of a people's judge, as Judge 10 shared: "It's hard to judge in a traditional way when the country is on fire and we are in the middle of that fire. I was there from the first day of the protests in July 2017, but anonymously. However, it is not enough to remain anonymous. People should see the judges out there." The new paradigm recognizes that public confidence in judges attacked by the ruling party can only be maintained if the judges take the risk of a public stand to defend their independence. This struggle is ultimately to defend citizens' rights, as independent courts serve the interests of citizens (Judge 2).

Judges had to become people's judges to reach ordinary people in the society. Many began to appear in public. It was a mistake of judges before 2015 that citizens were not told what a court was, the rule of law, and that they were shut out of society, leading Judge Irena Kamińska to introduce the term "caste" to refer to the judges. It became necessary to unite and speak out loud about what is wrong. That is why communication is important to help defend the rule of law (Judge 14).

The behavioral change could be slight and still facilitate the idea of a people's judge. In her first interview with the author, Judge 7 described her own transformation:

*As a result of the attacks on the judges my way of conducting a trial has changed. I freed myself from the shackles of what I was taught—that the judge only issues a ruling; that he does not talk to the parties; does not allow himself to be human, does not notice that people have emotions. This distances us from people. People are afraid. On top of that judges speak a complicated language. So I allow myself to joke. The witness is upset. I ask him his name and surname, age, and whether he is in court for the first time. When he confirms, I promise he'll get the best "Brave Patient" sticker [for being such a brave witness]. I shortened the distance. I don't talk to the parties as if we were at a social gathering, but I am trying to show that I am human too. A more human, friendly attitude.*

Another judge explained the new interactions between a people's judge and ordinary people by noting:

*Our slogan is: today we, tomorrow you. So we left the courts together. You, as ordinary citizens, sensitize us to your needs. We cannot necessarily support you as judges by being present on the streets in the same way as other citizens can. But we will help you by being more empathetic. There is no border between those who help and who are helped. We help citizens on the judges' bench. It is a mutual interaction that is part of what we have inherited from [Solidarity]. (Okręgowa 2021)*

The "Freedom of Choice" video by Iustitia (2021) emphasized the judges' mission to defend democracy. This mission must be also implemented outside of the courtroom when necessary:

*We took an oath to protect freedoms and rights.... Today we protect the freedom of choice by wearing gowns and T-shirts [the latter is in reference to judges going out on the streets to meet citizens]. We talk to people, we say who we are and we explain the meaning of our service. Education is the foundation of free choice, free elections. I am a judge, I am a citizen, I choose freedom. Free People, Free Courts, Free Elections.*

Judge 24 reflected on how they left the courtrooms to fight on equal footing against the government's slander campaign:

*Judges left their comfort zone and began to talk to people in places where they were. They had to go out to places they were not used to visiting, talking with protesters, going to local cultural centers, traveling around the country, and going to music festivals. They met ordinary people who do not always have to understand the institutions of democracy and the connections between them. This is how judges disarmed the false narrative that was being waged against them.*

And Judge 20 discussed their work as a people's judge:

*I consider myself a people's judge who takes part in the public debate on changes in the judicial system, criticizes these changes that are unfavorable to the functioning of the judiciary. In that sense our resistance is substantive, not physical.*

The rapidity and severity of the assault on judicial independence influenced some judges' decision to move toward more the public role of a people's judge, as noted by Judges 19 and 17, respectively:

*At the beginning, I also came out of such attitudes that the activity of the judge in the public space should be more restrained. But then the government began their "good change" and I decided that you cannot approach it in such a [traditional] way that I will not participate because I have my dilemmas. The lack of public display of my position leads to these changes progressing faster. The pace of dismantling of the legal protection system is happening so quickly that I feel my response is needed now. This is why [I am leaving a court bench] and attending those gatherings.*

*First of all, I am a human being, then a citizen and then a judge—in this order. If something poses a threat to humanity, I have to act like a human being. If something poses a threat to citizens—I have to act like a citizen. And if something poses a threat to judges— I have to act like a judge. There are situations when this is the only and effective method to prevent a state catastrophe. Borders are shaped by what is at stake. When constitutional democratic mechanisms are able to prevent the escalation of conflicts in accordance with the law, the scope of the protest is limited. When that mechanisms stop working, there are no such boundaries. [Whether and how judges act and go out to the public] are determined by the threat.*

## Judges' Freedom of Expression

The civic approach necessitates a clear distinction between formal judicial duties and active participation in public debates, particularly through the professional self-governance of judges. This distinction helps avoid conflicts arising from the dual roles of a judge as an official and a citizen (Skuczyński 2016, 157–9).

In times of a rule of law crisis, judges should actively engage in the public sphere, particularly in matters pertaining to the preservation of judicial independence (Najda and Romer 2007). Judges demonstrate their commitment to preserving their independence with the key attributes of a good judge: courage, a sense of responsibility, and the willingness to defend one's arguments (Skuczyński 2016, 159).

Judges are advised not to isolate themselves but rather to skillfully present their arguments to counter political attacks (Łazarska 2019). However, this should not influence their judicial responsibilities. According to Ewa Łętowska (2019), judges are permitted to discuss and critique judgments from a perspective of fair and professional use of the law and the judge's role, as long as their expression is impeccable and elegant. Judges may speak about court operations, judicial independence, the administration of justice, and personal integrity. Considering its societal role and general interest, freedom of expression in defense of the judiciary should not be restricted (Jaskiernia 2011; Kamiński 2017), especially when judges respond to criticism with restraint (Judgment of the ECHR 1995). Judges should refrain from engaging in activities that align them with a specific political option, expose them to political attacks, or compromise their dignity (Commentary 2007). They are prohibited from being members of political parties and should avoid situations that could spark public controversy, such as public meetings with politicians (Joint Opinion 2005). Judges must carefully consider their potential public involvement and avoid making statements or engaging in behavior related to politics (Commentary 2007, §136).

The ECHR has affirmed through its case law that when a matter has political implications, a judge's freedom of expression cannot be restricted. The division of power is subject to political debate in a democratic society, and the public has a legitimate interest in obtaining information about the judiciary (Commentary 2007, §138). The fear of disciplinary proceedings and speech restrictions can have a chilling effect on freedom of expression, particularly discouraging judges from making critical remarks about public institutions or policies. This may hinder their willingness to engage in public debates related to the administration of justice or the judiciary. Such an effect is detrimental to society.[4]

The evolving boundaries of what judges can and should do to resist authoritarianism are being shaped at the European level by the CJEU and the ECHR (Activist 2, second interview). Under normal circumstances, judges operate as officials without fear for their independence, and there is no attack on the rule of law. However, according to Koen Lenaerts, President of the CJEU, "judges should not express themselves, through whatever medium, in a manner which adversely affects the public perception of their impartiality. This does, however, not

---

4    Judgments of the ECHR in *Baka v. Hungary* (2014), *Kudeshkina v. Russia* (2009); *Wille v. Liechtenstein* (1999). See also: Joint opinion of the Venice Commission and OSCE/ODIHR on the draft amendments to the legal framework on the disciplinary responsibility of judges in the Kyrgyz Republic, CDL-AD(2014)018, §34 and Commentary on The Bangalore Principles §138.

prevent them from explaining the basic requirements of the rule of law" (Wójcik 2020). Judges have freedom of expression concerning the basic values of the EU legal order, such as democracy, the rule of law, and fundamental rights. Some limitations do exist. For instance, judges should avoid commenting on specific government policies, but they have the right to speak out when significant changes occur in the justice system and human rights protection. But they can defend their positions through media commentary, publishing scholarly articles, and are not confined solely to writing judgments.

## Resistance Emerges Against the Populist Onslaught (2015–2017)

During the initial stages of the constitutional crisis in Poland, judges mostly remained silent, either refraining from making public statements or speaking through court spokespeople or official bodies such as the board of judges and general assemblies. The first signs of resistance began to emerge through protest resolutions adopted by general assemblies in regional and appellate courts. The majority of judges supported these resolutions, while dissenting voices were rare (Bojarski 2021). Some judges expressed their concerns and analysis of the situation as professors of law or legal experts at international forums, presenting their perspectives on the crisis and possible paths forward. They were not yet ready to fight openly.

For each judge, the moment to join the resistance was different. For some, the turning point was the constitutional crisis and the takeover of the Constitutional Tribunal between 2015 and 2016. Only a few judges spoke against the government amendments concerning the Constitutional Tribunal, including its president, Andrzej Rzepliński, who represented the body. At that time, judges did not take any significant protest actions. "We were not sufficiently organized or had no idea how to fight," said Judge 2.

Most of the judges did not see the real danger in the ruling party's dispute with the Constitutional Tribunal. Moreover, previous conflicts between the Supreme Court and the Constitutional Tribunal created a sense of detachment among judges regarding the possibility to defend 15 politically elected justices. "Nobody wanted to die for the Constitutional Court," said Judge 1 (Second interview). Similarly, when talking about the fate of the tribunal and reaction of the judiciary, Judge 2 noted in a second interview:

> We did not go to the barricades with bayonets for the Constitutional Tribunal, because we saw the body as being already quite politicized- although compared to what is now, it was just an innocent play. I still remember the situation when Iustitia wanted to speak in the Constitutional Tribunal and was treated as an illegal trade union. We only took the position that it was an attack and the persons appointed to the positions of the judges of the Constitutional Tribunal could not be seated effectively [but did not do anything beyond that].

Judge 7 shared, "We saw the great evil of taking over the Tribunal, but the scale of the Tribunal's defense was not like that of the Supreme Court's later one."

The Tribunal judges were also criticized for not doing everything they could to resist. According to Activist 1, if the judges of the Constitutional Tribunal who were not sworn in by Poland's President demonstrated their independence and authority by sending their oaths in writing, it could end up with the occupation of the Tribunal.

Between 2015 and 2017, judges replied only by resolutions of the self-judicial bodies like the Boards of Judges and General Assemblies or by organizing congresses.

Judge Waldemar Żurek was one of the first judges to openly oppose the democratic back-sliding that began in 2015. As spokesperson and member of the National Judiciary Council, as well as a member of the judicial association Themis, he "felt obliged" to speak out and respond to the government's decision to withhold the publication of judgments from the Constitutional Tribunal that had declared the PiS party's new legislation concerning the Court and the nomination of three judges unlawful. As Judge 1 said, this "was the moment when one had to stand up with the judges of the Constitutional Tribunal." Judge 16 had a similar awakening to Żurek:

*When the Constitutional Tribunal was taken over I had to react. I started hanging information concerning this subject—such as a wall newspaper—in the court. Someone bought a pin board. We hung all the information on this topic so that it would reach everyone, starting from those who were walking along the corridor.*

Generally, however, judges missed the opportunity to protest in the beginning of the constitutional crisis. Judge 23 shared:

*We didn't know everything we know now. It went too smoothly. It's like stepping into a river—at some point you can see that it's the only way. When you exceed a certain level, you stop being afraid. Our actions progressed and became more radicalized. Just like overcoming the resistance to going out to people, to the streets. This is the place for judges. Man stops being afraid and goes where he needs to."*

"It is easy to look at some actions retrospectively from the perspective of 5-6 years," shared Academic 1. At the time, the potential effects of the proposed reforms were not fully understood. The laws concerning various institutions underwent significant transformations, including the public prosecutor's office, common courts, the Constitutional Tribunal, the Supreme Court, and the National Council of the Judiciary. But the justifications were rational and were acceptable to the public. However, the long-term implications became clearer with time. "It's the attitude of the rabbit in front of the snake: hypnosis and helplessness in the scale of destruction. Judges will always be reactive. The court never works ex officio. The court is always waiting for the case. The judge will not react by himself until there is a case."

The crisis prompted a timid response in the form of the Extraordinary Congress of Polish Judges on September 3, 2016. Over 1000 judges gathered in Warsaw to address the ongoing tension between the government and the Constitutional Tribunal. The congress discussed the new prosecution law and the potential impact of reforms on judicial independence. Three resolutions were adopted: urging the executive and legislative branches to engage in genuine dialogue with the judiciary, calling on the government to respect and publish the Constitutional Tribunal's judgments, and expressing concern over proposed amendments to the Law on the National Council of the Judiciary (Resolutions of the Extraordinary Congress, Nos. 1, 2, and 3 2016). The judges also expressed solidarity with judges facing unlawful dismissals in Turkey at the time (Resolution 2).

The judges' resolution proposed several measures to counteract the gradual limitation of judicial power. These included transferring administrative supervision of common and military courts to the First President of the Supreme Court, prohibiting the delegation of judges to work in the Ministry of Justice, and establishing a nationwide body of judicial self-government to represent the entire judicial community. To safeguard the citizen's right to an independent judiciary, they also demanded the principle that courts can only be established and abolished by statute, limiting political influence on the selection and appointment of judges (including those of the Constitutional Tribunal), and expanding the powers of judicial self-government. The judges appealed to society and the media for support in maintaining a balance between the three branches of power (Resolution 1).

This congress was an important event, if not for direct actions to disrupt the government takeover of the Constitutional Tribunal, for a psychological impact. As Judge 8 recalled, "For the first time, the judges counted themselves. A thousand judges came to the Palace of Culture and Science. From that moment on, we felt like a larger and more united professional group."

## The Year the Judges Rose Up (2017)

In July 2017, the ruling party's attempt to take control of the Supreme Court, common courts, and the National Judiciary Council through legislation led many judges to change their minds about positivism, and the resistance quickened its pace. More judges joined demonstrations, particularly in response to the increasing attacks on the common courts. Judge 13, expressing a common sentiment among those interviewed for this study, shared that the resistance really began "when the three court bills were passed. It was a turning point. We realized that the Constitutional Tribunal [by then captured by PiS] was not the only guardian of the Constitution." The whole judiciary system stood behind the constitution and was threatened by the populist assault.

Judges now understood that the resolutions they had been issuing to criticize the government's capture of the judiciary "were worth nothing. We could not watch with crossed arms, doing nothing, as the judiciary is being demolished" (Judge 20).

That summer, Poland experienced widespread civic protests against the new judiciary laws, with demonstrations taking place in over 180 cities. These initial protests were primarily organized by concerned citizens, and judges participated in them as ordinary citizens rather than in their official capacity. The involvement of civic movements provided further encouragement and support to the judges. As Judge 22 shared:

*At the beginning the judges stood aside. But with more and more demonstrations, we started to mix with the citizens. We also didn't know how the citizens would react— whether they would accept us in their ranks or not. But people cared that the judges protested with them. The citizens who fought for the courts wanted us the judges to be there with them.*

When the judges started attending demonstrations, people's praise further encouraged them. "I was in a green reflective vest," said Judge 23. "People came up and said they were happy to see me with them demonstrating. I found that what we were doing was important. It was a turning point."

The first event that mobilized the judges was a Chain of Lights in front of the Supreme Court organized on July 16. This event, initiated by Iustitia and Action Democracy, would spark a series of local protests held in front of court buildings across the country. Thousands of people participated in these protests. "The decision was made to meet with candles and create a human chain around the Supreme Court's building," shared Judge 2:

*Meanwhile, 17,000 people came to Krasiński Square. Euphoria. The sight of 17,000 people with candles. One of three events that I will remember the most. The words 'This is our court' appeared on the Supreme Court building. The point was to make the public aware of the fact that the fight is not about judges, but about everything. Judges owe a debt of gratitude to society, but in fact all of them do because the game was about the rights of every human being pursued before a court.*

On July 24, the Supreme Court judges went to the protesters that gathered outside to thank them for their support. The protesters handed white roses to the judges. That evening, representatives of the Court visited the protesters to thank them for their demonstrations of support over the previous days. Krasiński Square was full, and the people joined in singing the national anthem. When President of the Supreme Court Małgorzata Gersdorf came outside, the crowd chanted, "Thank you. Thank you."

**FIGURE 1.** In the July 2017 "Chain of Lights," protesters hold posters that read "Constitution."

*Source: Paweł Rochowicz.*

## Judges' Resistance Actions in 2017

On November 24, 2017, assemblies across Poland demanded the withdrawal from the Sejm of the presidential bills on the National Council of the Judiciary and the Supreme Court from the Sejm. These assemblies were accompanied by protests in 123 other cities, both in Poland and abroad (Chrzczonowicz 2017). Iustitia (2017) appealed to judges to participate in the demonstrations. One of them was held in front of the Presidential Palace in Warsaw, where demonstrators chanted slogans such as "Free courts, free elections, free Poland." At 7:00pm, protests began in 123 locations, including international cities such as Chicago, Dublin, Copenhagen, London, and Zagreb. Constitutional law professor Marcin Matczak delivered a speech in front of the Presidential Palace, emphasizing the significance of the changes to people's lives and their right to determine their representatives. He called for the defense of common values, the courts, and individual rights, urging the crowd to stand firm and prevent the violation of the constitution:

*This change is closer to our life, because it may break our right to decide who is to represent us. Here we can no longer shrug our shoulders and say, 'These are some other people.' It's us. It is our life, our freedom, our dignity, our right to make decisions that can be violated by these laws, he said and continued: So let us not allow the constitution to be broken and let us not allow ourselves to be broken. Let us steadfastly*

35

*defend those common values around which we have gathered. Let's defend the courts and defend ourselves.* (TVN 2017)

That day, protests were held in front of courthouses in Gdańsk, Gdynia, Sopot, Słupsk, and Wejherowo, with approximately 500 participants gathering at the district court in Gdańsk. Representatives from organizations such as KOD, Dziewuchy Dziewuchom, and Obywatele RP were present. In Cracow, a protest under the slogan "We defend free courts!" occurred on the Main Square, with demonstrations taking place in 12 towns of the Małopolska region.

In Poznań's Old Market Square, around 1,500 demonstrators chanted that they would not hand over the judiciary power to one party. Judges who participated in the protest stated

---

### Box 2. Judge 16 Recalls the 2017 Resistance

A breakthrough came in 2017 and an attempt to take over the Supreme Court. Three acts were intended to take over the judiciary. This awakened a wide social mass—we decided that we must reach proportionally for more tools to block it. This required taking another step forward. I knew that you had to go out into the streets, but the judges stood aside, a little further, so as not to show themselves, they did not speak because it was a time when politicians were still pushing their way. It was also the case that we agreed with citizens in Gorzów, that we divide the demonstration into two parts—there are 20 minutes for lawyers, and in the second part, when politicians, we leave aside. The change was big, because I remember that there were 20-30 judges in front of the courts, 50-60 in Gorzów itself. Judges and their families came. There were also lawyers, prosecutors and court employees.

The nature of the chains of light (invented by judge Bartłomiej Przymusiński)—they were sublime in character—everyone could join.

We joined in 2017. It was difficult for us judges to break down to go out on the street—an action that goes far beyond our office. It cost us a lot to overcome the shame and inner resistance to take to the streets. Beyond an ethical question: is it appropriate for us or not there was also a strategic one: Will we harm it or help? Or with regard to the media: what to say, how to say—after all, we have not been trained.

Professional attitude—talks spreading the judge's ethos (values) and changing the judge's attitude towards citizens (opening up this environment, changing habits—justifying judgments, explaining the motives of verbal judgments in the courtroom, paying more attention to the rights of a party, witness during a court trial to they were not broken).

Judicial self-governments—we had to act as one. Resolutions were usually passed unanimously or by a majority. In 2017, going out to the streets plus media activity.

---

that, in their view, nothing had changed since July, and they regarded it as "the end of independent judges and the judiciary in Poland."

In Wrocław, several hundred people marched from the court buildings on Plac Wolności, carrying banners with slogans such as "Not for Pisocracy!" and chanting phrases like "Freedom, equality, democracy" and "Wrocław is the stronghold of democracy."

In Łódź, several hundred protesters gathered in front of the Regional Court building on Dąbrowski Square. Some held candles, white roses, and flags of Poland and the European Union. Copies of the Constitution were distributed. Banners read "Do not sleep, they will rob you of democracy" and "Courts free from politicians." The speeches argued that "by defending the independence of the judiciary, we defend our freedom, equality and democracy" (TVN 2017).

Two weeks later, on December 6, 2017, judges from the District Courts of Myslenice and Krakow issued an appeal to the state authorities, urging them to stop undermining the foundations of a democratic state governed by the rule of law. They called for an end to the subordination of the judiciary to political decision-making centers and the campaign of slander against judges. The judges also called upon the citizens of Poland to defend the constitutional legal order within the boundaries of applicable law. "Without independent courts, there is neither democracy nor an adequate level of protection of civil rights and freedoms, especially the right to a fair trial, and no respect for human dignity" (Iustitia 2017).

For some, the turning point was the removal of presidents and vice-presidents of the common courts between 2017 and 2018 (see Box 2). Some of them were fired by fax. On November 23, 2017, Iustitia appealed to judges not to accept the nomination on the functions of the presidents of the courts:

*Our appeal not to accept any posts from the dismissed officials in this way remains valid. One cannot accept the attitude that it would be better to be me than a person unknown to the environment. Such justification cannot be approved of, because by taking up a function released in such circumstances, it enables and legitimizes the actions of the Minister of Justice, undertaken in breach of the constitutional principle of the independence of the judiciary from other authorities. (Iustitia 2017)*

In response, some newly nominated court presidents resigned (Iustitia 2017).

Academic 1 shared:

*You had the impression that this was the end of the action. When we react to an unknown and unexpected situation we don't know how to behave. What is happening with the judiciary has never occurred to anyone before. This is a situational shock. 1.5 years is the time it takes for everyone to realize that the unimaginable is reality. There has been a paradigm shift. The judges quickly understood what was happening and what the consequences would be.*

*The awakening occurred when people went out into the street, and the judges went out to the people standing in the street. The judges expressed their solidarity with those who protested. In the beginning, it was a presence. There was more silence than communication instead of being present on matters relating to the judiciary. Judges publicly began to speak about the effects of changes in the legislation. The scale of the demonstrations in July 2017 was surprising.*

*The judges began to understand that there was no communication between the public and the judges. Moreover, they found that most of them could not talk to people on the street.*

*Then, repressive measures against rebellious judges began. Defamation action at the level of very strong emotions against the judges. At the same time, judges from Iustitia and Themis, activists from KOS organized themselves with the participation of advocates, legal advisers, Lex Super Omnia, and OSSSA. In this process, the press conferences in front of the courts were organized by KOS and very short blunt speeches by judges, prosecutors, lawyers, and academics.*

*The positions were expressed by the self-governments of courts of all instances—general assemblies of courts, as long as they existed. Then positions and signatures for opinions. He will stand next to or together with people in need—next to judges harassed by political authorities. Taking systemic positions in relation to new statutory regulations.*

To some extent, Polish judges benefited from the lessons learned from executive overreach in Hungary. Observing the consequences an authoritarian-leaning government could have on an independent judiciary lacking internal resistance, they were careful to avoid the mistakes made by their Hungarian counterparts.

Since the early 2010s, the judiciary in Hungary has experienced blatant political interference, including the mandated early termination of the President of the Supreme Court, forced retirements of judges, and the establishment of a centralized court administration model susceptible to political control and interference, lacking sufficient institutional guarantees of independence. Prime Minister Viktor Orban and his allies consistently assail the courts and judges, labeling them as "the judicial state" (Curia 2018) and criticizing their competence, particularly when their rulings touch on matters related to free and fair elections, an area Orban considers his party's domain.

The Polish Sejm passed a bill amending the Law on the Structure of Ordinary Courts and Certain Other Acts (Sejm form no. 1491). On July 12, 2017, the Sejm received a members' bill on the Supreme Court (Sejm form no. 1727). The Act introduced changes regarding, among others:

- increasing the influence of the Minister of Justice on the appointment of court presidents and vice-presidents;

- the introduction of new tools of external and internal supervision over the administrative activity of courts;

- the submission and publication of asset declarations of judges;

- the introduction of the ability to delegate a judge to the Ministry of Foreign Affairs and the President's Chancellery;

- changes to the system of appraising the work and planning the professional development of judges.

On July 24, 2017, the President of the Republic of Poland signed the act.

Despite these challenges, Hungarian courts have continued to render decisions demonstrating their independence. They have addressed cases involving discrimination against the Roma minority, workplace discrimination, administrative lawsuits for legal gender changes (Szabó 2019), and the disclosure of public information (Fleck 2018).

However, Hungarian judges deliberately maintain political disengagement, striving to uphold the perception of being apolitical and impartial professionals. Consequently, they primarily express their opinions through court judgments rather than publicly sharing their views or responding vigorously to overt political attacks. Despite issuing open letters, these actions are considered insufficient resistance against the unprecedented assault on the rule of law and judicial independence.

Due to the "unjustifiably narrow interpretation of judicial free speech and the self-image of the apolitical judge" prevalent in the Hungarian judiciary, the potential for resistance at both individual and organizational levels is low (Fleck). This has resulted in significant self-restraint among Hungarian judges. Consequently, the likelihood of more assertive, disruptive, visible, and widespread forms of resistance emerging within the Hungarian judiciary remains minimal, as long as the culture of self-restraint and the traditional understanding of the judge's role persist unchanged.

When Polish judges met with their Hungarian counterparts, they were taken aback by the differences in their experiences regarding the rule-of-law crisis and judicial resistance. Judge 8 recalled the meeting, stating, "We know what is happening in Hungary, and there is no resistance there." The Hungarian judges appeared fearful, to the extent that the meeting location was kept secret until the last moment. This fear was indicative of the lack of solidarity and support among Hungarian judges, who are relatively fewer in number and financially secure compared to their Polish counterparts. Judge 8 emphasized the absence of solidarity and noted that even internationally active judges lacked support. The lack of resistance in Hungary resulted in delayed action from the European Union, unlike the swift reaction to the protests in Poland in 2017, which left a strong impression on figures like Timmermans and the European Parliament. Judge 7 added that during the meeting in Hungary, it was discovered that Hungarian judges weren't even registered at the hotel, indicating their reluctance to be associated with the Polish judges perceived as rebellious. The judiciary community's lack of a unified stance and the EU's delayed reaction facilitated the Hungarian regime's handling of the situation concerning judges.

### Judicial Resistance Continues (2018–2023)

In April 2018, a new law came into effect requiring individuals who turned 65—including First President of the Supreme Court Małgorzata Gersdorf—to seek permission from the country's president to continue their service for a 3-month extension. Out of the 27 affected judges, only 16 applied for permission to remain in their posts, while 11, including Gersdorf, refused. They argued that the legislation violated constitutional guarantees of judicial independence and the constitutional provisions that secure a six-year term for the supreme court president. In a symbolic and inspiring act of resistance, Gersdorf simply turned up for work.

On July 4, holding a white rose and supported by a crowd of anti-regime protesters, Gersdorf entered the Supreme Court building after a brief speech in which she said she would support supreme court judges resisting government attempts to take control of Poland's highest judicial body. She said, "I'm not engaging in politics; I'm doing this to defend the rule of law and to testify to the truth about the line between the constitution and the violation of the constitution" (Davis 2018).

According to Activist 4, "the First President of the Supreme Court prominently turning up for work after the forced suspension was a key moment in the entire history of resistance against democratic backsliding of the state that revealed a steadfast determination. Such gestures were not expected from judges—to resist the authorities—and this was met with great appreciation. This image of defiance inspired judges in their fight in the months that followed."

On November 19, 2019, the president of the court refused to make a room available for a meeting organized by judicial self-governments, but the ombudsman provided a room for the judges to meet (Ombudsman's Office 2019). During this meeting, the first ruling of the CJEU was released. On this day, the rules of the game changed. The discussion changed from a political to a judicial, purely legal one, fundamentally important in the individual and institutional dimensions (the ECHR and CJEU, respectively). One of the preliminary questions came from the Supreme Court concerning the system of justice and destructive elements of the deformation of the justice system, submitted by higher courts in Warsaw, Katowice, and Łódź (Academic 1).

For most of the judges, the civic movement for the protection of democracy did not influence how they became involved, but it did strengthen their resolve. As Judge 24 commented, "It gives me the strength to take more intensive actions. I am glad that the society is so determined."

## Changes in the Way Judges Perceived Their Function

Other judges had more personal journeys to resistance. For Judge 24, the moment to resist came in November 2017, when she decided to take a lawsuit against the minister of justice for the protection of personal rights after she was dismissed from her post as the president of the Cracow Regional Court. The dismissal was made in an atmosphere of suspicion. In the official statement on the ministry's website, they falsely connected her with an ongoing investigation and allege bad management of the court (Mazur 2020). "We did not even know who had what political views at the time of the attack on the Constitutional Tribunal or illegal voting in the Column Hall,"[5] said Judge 16:

> There were also conversations with people that there was nothing to be afraid of. But the first signatures we collected in 2016 in protest against the takeover of the Constitutional Tribunal were signed by people who voted for PiS but did not consent to the ruling party's actions. People who, in line with their political views, would not have to, still got involved. After two years, those who remained silent started using sinecures.[6] Certainly, there was an external department inside the community right away when the Constitutional Tribunal was killed. In September 2016, I went to the first convention of Polish at the Palace of Culture and Science. I persuaded a few people. I immediately

---

5    This latter point concerns the famous voting in the Column Hall. MPs from the opposition blocked the Sejm, so PiS moved the meeting to the Column Hall and did not allow them to vote on the budget. There was a criminal investigation that was discontinued. Judge Igor Tuleya, who adjudicated the appeal against discontinuation, decided to reveal information from the investigation to journalists, which they used to start criminal proceedings against him. He was suspended, his remuneration cut and immunity waived.

6    For example, accepting posts, getting functions, and securing promotions.

*got to Iustitia's media team. (I have always been a member of Iustitia, previously orga-*
*nizing trainings, trips, and even reactions against the liquidation of small courts.) I nat-*
*urally threw myself into a big bag of activities. I certainly acted personally and activated*
*the judges (about 30 to 35 in my city) and they got involved in the next changes and*
*the National Council of the Judiciary. We already knew who got sick.*

Judges were beginning to change the way they understood their own roles. As the judge
continued:

*There was a great discussion after the results of the Court Watch Foundation research.*
*In 2016, there was a big change in the way we thought about our function, our social*
*function and responsibilities. We got bludgeoned in the head. To win over society, we*
*would have to behave differently in the courtroom. It worked.*

The Court Watch Foundation has been monitoring courts in Poland since 2010. The Civic
Monitoring of Courts program consists of trained foundation volunteers participating in court
hearings. They do not represent any of the parties, but observe the course of the proceedings,
with particular emphasis on the work of the court, its judges and court employees, and the
manner in which the rights of participants are exercised, how they are treated, and under what
conditions they are brought before the court. As part of the Civic Monitoring of Courts, more
than 3,000 volunteers have visited over 40,000 court hearings in the first 12 years of the
Foundation's operation, which is the largest collection of data on judicial practice in the world.
Each year, the monitoring effort culminates in reports with recommendations to the courts.

For example, in the report from 2021, the Court Watch Foundation recommended the
following for judges:

- Judges should remember that apologizing or explaining the reason for delaying the
  start of a hearing is not only an expression of respect for the participants, but also
  relieves tension and builds the authority of the court, which results in the correct course
  of the hearing. It should always be remembered when the delay exceeding the usual
  few minutes was caused by the court (also in the event of an extension of the previous
  hearing) or if any of the participants may not know the reason for it.

- Judges should pay more attention to the correct and comprehensible instruction of
  witnesses and parties giving evidence or being interrogated.

- Judges should also pay due attention to announcing judgments in an accessible
  manner that leaves no doubt as to their content.

- The need to maintain discipline in a courtroom may not involve aggressive or disre-
  spectful attitude towards the participants of the hearing. On the contrary, it is

forbearance and personal culture, combined with commitment and control over the course of the trial, that build the authority of the court (Pilitowski and Kociołowicz-Wiśniewska 2021).

## Judges' Associations: The Engine Behind Judicial Resistance

Iustitia is the dominant judges' association in the Polish judiciary, boasting more than 3,500 member judges from all branches of the judiciary and comprising more than one-third of all judges in the country. The second, much smaller judges' association is Themis, with around 200 member judges also from all branches of the judiciary. These associations were established in the early 1990s. Prior to the government assault on the independence of the judiciary, these associations, as one interviewee shared, were only industry groups and social clubs that issued opinions about judiciary reforms and protected their group interests (Activist 4).

The associations were well-positioned to play a key role in judicial resistance—particularly Iustitia, given its size. Their cornerstone principles and work have been a democratic rule of law and the independence of courts and judges. Their organizational infrastructure helped coordinate various activities in a decentralized but targeted and concerted manner (for example, Iustitia has 32 autonomous branches across Poland). The associations also hold institutional knowledge of public communication, media outreach, experience dealing with policymakers, the ministry of justice, and domestic civil society groups. Furthermore, they have also been active on the international stage, having extensive contacts with judges across Europe. Both associations are members of the International Association of Judges (IAJ), the European Association of Judges (EAJ), and the Association "European Judges and Prosecutors for Democracy and Freedom" (MEDEL). Iustitia has also been active in solidarity actions with the repressed judges in Turkey.

A particularly important role in judicial resistance has been played by the member judges of Iustitia and Iustitia President Krystian Markiewicz. Becoming president in April 2016, his three-year mandate was subsequently extended twice, in 2019 and 2022. He is one of the faces of protest against changes in the Polish judiciary and has been a thorn in the side of the regime, illustrated by 55 disciplinary charges he has incurred from the disciplinary spokesman Przemysław Radzik. All charges concerned one letter sent to 55 people—one case for each recipient (Siedlecka 2019b). Markiewicz decided not to appear at his summons, considering them to be deprived of legal grounds. He was the target of an attack by a troll group associated with the ministry of justice (dubbed the "hate scandal" (Jakubowski 2022). He was one of the main initiators and organizers of the Social Codification Commission, the 2016 Extraordinary Congress of Polish Judges in Warsaw, the 2017 Congress of Polish Lawyers in Katowice, the 2019 Second Congress of Polish Lawyers in Poznań, and the 2020 March of a Thousand Gowns in Warsaw (Rzeczpospolita 2017; Szymaniak 2016; Radio Katowice 2017; Siedlecka 2019; Szczęśniak, et al. 2020).

Markiewicz recognized that the success of the resistance rests in the collective. "It is impossible to fight alone," he said in an interview with the author. He saw that a large organization such as Iustitia could bring considerable leverage in favor of the resisting judges. At the same time, Iustitia and its visible leader are driven by the work at the foundational level—"organic work," as Markiewicz observed in a reference to the Polish nonviolent grassroots resistance against partitioning empires in the 19th century.

*Because judges serve citizens who see them as the defenders and guarantors of their rights, this justifies judges' engagement in the public sphere.*

As one judge shared, "Iustitia has grown a lot, but there is a certain comfort of work because people are organized (such as the media team, local initiatives) so that the president of Iustitia himself does not know anything about some matters. It is a heavy organic work that cannot be seen: the preparation of certain matters, preparing the analysis of statistical data. Another team reports on judges under pressure, others deal with the PolAndRock Festival, study trips to Brussels and Luxembourg" (Szczęśniak, et al. 2020).

On its website, Iustitia informs its readers that because judges serve citizens who see them as the defenders and guarantors of their rights, this justifies judges' engagement in the public sphere and necessitates their collaboration with social partners. It fights for a strong, independent judiciary not for judges, but for society.

Judge 4 acknowledged the assistance and role of Iustitia in helping them become and stay engaged:

> *I was a regular member of Iustitia paying dues. Then I got involved a lot. I met many people, great people who put everything on one card. This was a group of serious, decent people. It gave me a lot of courage to participate in the demonstrations.*

One of the crucial roles was to support repressed judges in their struggle. As Judge 2 shared, "The judge will not fight alone. Paweł Juszczyszyn has three children. How long could he stand alone? This shows the role played by the judiciary associations."

Other judges appreciated Iustitia members' help in shaping their media and communication skills and strategies.

> *We talked as Iustitia's communication team with Igor Tuleya and Paweł Juszczyszyn on how to communicate with the media. The team's task is to establish Iustitia's strategy for contacting the public. We are responsible for day-to-day contacts with journalists,*

*for interviews, preparing judges and training them. We run social media. Iustitia has developed a lot in the last five years. Back then, we had about 1,000 followers. Now Iustitia has 64,000 followers on Facebook.* (Judge 13)

*Iustitia's media team builds the image of judges who not only adjudicate but participate in the public debate on the rule of law, perceive the threat posed by the rulers, and participate in educational campaigns at schools to explain various issues (such as hate speech and drugs). It also works at the social media level. It has contacts with journalists of all media (radio, newspaper, television).* (Judge 12)

To offer legal and organizational assistance to current and former judges, Iustitia changed its statute to allow judges to remain or become Iustitia members even after losing their judge status. "Now even a person that is not a judge can be a member of the association, an idea that was suggested by a colleague based on the experience of the former Yugoslavia," said Judge 2. It was important that resisting judges who might have been thrown out of the profession knew that they could count on the protection of the association and remain its member to continue the fight for the independence of the judiciary.

Iustitia was approached by international media outlets, such as the BBC and CNN, who treated the information contained on their website as a primary source. Meanwhile, TVP, the Polish state-owned public television who was at that time "a propaganda mouthpiece" of the regime (Lasocki 2021), had to pay the BBC to quote the prime minister's words (Judge 12).

Themis, a much smaller association compared to Iustitia, undertook a number of activities between 2016 and 2022 in support of the resisting judges and to advance resistance against the government. Themis's work led to the publication of detailed reports on controversial reforms to the justice system (Mazur 2019, 2020, 2021, 2022). They also published critical opinions of the association's management board on the government-initiated changes in the judiciary, the response of the Polish authorities to the CJEU judgment of November 19, 2019, and press articles on the current situation of Polish judiciary (Themis 2020; Gałczyńska 2019).

According to Judge Dariusz Mazur from Themis, "the current situation related to the attack of political authorities on the judiciary has posed new challenges for the association, which they try to meet, among others:

- By publishing articles devoted to the independence of the Polish judiciary in both Polish and foreign press,

- Participating in national and international conferences and seminars devoted to judicial power,

- Commenting in the independent media current situation of the Polish judiciary,

- Organizing, on the one hand, training for judges and, on the other hand, events aimed at legal education of the society, especially the youth,

- Supporting politically persecuted judges and prosecutors, both by organizing demonstrations of support for them and by providing them with professional legal assistance in disciplinary proceedings against them,

- Participating as amicus curiae in proceedings before the ECHR concerning the Polish judiciary" (Mazur in communication with author).

Iustitia and Themis have also worked together. Together they organized, along with other organizations, the Extraordinary Congress of Polish Judges, in September 2016. In fact, they have been partners for civil society orgaizations for many years. As Łukasz Bojarski found out, the cooperation between judicial associations and CSOs started in the 1990s. By 2015, member judges already knew the CSOs very well (Bojarski 2021). But what happened after 2015 is that the cooperation was even broader. "We started to work closely with judges' associations. Since July 2017, we have been constantly cooperating, maintaining day-to-day contacts," said Activist 3:

*After 2015, monitoring and advocacy—the cyclical collection of information on the scale of violations, studies with the participation of judges and prosecutors, or monitoring how legislation influenced the functioning of the Constitutional Tribunal, courts, and prosecutor's office—have ceased to be effective. Strategic litigation was about finding legal representation for affected judges and prosecutors.*

The new instrument that helped NGOs express their independent view on crucial problems concerning the rule-of-law crisis in Poland was the amicus curiae brief to the ECHR. The amicus curiae brief is an essential tool used by the Helsinki Foundation (HFHR) in strategic litigation, that is, conducting court proceedings of public interest to change practices or laws that violate rights and freedoms of an individual. An amicus submission enables NGOs to express their views in judicial proceedings and draw the court's attention to human rights concerns. The impact of amicus curiae briefs in the work of HFHR is confirmed by statistical data. In 2018–2019 alone, the Foundation made 61 submissions of this kind. Addressing the human rights problems affecting the countries where the HFHR operates and following the rapid changes in the legal systems, the Foundation has been preparing amicus curiae briefs in particular in cases concerning the rights of persons deprived of their liberty, the right to an independent court and the right to a fair trial, the rights of refugees and migrants and protection against discrimination.

## Size and Demographics of Judicial Resistance

Half of all judges are unequivocally critical of the government reforms in the judiciary, though many remain unengaged (Judge 4). In a survey conducted by the Helsinki Foundation of Human Rights titled "The Time of Trial: How do Changes in the Justice System Affect Polish Judges?", the overwhelming majority of interviewed judges (37 of 40 judges) expressed concerns that the judicial reforms of the past four years have, at best, compromised and, at worst, seriously undermined the systemic guarantees of judicial independence. These concerns stem from changes in disciplinary proceedings, the establishment of the government-controlled Disciplinary Chamber of the Supreme Court, restrictions on the role of courts' governing boards, marginalization of judges' assemblies, and institutional changes affecting the National Council of the Judiciary Council (NCJ) aimed at capturing it by the ruling regime.

The judges also highlighted that although the constitution still guarantees judicial independence, in practice, this protection is perceived as illusory. The activities of the Constitutional Tribunal since 2016 were also assessed negatively by almost all interviewed judges, citing doubts about the status of three Tribunal judges appointed by the ruling party and its president, the working methods of the Tribunal, its judicial efficiency, and lack of credibility. None of the interviewed laywers expressed definite enthusiasm for the activities of the NCJ. They also negatively assessed the new framework of disciplinary procedures, which, "on one hand, limited judges' right of defense and, on the other, strengthened the position of disciplinary officers and the Minister of Justice in these proceedings" (Szuleka, Wolny, Kalisz 2019, 43–53).

This is corroborated by Judge 19, who said that the majority of judges choose not to publicly support either side. They prefer not to articulate their stance openly. "If you cannot see me, you cannot hear me, it is better because it can be used against me later."

Judge 10 shared that between 1,000 and 2,000 judges are involved in different projects and actions that are part of the resistance campaign, with the regularly engaged core constituting around 10 percent of the total judiciary (also mentioned by Judge 16 and Lawyer 7).

The most active judges are those age 40–50 years and those who began their judicial careers after 1989 (Judge 5, 2nd interview; Judge 8; Judge 22). Judges that are closer to the retirement—55 and over—tend to be less involved and showed greater degree of conformity (Judge 5; Judge 1). However, there are retired judges who join resistance actions such as street protests (Judge 5). Younger judges are generally less involved in resistance. Most work in the district courts and are overwhelmed. They also care more about promotion at this stage of their career and tend to be overburdened with family matters (Judge 3). Women judges involved in resistance are 40 and over. By this age, their children are older, which allows their involvement in social life again (Judge 8).

Interviewees supplied anecdotal evidence regarding the involvement or abstention from resistance among judges in specific courts. One judge stated that the civil department at the District Court in Warsaw is experiencing a lack of participation, with only one judge attending demonstrations out of the seven departments (Judge 4). In the Katowice District Court, it was mentioned that 30 judges were supporting the resistance, while 20 remained neutral (Judge 9).

In one of the smallest courts, which have seven judges adjudicating, three judges openly opposed the president of the court who wanted to benefit from the so-called "good change," which was the 2015 campaign slogan of the PiS. The other judges wanted to be neutral, but one of them signed the appeals (Judge 11). Some of judges go to protest in front of the court together with two to three colleagues from the II criminal department against more than 40 judges in the court (Judge 14). Appeal court judges are less involved. They sign letters, appeals, post photos, but do not initiate actions (Judge 1).

In addition to resisting judges and those who remain uninvolved or sit on the fence, there are also judges who support the government or its policies. It is estimated that this group comprises approximately 10–15 percent of judges. These supportive judges can be further divided into two groups. According to Judge 11, "the first group includes the so-called followers who are convinced that the change is good (they accepted the propaganda without much reflection). They felt aggrieved and have exorbitant ambitions. The second group consists of careerists who want to cynically benefit from the situation professionally."

There is also the group known as neo-judges—those who applied for promotions and participated in the competition boycotted by other judges and were nominated by the neo-NCJ. As of March 2023, it is estimated that there are around 3,000 neo-judges. The reasons behind their decisions to compete vary. Some seek promotion because it is their turn and they do not want to wait until the rule of law crisis ends. Others compete for promotion because they believe they would not have a fair chance in an open competition. There are also those who seek promotion because they are loyal to the system. However, there is currently no research concerning neo-judges. As Judge 8 shared, "There are judges who keep silent because they signed letters of support for members of the neo-NCJ."

# Chapter 4. Professional Groups in Support of Judicial Independence

Judicial resistance in Poland would not succeed without a support of a great coalition of allies. We can mention here not only civil society organizations but also associations of prosecutors (LSO), human rights foundations (like HFHR) or even a constitutional body like the Polish Commissioner for Human Rights and their office. However, one of the most important actors was Free Court Initiative, group of lawyers that not only educated about the importance of rule of law but also were present in the media from the beginning. The archival role of the AO is also very important to understand the phenomenon of the populist overhaul of the PiS and judicial resistance. Finally, the coordinating body, KOS—a collaborative effort of 12 organizations of judges and prosecutors, as well as NGOs and social initiatives defending the rule of law in Poland—was crucial in organizing and conducting all resisting actions.

## Action Democracy (AD)

The Polish NGO Akcja Demokracja ("Action Democracy" or AD) was launched in 2015 to mobilize a social movement on various social issues. Activities are carried out through billboard campaigns and demonstrations. For example, AD placed posters in the center of Warsaw with diametrically opposed statements of the Kaczyński brothers[1] about the National Council of the Judiciary. On one there is a statement by Lech Kaczyński that "the postulate to create the National Council of the Judiciary was an important step on the way to making Poland a democratic state ruled by law." On the other are the recent words of Jarosław Kaczyński that "the National Council of the Judiciary is a post-communist institution." In this way, they showed the hypocrisy of the ruling party. In this campaign, AD expressed opposition to the pending reform of the judiciary (Wirtualnemedia 2017).

AD also organized the Chain of Lights protest against the changes to the Supreme Court introduced in 2017, calling on citizens for mass protests (Miecik 2017). In April, supported by donations from activists, they bought billboards in five cities (Kraków, Poznań, Łódź, Warsaw, and Włocławek), on which they directly asked PiS deputies sitting in the Parliamentary

---

1   The Kaczynski brothers were identical twins. Lech Kaczyński was Poland's President (2005–2010). On 10 April 2010, Lech Kaczyński died, along with his wife, in the crash of a Polish Air Force jet that occurred while landing at Smolensk North Airport in Russia. Jarosław Kaczyński was the Prime Minister (2006–2007) and is the Head of the Law and Justice Party.

**FIGURE 2.** AD projected the message "This is our court" on the Supreme Court building during the Chain of Light protest.

Committee on Justice and Human Rights whether they would execute the sentence on Polish democracy.

The organization also collected 72,594 signatures online for the petition "Courts free from politicians!" By May, their activists brought 233 yellow cards to the Sejm addressed to all PiS MPs. The card contained the content of the appeal, information on how many people had signed it so far, and a warning: "The destruction of the independence of the judiciary through unconstitutional changes to the act on the National Council of the Judiciary may also turn against you in the future" (Akcja Demokracya).

They held more protests in 2018, launching the slogan "All lights on the president" at the Presidential Palace in September (Newsweek 2018). Those gathered demanded that President Andrzej Duda listen to their voices before making the final decision on the draft laws on the Supreme Court and the NCJ (Bartkiewicz 2017). Furthermore, AD appealed to the Supreme Court judges to stay at their posts to defend rights despite their mandate being shortened (Akcja Demokracya).

On November 12, 2019, the CJEU issued a judgment with guidance on how to remove political nominees from the Polish NCJ and the Supreme Court (Akcja Demokracya 2019). In response, AD activists brought several dozen empty suitcases to the Supreme Court with a message to the judges from the Disciplinary Chamber who were illegally appointed by the neo-NCJ that they should cease their work and start packing.

## Committee for the Defense of the Democracy (KOD)

On November 18, 2015, Krzysztof Łoziński published an article in which he urged that after PiS took hold of power and launched its anti-democratic initiatives, a Committee for the Defense of Democracy (Komitet Obrony Demokracji or KOD) should be established. The following day, Mateusz Kijowski set up a Facebook group under the name. Seeing a large response—30,000 users signed up within three days—the founding group discussed creating a social movement. Meanwhile, they launched a website and published a manifesto inviting everyone valuing democracy to join. In the manifesto they wrote, "Democracy in Poland is under threat. The actions of the authorities, their disregard for the law and democratic customs force us to express our firm opposition.... We do not agree to breaking the Constitution and introducing authoritarian rule using the abusive mechanisms of democracy" (KOD nd).

On November 26, the members of KOD released "A Letter of the Citizens of the Constitutional State to Andrzej Duda, the President of Poland" asking him to swear in three of five judges to the Constitutional Tribunal. KOD argued that those three were duly elected by the previous parliament. As the disagreements between PiS and the Constitutional Tribunal continued, KOD called for protests against what it saw as a breach of the constitution that violated democratic norms and the separation of powers between the legislative, executive, and judicial branches.

On December 12, KOD organized the first demonstration against the takeover of the Constitutional Tribunal, in which 50,000 demonstrators participated. Parallel demonstrations were also held in other major Polish cities, including Poznań and Szczecin (with 2,000+ participants each), Wrocław (approx. 2,000), Lublin (500), and Bielsko-Biała (200). The following day, more than 3,000 people demonstrated in Gdańsk.

Early in 2016, KOD organized demonstrations calling for the protection of the free press (in 20 cities on January 9 and 40 cities on January 23). The following month, 70,000 people protested in the "We the People" demonstration on February 27. The "We Are and Will Remain in Europe" demonstration took place on May 7 at City Hall in Warsaw, with an estimated 240,000 protesters. Three years later, on December 16, 2019, a quarter of a million protesters demonstrated in small towns against the government's muzzle act targeting independent courts. Most protests are accompanied by smaller demonstrations by KOD cells in European capitals and around the world, notably in Brussels, London, Paris, Berlin, and the United States.

## Free Courts Initiative

In 2017, on the wave of protests in defense of independent judiciary, a group of four lawyers—Sylwia Gregorczyk-Abram, Maria Ejchart, Paulina Kieszkowska-Knapik and Michał Wawrykiewicz—launched the Free Courts initiative. As they shared in an interview with the author, "We were angry about what was happening in Poland. And not everybody understood what was actually happening. Nobody tried to explain to the public what was happening to the courts. The real goal was to educate others."

The goal of the Free Courts was to educate citizens on the rule of law and what was happening to the independent courts. As part of the initiative, short videos were recorded explaining the significance of an independent judiciary and its importance for every citizen. The Free Courts initiators invited famous people to appear in the videos, from actors, lawyers, and doctors, to journalists and artists. The videos explained what would happen when a judge ceases to be independent while referencing examples from everyday life. "We made these videos as lawyers which achieved incredible success. These videos had more than 400,000 views," said Lawyer 5.

The Free Courts initiative released around 1,000 movies, clips, infographics, live broadcasts, studio programs, and podcasts, and close to 80,000 people follow the #FreeCourts Facebook page at the time of this writing. Since 2020, they have been present on YouTube, where they regularly publish films concerning attacks on the rule of law in Poland. They are also active on Twitter and in the mainstream opposition media—such as Gazeta Wyborcza, Onet, Oko Press, and TVN—where they are invited as experts to comment on current legal issues, including how the regime's policies and actions undermine the independent judiciary and how this affects ordinary citizens.

The lawyers from Free Courts also prepare reports about the rule-of-law backsliding in Poland. In their report *2000 Days of Lawlessness*, they show step-by-step how the government brought about the destruction of the rule of law, including "a record of all legislative changes and other decisions taken by the executive and legislative authorities to politicize the judiciary." The report also shows that none of the steps taken since 2015 intended to implement a genuine and credible reform of the judiciary. "Knowing what work has been done will be crucial when the time comes to repair what has been destroyed," notes the report (Gregorczyk-Abram, et al. 2021). At one event, the *2000 Days of Lawlessness* report was displayed on the lawn in front of the Supreme Court. The description of violations of the rule of law covered 87 meters (FreeCourts 2021).

*None of the steps taken since 2015 intended to implement a genuine and credible reform of the judiciary.*

Since 2017, Free Courts have been co-organizers of dozens of demonstrations and protests in defense of the rule of law and the repressed judges. Their campaign "Europe, Do Not Let Go" appealed to the European Commission to refer a complaint to the CJEU in the case of unconstitutional forced retirement of Supreme Court judges over age 65. This appeal led to the EC submitting the complaint to the CJEU and resulted in the interim measures allowing retired judges to be restored to work.

The initiative founders regularly present the position of the Polish legal community on the government's activities to EU institutions. In Poland, they met with diplomatic representatives of EU countries to explain the situation in the courts. They regularly comment on matters related to the Polish and European judiciary in the foreign press. "We provided the lawyers of the EU Commission with the legal arguments on the merits," said one of the co-founders in an interview with the author.

Free Courts members attended CJEU proceedings in Luxembourg initiated from the preliminary ruling requests regarding the independence of the judiciary, including proceedings concerning the status of the Polish National Council of the Judiciary. They also represented Polish judges in the ECHR regarding individual complaints against the Polish state.

Domestically, when the regime began their campaign of repression, Free Courts supported the judges in the courts, formulating preliminary rulings and acting as defense lawyers in disciplinary proceedings before the Supreme Administrative Court. The "Free Courts" represented Professor Małgorzata Gersdorf, former First President of the Supreme Court, in the trial against Stanisław Piotrowicz of the ruling party who called judges "thieves." They also represented Professor Wojciech Sadurski in a well-known case regarding freedom of speech initiated by the ruling party after he called them an organized criminal group.

The initiative originated the "Constitutional Week" project, which, since 2016, takes place every six months in schools across age groups throughout Poland and is organized by Association pro Memoria of Professor Zbigniew Hołda. It was organized to protest the unconstitutional takeover of the Constitutional Tribunal. Each annual edition of the project engages around 600 lawyers who conduct classes on governance, constitutional issues, and matters related to the European Union for approximately 30,000 children in more than 700 schools.

Free Courts has also organized extra-curricular educational events. For instance, at the Academy of Fine Arts' Woodstock festival, Gregorczyk-Abram and Wawrykiewicz conducted classes for youth addressing the risks of withdrawing from the EU given the government's policies.

The Free Courts initiative received numerous awards for its public activity. In 2018, they were awarded with the Teresa Torańska Newsweek award; in 2019, with the Anna Laszuk TOK FM radio award for "exceptional impact on the ground." In 2020, they received the European Citizens' Prize awarded by the European Parliament for expressing values enshrined in the Charter of Fundamental Rights of the European Union (Wolne Sądy 2024).

## The Citizens of Poland (ORP)

Obywatele RP ("The Citizens of Poland" or ORP) is an informal anti-fascist movement in Poland opposing the PiS-led government. ORP were actively engaged in protests against the unconstitutional judicial reforms in July 2017 (Flückiger 2017). They blocked extreme right-wing rallies and demanded the delegalization of organizations promoting racism and xenophobia. The movement also established ObyPomoc, a network of support for those prosecuted for pro-democracy and anti-fascist activities, and arranged for their pro bono legal aid (Obywatele 2018).

## The Osiatyński Archive (OA)

The Osiatyński Archive (OA) was established in 2017 in memory of the late constitutionalist and human rights defender, Professor Wiktor Osiatyński, in order to fulfill his idea of creating a "chronicle of unlawfulness" (Archiwum Osiatyńskiego 2024). The OA Council is composed of top Polish lawyers, including former judges of the Constitutional Tribunal and the Tribunal of State, legal scholars, judges, attorneys, and civil society activists. The OA consists of several initiatives, including the Archive, RuleOfLaw.pl, the Alphabet of Dissent, and Debates.

The Archive is a growing collection of documents, draft laws, analyses, and opinions. Through it, the OA has been monitoring, analyzing, and explaining all events connected with the rule-of-law crisis in Poland since December 2017. It also covers the conflict between the EU and the national government concerning the democratic backsliding in Poland. The Archive documents attacks on judicial independence, including all repressive acts against judges and prosecutors. The OA also aims to discuss genuine changes to the justice system that are needed to guarantee adherence to democratic rule of law. One OA member, Activist 4, reflected:

> Nobody expected the amount of work that needs to be done to keep a finger on the pulse—the initiative of analyzing and documenting the aggression against the rule of law. The need to explain what the authorities were doing to the independent judiciary was tremendous.

Another important initiative of the OA is the Rule of Law in Poland website (www.ruleoflaw. pl) that provides English-language information about the rule-of-law crisis to inform public opinion abroad. Before this initiative, there was no information about developments in Poland in English, and foreign media was not always able to understand the complexities of what was happening to the judiciary and opposition to it. The website now provides accurate and timely information to the foreign media and the EU institutions.

The Rule of Law in Poland team consists of Anna Wójcik and Patryk Wachowiec. They read lawyers' texts and follow what is happening. They publish news about the rulings of the ECHR, the CJEU, the statements made by politicians, and tweets from experts. They maintain contact with constitutional lawyers, international, EU and national legal experts.

Through the Alphabet of Dissent initiative, the OA has published profiles of more than 250 individuals and initiatives against the regime to acknowledge their work and promote civil activism. Through the Debate initiative, the OA provides a platform for expert analysis and commentary.

## The Human Rights Commission (HRC) of the Polish Bar Association

Polish attorneys have played a significant role defending judges. The Human Rights Commission (HRC) of the Polish Bar Association was particularly active from the start of the rule-of-law crisis when they shared opinions to cases concerning the constitutionality of the amendments of the law on the Constitutional Tribunal. The HRC also held meetings with representatives of international organizations who came to Poland to monitor the situation.

The HRC created a team of attorneys to represent judges and prosecutors pro bono in explanatory and disciplinary proceedings. It was a grassroots movement to help the oppressed. As Lawyer 3 shared:

> *There are 6,000 lawyers in Poland. There are 30 to 50 of them to whom a judge may turn for pro bono help. Defense tactics depend on the proceedings launched against the judge. As part of all these instruments, in almost all proceedings, we are requesting the exclusion of a judge of the Disciplinary Chamber, as we believe that the disciplinary officer, the Disciplinary Chamber, was appointed in a manner that does not ensure the independence of the system.*

Some lawyers, like Mikołaj Pietrzak, had previous experience in defending judges. The first case that Pietrzak took as a defense attorney was of the Constitutional Tribunal judge, Jerzy Stępień, who was charged with violating the dignity of a judge by participating in a political rally. In 2017, Judge Stępień appeared at the Freedom March organized by the Civic Platform and KOD. During the court hearing, attorney Pietrzak referred, inter alia, to the case-law of the Strasbourg-based ECHR in the case of *Kudeshkin v. Russia*, where the Court held that the statement of a judge that is a public criticism of phenomena adversely affecting the independence of the judiciary is one of the important issues of public interest which should be open to free debate in a democratic society. He also referred the ruling in the case of *Baka v. Hungary*, in which the court stated that critical opinions expressed by a judge in a debate on matters of public importance require protection (Baka, the judge in question, was President of the Hungarian Supreme Court). Pietrzak argued:

> *The knowledge and experience of retired judges of the Constitutional Tribunal and their reflections on constitutional issues—necessarily related to the functioning of the state in many of its aspects—can and constitute an extremely valuable contribution to the debate on public matters and matters important to the whole society. Retired judges of the Constitutional Tribunal should be perceived as natural participants in the discussion of the most serious matters concerning the state system and the rights and freedoms of all citizens.* (Siedlecka 2018)

The resisting judges were a relatively small group. "They need help our help," said Lawyer 5. "They needed experienced people who would explain why there are independent judges, why there is injustice, why the attack on the judicial independence should concern greatly ordinary people and future generation." They continued:

*For the judges, the repressions were unimaginable. Suddenly they realized that they could not defend their independence without assistance from outside. A group of resisting judges required help very quickly. We knew they had to be helped in the best possible way. Each of the involved attorneys took their favorite judge to defend. What distinguishes lawyers from judges is that lawyers have a glorious history. We have mentors, role models, references. Attorneys helped those repressed during the Solidarity years. And now the judges have been put to the test—what they have done is fantastic, and we needed to defend them.*

According to Lawyer 7, one of the attorneys that defended judges, before the rule-of-law crisis there was no channel between judges and other legal professions allowing for the articulation of views and observations.

*We started meeting together because we had no other choice. If a judge is charged in disciplinary proceedings or a judge who is threatened with lifting immunity for reasons that do not indicate an offense, it is the duty of the community to stand for such a man. I specialize in criminal and disciplinary law and offer what I know best. I enter into relationships with the judge who is involved in the case and with judges who are co-defenders. There are a number of judges specialized in defense in disciplinary proceedings. We exchange experiences, observations, reflections on topics that go beyond what is the subject of a specific case and this brings people closer.*

Lawyer 1 shared:

*Cooperation with the judges is extremely interesting and completely new. We did not know the judges from this side. They didn't know us either. A new relationship was formed with the judges after we marched with them during the March of 1,000 Gowns or represented them before the ECHR. The experience of the judges of the resistance and taking up the fight completely changed their optics. They gained the experience of being the plaintiff, the defendant, the accused.*

### Lex Super Omnia and Resisting Prosecutors

Though relatively small in number, a group of prosecutors stood up for judicial independence and against the changes to the judiciary spearheaded by the ruling party. On January 26, 2017, the prosecutors registered their association, Lex Super Omnia. Presently, it's comprised of 270 prosecutors—not many, considering there are 6,000 prosecutors in Poland. Prosecutors are much more vulnerable than judges as they risk immediate repression. The profession is more hierarchical, and they cannot contest the decisions of their superiors. It is also much more difficult to convince a prosecutor to resist. The chilling effect is very big. And so, most of the prosecutors do not engage in resistance.

The first tool for resisting prosecutors is filing a lawsuit. For example, prosecutor Katarzyna Kwiatkowska sued the National Prosecutor's Office and the Warsaw-Praga District Prosecutor's Office, demanding PLN76,000 compensation for violating the prohibition of discrimination and unequal treatment. She indicated the activity in Lex Super Omnia as the reason for the discrimination (Łukaszewski 2021). She simultaneously faced a countersuit submitted by the National Public Prosecutor's Office (NPPO) demanding PLN2,000,000. According to the prosecutor's office, her interview in Gazeta Wyborcza contained "insinuations that the management of the National Public Prosecutor's Office was committing crimes and other violations," and such statements allegedly "undermine the authority of the National Prosecutor's Office and harm its good name" (Łukaszewski 2021; TOK FM 2021).

*The first tool for resisting prosecutors is filing a lawsuit.*

When judges started protesting in 2017, the prosecutors joined the street demonstrations and protests. When five prosecutors took gowns from the prosecutor's office for use in the March of 1,000 Gowns, the office weighed charging them with misappropriation. "I do not agree as a citizen and a public prosecutor with what is happening currently with the judiciary," said Prosecutor 1.

*As a prosecutor, I really care about the cases being adjudicated by the independent judges. I'm not afraid of the consequences, I thought it over. It is worth participating and supporting judges in their protests.*

Prosecutors also joined judges in the Tour de Constitution where they drove around Poland to meet and talk with citizens about the meaning of the constitution and the current legal challenges. Prosecutor 1 continued:

*[Formerly] we committed the sin of omission. We did not care about legal education or the level of legal culture. Now I am participating in accelerated legal education courses for all citizens. I translate the constitution to people, more and more people read the constitution.*

Prosecutors continue to resist by speaking in the news media. They present their views and assessments regarding specific regulations and comment on reports issued by Lex Super Omnia. As Prosecutor 2 shared:

*In my case, because I like the media, I am a licensed PR person. The limited reach of Twitter allows me to do this, to rectify distortions and lies, and to promote the activities of my association and my fellow judges' associations. Citizens are very surprised that the prosecutor is a normal person and is not a bronze, figure wearing an intimidating robe but he can joke and laugh. I just have to be careful not to give legal advice on specific cases and not to comment on proceedings that I do not know. I'm a person like you—it's about overcoming the fear that I don't have the right to speak out without my boss's consent. We can participate in radio and television broadcasts, conduct social media only with elementary dignity and respect for human rights. I know that my association has become more recognizable thanks to my activities.*

Prosecutors also cooperate internationally with the Venice Commission, preparing written positions comparing current and previous regulations. They take part in meetings at the European Parliament or with Commissioner Vera Jurova, where they present their position regarding the prosecutor's office. They also cooperate with MEDEL.[2] As Prosecutor 1 shared: "In this way, we show how Polish prosecutors are treated, how the proceedings are manipulated, and how the prosecutor's office has become a tool for the ruling party."

Previously, the norm was that a prosecutor could not express himself in public without the consent of his superior. The members of Lex Super Omnia overcame this by daring to speak out in public. Prosecutors began taking an active part in meetings with young people. Because there are many academics among the prosecutors, there is a thriving group of prosecutor-educators. Moreover, the prosecutors established contacts with NGOs in various cities and passed their message to schools and social organizations where they had the opportunity to speak.

In January 2021, seven prosecutors from Lex Super Omnia were relegated far away from their previous posting and place of residence. They were given two days to pack their life and move to cities located 300 km from their home, where they were about to spend the next six months separated from their families. But as Prosecutor 1 shared:

*Repressions do not make a negative impression on us. The amount of harassment motivates me more to fight. I will fight to the end to eliminate lawlessness. The National*

---

2    Magistrats Européens pour la Démocratie et les Libertés (MEDEL) was founded in Strasbourg in June 1985 by eight trade unions and associations of judges and prosecutors from Belgium, France, Germany, Italy, Portugal, and Spain. After the fall of the Berlin Wall and the disappearance of the Iron Curtain, MEDEL was strongly committed to supporting the establishment of independent judicial institutions that respect the rule of law in the former Eastern Bloc countries. The association gradually expanded, welcoming new organizations of judges and prosecutors from Bulgaria, Cyprus, Czech Republic, Greece, Moldova, Montenegro, Poland, Romania, Serbia, and Turkey.

*Public Prosecutor's Office shows helplessness, weakness, high emotionality, and does not know how to deal with resisting prosecutors. I am ready to be discharged from my profession for what I am doing.*

### The Justice Defense Committee (KOS)

The Justice Defense Committee (KOS) has born out of a case concerning Judge Czeszkiewicz (Judge 1, second interview). The judge had acquitted activists from the Committee for the Defense of Democracy (KOD) who were accused of disrupting an exhibition about General Anders. This did not fare well with the judge's superiors, and he was presented with disciplinary charges by the deputy disciplinary spokesman. Judge Czeszkiewicz acknowledged:

*Everything seems to be happening because I handed down the first acquittal of KOD activists. My problems in court began after this sentence.... As a judge, I want to be as far away from politics as possible. Charges are being brought against me because politics has entered the court. This is happening because the presidents of courts are nominated by the minister of justice.* (Jałoszewski 2018)

KOS is a collaborative effort of 12 organizations of judges and prosecutors, as well as NGOs and social initiatives defending the rule of law in Poland. The committee was established to work together when the impartiality of judges and the independence of lawyers came under threat. It was established on June 4, 2018, the 29th anniversary of the historic 1989 elections, which marked the start of Poland's road to freedom and democracy. The agreement was signed by representatives of the Professor Zbigniew Hołda Association, Iustitia, Themis, the Association of Prosecutors Lex Super Omnia, the Free Courts initiative, The Helsinki Foundation for Human Rights, the Institute for Law and Society (INPRIS), and the Osiatyński Archive.

The committee's objectives include monitoring cases of pressure being exerted on judges, lawyers, and legal professionals, informing the public about these cases, offering defense and support to those harassed, and broadly supporting the rule of law and an independent judiciary to ensure the protection of civil rights and freedoms. The main goal of KOS is to help repressed judges by contacting legal defenders on their behalf (Judge 11). KOS became the "central platform of cooperation between civil society organizations and judicial associations" (Bojarski and Lukasz 2021). Through KOS, aid for judges became institutionalized.

KOS was designed to ensure better communication and division of tasks between parties so that everyone could contribute from their strengths. KOS meetings take place once per week with an agenda prepared in advance (Lawyer 2). They also hold a group on WhatsApp. "KOS was supposed to ensure better communication and a better division of tasks so that everyone could find their place in what they do best," said Activist 4. Meanwhile, for external messaging, "It was decided that signing by coalitions of experts would be more important and would be better communicated in the media."

KOS conduct strategic litigation in almost every case concerning judicial independence in Poland. When a judge becomes a party to disciplinary proceedings, KOS initiates contact to offer pro bono legal aid. In addition to pursuing its own cases, they also use their cases to establish case-law before the domestic and European courts. They also provide expert advice and support to judges and prosecutors engaged in litigation and case-building with the CJEU and ECHR. They have also been archiving all examples of repressive acts against judges and prosecutors.

The success of KOS stems from its genuine solidarity among lawyers, activists, prosecutors, and judges, as noted by Activist 2. Judge 16 highlighted the organization's inspiration drawn from the Solidarity Movement of the 1980s, following the pattern of KOR. Lawyer 6 described KOS as an effective platform providing defense and representation in disciplinary courts, with judges receiving significant assistance in finding lawyers for those in need. Judge 2 emphasized the cooperative relationship between Iusititia and KOS, noting the provision of a list of proxies. According to Judge 27, involving various entities such as NGOs (including KOS and Free Courts) and the Supreme Bar Council in proceedings ensured transparency. Furthermore, many individuals affiliated with KOS from diverse organizations supported judges asking preliminary questions, as noted by Judge 20.

## Polish Commissioner for Human Rights

The Commissioner for Human Rights holds the constitutional authority for legal control and protection and operates independently from other state authorities. Appointed by the Sejm and approved by the Senate for a five-year term, the Commissioner safeguards human and civic freedoms and rights specified in the Constitution and other legal acts. In fulfilling this role, the Commissioner investigates actions undertaken or neglected by entities, organizations, or institutions responsible for observing and implementing human and citizen rights and freedoms, ensuring compliance with the law and principles of social coexistence and justice (Commissioner 2012).

Polish Commissioner for Human Rights Adam Bodnar and his Office emerged as allies of judges in their resistance efforts. Bodnar and the Office received the Rafto Prize in 2018 for their significant stance against political developments in Poland. The Ombudsman played a crucial role in defending judicial independence and minority rights, with Bodnar being recognized as "a significant advocate of democracy, defender of minorities, and fundamental human rights" (Rafto Foundation 2018). Bodnar expressed gratitude, stating that the award symbolizes support from the international community for Polish civil society, academia, judges, and lawyers striving for the rule of law, judicial independence, pluralism, and protection of minorities in Poland.

One of the Ombudsman's responsibilities was to engage in national cases submitted with preliminary questions to the Court of Justice of the European Union, providing arguments for protecting the independence of judges. These opinions were often referenced by spokesman Tanchev, with the "Miasto Łowicz" case being the sole loss. Lawyer 8 explained, "It was a lose–lose case due to the lack of an EU element," but we aimed to alter the CJEU's approach to the issue, raising its profile to prompt meaningful commentary that judges could adhere to. "In this way, thanks to the CJEU, we developed standards of independence of judges, showed the full picture of the situation in Poland and were able to point out shortcomings and lies on the part of the government. The Ombudsman was the only entity that could speak on behalf of judges during hearings before the CJEU."

Furthermore, the Ombudsman inspired attorneys and judges on the direction to pursue. A significant task involved submitting amicus curiae briefs to the European Court of Human Rights, enabling participation in hearings such as the Grzęda v. Poland case. Consequently, the Ombudsman contributed to shaping CJEU and ECHR standards regarding the rule of law. In disciplinary or criminal proceedings, the Ombudsman couldn't intervene directly but monitored state authorities' actions, providing vital insights into the realities faced by judges in Poland. This comprehensive approach allowed the Ombudsman to present a nuanced picture to the CJEU, underscoring the importance of these details in understanding the broader context.

Lawyer 8 emphasized that although the Ombudsman couldn't directly intervene in disciplinary or criminal proceedings, monitoring the actions of state authorities allowed him to provide crucial insights into the realities faced by judges in Poland. This comprehensive approach enabled the Ombudsman to present a nuanced picture to the CJEU, emphasizing the importance of these details in understanding the broader context.

On April 22, 2021, Ombudsman Adam Bodnar actively participated in a protest supporting Judge Tuleya, who faced the possibility of having his immunity waived. During the protest, Bodnar expressed his concerns, stating, "The Disciplinary Chamber in an EU member state that calls itself a law-abiding state decides whether a judge is to be led away in handcuffs. This is what the whole procedure boils down to. This is a shame for our country. I am very glad that citizens are defending the judge. That they are with him and were there yesterday, and were there many times earlier, when previous proceedings regarding the lifting of immunity were held" (Biuletyn Informacji 2021).

# Chapter 5. Impact of Judicial Resistance

Had it not been for the resistance, the ruling party would have successfully implemented their undemocratic agenda. Instead, in July 2017, the judges' resistance led the Polish president to veto the bills concerning the National Council of the Judiciary and the Supreme Court. Their resistance delayed the unconstitutional changes that would have undermined judicial independence (President 2017). As Judge 5 shared in their first interview:

> *Had it not been for the resistance, the judiciary would have been subordinated to the executive a long time ago. Had it not been for the wave of protests, President Duda would have signed the law on the Supreme Court, which would have been taken over as early as July 2017.*

## Polish Resistance Became a European Concern

The judges' resistance also reached European institutions. As their resistance became more resolute and earned the support of citizens, it made Europe more involved in Polish affairs. European lawyers and politicians began to follow what was happening in the country. Judge 22 shared, "All European and global legal organizations support us, and they have no doubts whose side is right."

The judges' actions made the defense of the rule of law not merely a national but a European issue. The judges understood that it was important to make Europe aware that by defending the rule of law in Poland, they were also defending it in their own countries. "What is happening in Poland can also happen in other countries" (Judge 22).

The resistance—its legal creativity as well as its public nature—elevated the matter to the international level. The European courts became actively engaged in defending the resistance efforts. Judge 1 shared, "The government is currently under pressure from the European Parliament. The rulings of international courts have had great influence." As Judge 5 said:

> *From the outset, we aimed our actions at publicizing these changes abroad. From 2017, we went on regular study visits to Brussels and prepared numerous reports in English informing the public abroad about what is happening in Poland. The European Union could not pretend they were not seeing it. Having it so plainly showed on a plate along with the media coverage—this constituted the real pressure force.*

As a result of the domestic judiciary resistance that reached out the European court, Judge 4 shared, *the status of the Disciplinary Chamber created by the ruling party was successfully undermined. The issue of the National Council of the Judiciary has become an international matter. All CJEU judges know the subject of the NCJ. There are appeals—this issue lives on in the European Parliament and in the forum of the European Commission.*

More precisely, the requests for the preliminary rulings by the resisting judges paved the way for the CJEU and ECHR to question the status of the Disciplinary Chamber, the NCJ, and the neo-judges. After the CJEU judgments, the Polish Supreme Court judges returned to adjudication. Judge 2 shared: "The great victory of Iustitia was that after the termination of the term of office was quashed [by the government], judges Gersdorf, Iwulski, Zawistowski, and many other judges of the Supreme Court returned and adjudicated."

"The most important questions for a preliminary ruling—which, paradoxically, had the greatest effect—came from my chamber," said Judge 25.

*It turned out that the submitted questions for a preliminary ruling, which have consequences in the form of judgments, are more important than statements and appeals. I do not underestimate what the judges do in their speeches, but the real effect is CJEU and ECHR judgments. The CJEU ruled that the Disciplinary Chamber is not a court. Greater effectiveness cannot be imagined. In the case of* Xeroflor w Polsce sp.z o.o. v. Poland, *the ECHR found that the quasi-judge leads the judgment to be invalid due to the composition of the bench.*

As Lawyer 8 shared, "The questions referred for a preliminary ruling by the Polish courts to the European ones keep getting better." As a result of Poland's judicial resistance, the judgments of the CJEU and the ECHR slowly accumulated and pushed the current rulers into defense. Lawyer 3 said, "We won. We have the backing and rulings of the ECHR, the CJEU. Even though we are still far from making real changes we now have adequate legal instruments to win."

Furthermore, the Polish case helped the CJEU and ECHR develop a standard for understanding the term "independent *court*." This is an achievement not only for Poland—populism can develop in any country. This resistance established the idea that the court must be treated as a fundamental guarantee against authoritarianism. "Today, despite the passage of many years, unlawfulness has been tamed to some extent, but not defeated" (Judge 27).

Polish judicial resistance became a European matter, and Polish judges became European judges. They understood that they must be independent to implement European law. As President of the Criminal Chamber in the Supreme Court Michał Laskowski said, "We feel like European judges, we know the judgments of the Luxembourg and Strasbourg courts. We adjudicate in accordance with the standards expressed in these judgments" (Ivanova 2021)

63

## Judges Engaged Citizens

Resistance changed the common understanding of the connection between judge and citizen. "When I travel around the places where there are courts, I introduce local judges to the local community: 'They are your judges.' We must be close to people, closer than any other authority. This is our social legitimacy. Now we need to document our legitimacy through the support of the people," said Judge 2, adding:

> We realized very quickly that we had to go beyond certain patterns and change the way we as judges communicate with society. The authorities wanted to gradually isolate the courts from the people and break up the judges themselves. It was necessary to get closer to people through various forms: PolAndRock Festival, Opener Festival, Academy of Fine Arts, meetings at the Legal Education Foundation, meetings at book fairs.

By engaging ordinary citizens, the movement raised awareness of constitutional rights, the right to protest, direct application of the constitution, EU law, and human rights standards. People now consider it important to go to demonstrations, and they are aware of their constitutional right to do so (Judge 4).

The crisis of the rule of law has resulted in increased interest in EU law. Courts could not wait for the CJEU to suspend something and began suspending the application of the undemocratic law themselves (Lawyer 8).

## Politicians Learned What Was at Stake

Another impact of the resistance movement is that politicians came to understand the gravity of the situation. Judge 2 shared, "I warned them about the consequences, and I managed to convince them. It is our duty to fight for the rule of law and speak out about it. I cannot imagine ignoring the world of politics." Judge 1 agreed, saying, "The resistance made the opposition aware of the importance of the rule of law, and they took it on their banners." In 2023, because of the resistance, the democratic opposition joined forces and won the parliamentary elections, forming a new government.

At the political level, a conditionality mechanism was established. The EU managed to connect monetary payouts to rule-of-law reforms, prompting EU countries to carry out the bloc's recommendations. In this way, €36 billion in frozen EU post-pandemic cash was blocked, leading the PiS government to attempt amending existing laws in order to unblock it.

"For the Polish government, the resistance of judges might not mean much, but the fact that the Disciplinary Chamber does not waive the immunity of Judge Wróbel—that Judge Morawiec is reinstated—this is all due to the resistance of citizens and the European Union," said Lawyer 2, continuing:

*Zbigniew Ziobro's forces weakened. He wanted to flatten the judiciary structure, but he cannot because the government is now in a crisis. This resistance manages to inhibit certain government antidemocratic actions. Resistance also works on people, especially when they see judges putting their professional lives at risk. We have a new partner in the entire human rights defensive pact in Poland in the form of the judiciary. It is a good ally. It has never been the case before that so many joint meetings and conferences took place involving different legal professions, and especially judges.*

## The Legal Profession Came Together

This resistance also changed the relationship of judges to lawyers and prosecutors. "Earlier, our relations were accompanied by distance and distrust," said Judge 4. "Now we have a shared commitment and trust established between resisting judges, and lawyers and prosecutors that support them. There has been a feedback loop for these professions."

The shared commitment and greater communication among legal professionals allowed for coordinated efforts against executive overreach. As Judge 5 reported in their first interview, "Since the summer of 2018, competitions conducted by the neo-NCJ have been virtually blocked for 1.5 years. General assemblies of the courts passed resolutions refusing to issue an opinion. It was a legal form of resistance. Only the muzzle act prohibited the adoption of resolutions critical of the National Council of the Judiciary or the Disciplinary Chamber."

## Judicial Resistance Pierced the Opponent

Resistance helped bring loyalty shifts inside the judiciary. A tangible success can be seen in decisions of the disciplinary spokespersons who could have been the legal henchmen of Minister of Justice Zbigniew Ziobro but instead chose to defend the prosecuted judges. Minister Ziobro wanted to prosecute Judge Gąciarek for organizing a demonstration in defense of Judge Igor Tuleya under the National Prosecutor's Office. The minister also wanted to discipline judges from Krakow—Maciej Czajka and Dariusz Mazur for putting up posters in the court in defense of the independence of the courts and in support of the prosecuted Judge Paweł Juszczyszyn. Disciplinary spokespersons operating at the courts of appeal have refused to institute disciplinary proceedings against them. They found that judges could protest and organize demonstrations to defend the independence of the judiciary. Disciplinary Spokesman Janusz Szarek, who is dealing with the case of Judges Czajka and Mazur, indicated that they spoke out on fundamental issues in which they have freedom of expression. He stressed that judges may speak in public to "protect the public and social interest in the protection of the independence of courts and judges, and the principle of separation of powers" (Jałoszewski 2020). In turn, in the case of Judge Gąciarek, Disciplinary Spokesman Rafał Kaniok, in his decision to discontinue, emphasized that the demonstration was in defense of the constitutional independence of the courts. "Therefore, the judge who organized such a demonstration cannot be effectively credited with committing a disciplinary tort consisting in conducting social activity contrary to the principles of the independence of courts and judges." Kaniok concluded Gąciarek did not break the judges' code of ethics (Jałoszewski 2022). The president of the court appealed the decision of the disciplinary commissioner to the disciplinary court. As of this writing, the case is still pending (Rzeczpospolita 2022).

In July 2021, neo-judges signed the appeal to respect EU law in Poland and to execute Court of Justice judgments. This letter was also signed by officials appointed by the neo-NCJ. As Judge 23 shared, "These people signed up, meaning that somewhere there are a whole lot of people who hesitate. Everyone has the right to become wise."

When Judge Iwulski was suspended by the Disciplinary Chamber and his immunity was waved, the resistence actions even led regime supporters to act in his favor. "The neo-judges in the Supreme Court wanted to sign the letter of support for Judge Iwulski, but they were not allowed to do so. You can see that they are starting to be afraid," said Judge 1.

In another success story, the resistance led to the discontinuation of criminal proceedings against one of the repressed judges, Beata Morawiec, who, after having been suspended for around 240 days with a 50 percent pay cut, came back to work with full pay (Bździkot 2021).

The most significant recent development of the resistance is the quashing of the suspension of Judges Igor Tuleya and Paweł Juszczyszyn and their return to work, as well as the liquidation of the Disciplinary Chamber of the Supreme Court. The erstwhile Disciplinary Chamber was replaced by the Professional Liability Chamber at the Supreme Court. Nevertheless, work is underway to transfer the disciplinary jurisdiction of judges to the Supreme Administrative Court. Other judges such as Piotr Gąciarek and Joanna Hetnarowicz-Sikora also returned to work after their suspension.

Another success is that Judge Andrzej Cichocki from the Gliwice Regional Court—one of the judges accused by the media of inspiring and organizing hate against judges opposing the authorities—eventually admitted that "the hate campaign took place" against resisting judges, and that he could not keep silent anymore. "I have enough, I have to live with it, so I want to at least tell you about it," Judge Cichocki said during an interview with the opposition media (Ivanova 2021).

Neo-judge Joanna Przanowska-Tomaszek became president of the Warsaw Regional Court after former president and Chief Disciplinary Spokesman Piotr Schab became president of the Warsaw Court of Appeal. Before she took over her duties, Piotr Schab had blocked the return of Igor Tuleya to work. However, Judge Przanowska-Tomaszek restored Tuleya to work, executing the judgment of the court that ordered his return.

President of the Supreme Court and neo-judge Małgorzata Manowska also protested the repression against two judges of the Warsaw Court of Appeal. In her letter to Piotr Schab, she appealed to rethink and revoke the decision of the Deputy President of the Court of Appeal in Warsaw regarding the transfer of Judges Ewa Leszczyńska-Furtak and Ewa Gregajtys from the 2nd Criminal Division to the 3rd Labor and Social Security Division. She wrote, "I believe that the transfer of experienced judges, especially at the level of the appellate court, harms citizens, parties to proceedings.... The above staffing decision leads to a righteous protest from the judiciary community" (Jałoszewski 2022).

Ultimately, the ruling party seems to sense defeat in their campaign against the judges. As Lawyer 7 shared:

*Resistance lasts so long because we resisted with legal instruments. We waited until the European institutions reacted. Nothing happens in a vacuum. Consistent resistance—including journalism, public statements, lawyers' trips to music festivals—each of these drops seen separately also led to a situation where we also managed to cause some kind of reflection not among the rulers themselves but in their electorate.*

*I follow the internet forums that supported the so-called reform of the judiciary by Minister Zbigniew Ziobro, and I must say that we can observe the effect of bitterness, the effect of frustration. I don't see some in-depth reflection, but these people have felt or have a sense of defeat and failure. This is quite important in the overall social dimension. At the moment, we can live with a feeling of—I am not sure whether it is a victory—but a feeling of satisfaction with a job well done. As long as we ensure the peaceful nature of the resistance, the sky is the limit.*

# Chapter 6. Catalog of Judicial Resistance Actions

In this chapter, the analysis of judicial resistance was conducted using Michael A. Beer's (2021) categorization of civil resistance actions. Polish judicial resistance was examined across various sections, including acts of expression (using the human body, engaging in material arts, employing digital technology, and using human language), acts of omission (such as political/judicial non-cooperation and social non-cooperation), and acts of commission (including political/judicial disruptive intervention, political/judicial creative intervention, economic creative intervention, social creative intervention, and psychological creative intervention). This approach not only highlights the creativity demonstrated by judges and lawyers but also underscores the multifaceted nature of judicial resistance in Poland.

## Acts of Expression

Becoming people's judges engaged with the public has been a conscious and deliberate shift in response to the authoritarian threat. In doing so, judges have employed various tactical choices classified as "acts of expression." These are the actions that require "saying" and

**FIGURE 3.** Polish lawyers support the judges during the March of 1,000 Gowns. One lawyer holds the Polish Constitution.

*Source: Paweł Rochowicz.*

can be divided between confrontational acts that protest and constructive acts that appeal or persuade.

Before the emergence of the resistance, Polish judges were known for their adherence to court decorum and a reserved public presence. They often relied on established legal scholars and retired practitioners like Ewa Łętowska, Andrzej Rzepliński, Adam Strzembosz, and Irena Kamińska to speak on their behalf. As of 2012, Iustitia questioned whether to even be on Twitter, and in apprenticeship classes, judges were instructed that simple public actions like eating ice cream were discouraged (Judge 9). Judges were taught to communicate exclusively through court sentences (Judge 14). But this was about to change.

News media became an important avenue for the judges' messaging. With the populist attack on the judiciary, resisting judges recognized the importance of their outreach and cooperation with the media to advance their goals. According to Judge 4, "I learned to live with journalists. We communicate information in a thoughtful way. We have developed rules of cooperation. I know how to deal with them, how to inform them. *The Washington Post* quoted me. It's impressive." Judge 8 shared:

*A lot of judges went out to people, got involved in educational campaigns—what is important is the message, explaining the verdict, understanding how the media work.... There was a need for a press spokesman that works at Iustitia to immediately report on the controversial verdicts. More and more people are realizing the importance of information policy.*

### TABLE 1.  Judges' Tactics Using Actions of Expression

| Resistance Behavior | NATURE OF TACTIC INDUCEMENTS | |
| --- | --- | --- |
| | **CONFRONTATIONAL (COERCIVE)** | **CONSTRUCTIVE (PERSUASIVE)** |
| **Acts of Expression (Saying)** | Protest<br>Communicative action to criticize or coerce | Appeal<br>Communicative actions to inform or persuade |

*Source: Beer 2021*

## 1.  Acts of Expression Using the Medium of Human Body

### 1.1   *March of 1000 Gowns*

On January 11, 2020, judges, prosecutors, and lawyers from 26 European countries united in a show of solidarity with Polish judges resisting the authoritarian control over the judiciary. In Warsaw, they marched in their robes, accompanied by enthusiastic applause from the local residents. Participating judges came from countries including Austria, Croatia, Denmark,

**FIGURE 4.** On the eve before Igor Tuleya's hearing regarding the possible waiver of his immunity, demonstrators hold letters spelling "Murem za Igorem," "Standing behind Igor."

*Source: Paweł Rochowicz.*

Estonia, Greece, Hungary, Italy, the Netherlands, Ireland, Germany, Norway, Portugal, and Romania. This demonstration attracted around 15,000 participants and enjoyed the support of other legal professionals such as prosecutors and attorneys.

The march started at 3 p.m. on Krasiński Square next to the Supreme Court building. The planned route included a march along the following streets: Miodowa, Krakowskie Przedmieście, Nowy Świat on pl. Trzech Krzyży, then along Wiejska Street in front of the Polish Parliament. The march bore the slogan: "The right to independence. The right to Europe." A prominent motive behind the March of 1000 Gowns was the enactment of the Muzzle law, which introduced disciplinary consequences for judges whose actions might hinder judiciary operations, question judge appointments, or for "public activities incompatible with the principles of independence of courts and judges."

Upon reaching the Presidential Palace, the march came to a halt, and judge Waldemar Żurek read out an appeal addressed to President Andrzej Duda. The appeal urged the president to embrace independent politics and highlighted that the Muzzle law would perpetually relegate judges to mere clerical roles (Lisowski 2020; Adamski and Łukaszewicz 2020).

Initially, expectations for the march's turnout were modest. "When we were organizing this march, the first president of the Supreme Court, Małgorzata Gersdorf said: say at least 200 people will come," mentioned Judge 2. However, the event exceeded expectations as

70

**FIGURE 5.** Cracow judges calling the entrance into force of the muzzle act as the Black Friday for the European judiciary

all legal professions—including judges, prosecutors, attorneys-at-law, and legal advisers—rallied together, alongside colleagues from other European countries. Judge 1 reflected:

> *It was an amazing event, a show of solidarity between Polish judges, prosecutors, lawyers, and legal representatives from other countries. It was a great staging of a historic march. It was an absolutely amazing moment, raising awareness about the necessity to defend the democratic rule of law and solidarity among legal professionals in the country and abroad in the common struggle against authoritarianism.*

Initially, "Supreme Court judges did not want to wear gowns. They were afraid. They needed 3 minutes to get into the atmosphere to put on these togas," Judge 2 revealed. Despite this initial hesitation, the march was eventually attended by notable figures including the First President of the Supreme Court, Małgorzata Gersdorf (although she did not wear the gown), and the spokesman of the Supreme Court, Judge Michał Laskowski.

Efforts were made to prevent judges from wearing their gowns during the March. The president of the Elbląg District Court, Agnieszka Walkowiak, instructed that the gowns be placed in storage, to be returned to the judges after the weekend (Interia 2020). However, some judges were resolute in their decision to march in their gowns, with Judge 22 mentioning, "I had no hesitation at all to march in a gown. Probably because this march was another kind of protest that was organized by lawyers."

Not all judge agreed with the street protests. For example, Judge 27 noted:

*I am aware that I will have to adjudicate. Often these demonstrations are political. There are demands on who should take power or lose it. The judge should not so much exercise moderation as think about what will be adjudicated in the future. The subject of protection is the administration of justice, something I do. I did not take part in the thousand-gown march because I would have protested in my own case.*

Though some judges were opposed to these marches, it is noteworthy that Supreme Court justices participated in the March of 1,000 Gowns and the street protests.

### 1.2 To stand with letters forming names of the prosecuted judges

Judges show solidarity by forming letters to spell the name of the targeted judge, symbolizing their support and unity. These letters are displayed prominently, either held by judges or placed on court windows, as a visible sign of solidarity and resistance.

### 1.3 Black Friday protest in front of the Krakow court

Judges in Krakow organized a protest against the "Muzzle law" on February 14, 2020, referred to as "Black Friday for the European Judiciary." They gathered with posters questioning the legality of judicial appointments by the pseudo-NCJ and the neo-judges on the Supreme Court. This protest was in response to the newly enacted law, which granted the power to remove or relocate judges and prosecutors based on compliance with European Court of Justice judgments. The law also allowed for the prosecution of judges and prosecutors for actions seen as obstructing the judiciary's functioning or challenging appointments. Spontaneous demonstrations supporting targeted judges also took place outside the court building.

### 1.4 Attending disciplinary proceedings related to repressed judges and adjudication of neo-judges

Judges demonstrated their solidarity with their repressed colleagues by attending disciplinary hearings initiated against independent judges. For instance, during the trial of Paweł Juszczyszyn, approximately 20 judges were present to show support (Judge 4). In Łódź, judges attended a disciplinary court hearing wearing T-shirts bearing the word "Constitution" (Judge 3).

"I didn't anticipate my colleagues attending all the hearings and standing up for me in the disciplinary proceedings," remarked Judge 24, who was facing prosecution. Judge 8 added, "Solidarity means that I sense the backing of the community. Numerous individuals turned up for a disciplinary case in Wrocław, which is heartening. The most disheartening

**FIGURE 6.** "Today Tuleya, Tomorrow You" action on June 8, 2020, in 150 cities against the possible waiver of immunity for Igor Tuleya (the hearing before the Disciplinary Chamber was scheduled for the following day).

Source: ruchkod.pl

thing would be to be left unnoticed." Beyond fellow judges, members of organizations like KOD and Obywatele RP also participated in the hearings, frequently gathering outside the Supreme Court during these proceedings.

By attending the hearings, the judges effectively remove the anonymity of the repression apparatus. Judge 17 noted, "We witness when the repressive apparatus sign their statements, they take responsibility for it. Our presence allows us to be witnesses and call it as it is—evil."

Moreover, the judges held media briefings following their attendance at disciplinary hearings against their colleagues. They not only supported their colleagues in court but also highlighted their struggles to the public (Judge 25).

When the disciplinary spokesman Radzik was assigned by the Minister of Justice to preside as a judge at the Regional Court in Warsaw, judges from the capital attended his initial hearings. This was due to their disapproval of Judge Radzik's assignment to the court by the Minister of Justice. The General Assembly of the Regional Court in Warsaw passed a resolution opposing

Radzik and Lasota's ruling. Judge 4 shared: "Eleven judges went to watch the hearing. The cases were trivial and Radzik was lost in simple judgments. It was scary because he would adjudicate in complicated cases concerning murder as an appellate judge."

### 1.5   Running in solidarity with repressed judges

In a show of solidarity, one judge decided to run on behalf of the repressed judges. This decision was communicated through social media, initially intended as a tribute to Beata Morawiec, Igor Tuleya, and Paweł Juszczyszyn. Unexpectedly, others began to express interest in joining the running protest as well (Szczygielska-Jakubowska 2020). T-shirts dedicated to Igor Tuleya were even created to support the cause. This act of support evolved from nothing into a significant movement. Engaging in these daily activities serves as a positive influence on the repressed judges. Their situation is not easy, with many days spent without being able to make judgments. Such actions help them feel connected, reminding them that there are people who care and are committed to reversing the negative consequences of these actions (Judge 12).

### 1.6   Gathering of judges in front of the Supreme Courts during indictment

During indictments, judges started gathering in front of the courts. However, they were cautious about terming it a strike or a protest. Krzysztof Zawała, the spokesman of the Katowice Regional Court, emphasized, "In no case should this meeting be equated with a protest. The meeting was convened in accordance with the law." In the Warsaw Regional Court, the meeting lasted around 40 minutes. This work stoppage received backing from pickets organized by the KOD, which took place in various locations including Warsaw and Gdańsk (Polsat News 2017).

The second instance of judges gathering during ongoing court proceedings occurred on June 9, 2020. Prior to this, members of Iustitia urged a halt to hearings on that day when the

FIGURE 7. Cracow judges protesting on the stairs of the Cracow District Court

Disciplinary Chamber was reviewing the request to lift judge Igor Tuleya's immunity. The call was to pause proceedings at 9:00 AM for 30 minutes in solidarity with Tuleya, who faced indictment due to a ruling. Iustitia also urged judges not involved in hearings that day to assemble outside the Supreme Court building. This work stoppage was accompanied by protests in 150 cities, each limited to 150 participants, under the banner "150x150, Today Tuleya, Tomorrow You" (Niezależna.pl 2024).

FIGURE 8. Demonstrators wear shirts that read "Konstytucja" (Constitution).

*Source: Twitter.com / MicWawrykiewicz*

## 2. Acts of Expression Using Medium of Material Arts

### 2.1 Konstytucja T-shirts

Independent judges who resisted cooperating with Zbigniew Ziobro's Ministry of Justice began wearing T-shirts bearing the word "KonsTYtucJA" ("Constitution"), emphasizing the Polish words *ty* ("you") and *ja* ("I"), signifying the importance of the Polish constitution for everyone. In 2018, on the occasion of Poland's 100th independence anniversary, judges took a group photo while wearing these T-shirts.

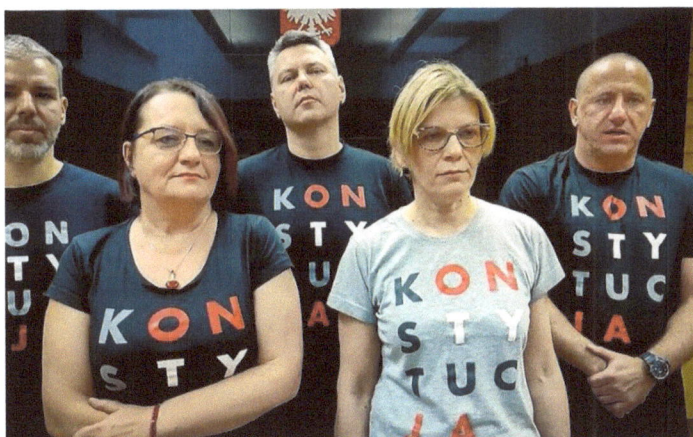

FIGURE 9. Judges Katarzyna Wesołowska-Zbudniewek, Ewa Maciejewska, Krzysztof Kacprzak, Paweł Maciejewski i Grzegorz Gała

*Source: YouTube*

In December 2018, the newly constituted National Council of the Judiciary, largely composed of judges aligned with the government, issued a resolution asserting that the "use by a judge of infographics, symbols that are or can be unequivocally identified with political parties, trade unions, and social movements, created by trade unions, political parties or other organizations engaged in political activity [is] behavior that may undermine the trust in the independence and impartiality of a judge" (Woźnicki 2018). In defiance of this directive, judges participating in the Civil Rights Congress in Warsaw in 2019 responded by taking a photo while wearing T-shirts spelling "Konstytucja."

On November 23, 2018, Judge Dorota Lutostańska of the Regional Court in Olsztyn upheld a decision to acquit individuals who had displayed T-shirts with the inscription "Konstytucja, Jędrek" on sculptures, "Jędre" being a nickname for Jarosław Kaczyński, the de facto leader of the ruling party. The judgment emphasized the lack of societal harm and the expression of views connected to constitutional values.

FIGURE 10. Judge Lutostańska and other judges from Olsztyn posing in the Konstytucja T-shirts.

Deputy Disciplinary Spokesman Michał Lasota called on Judge Lutostańska to explain her failure to withdraw from the proceedings, suggesting doubts about her impartiality. The General Assembly of Judges of the Olsztyn District expressed disapproval of the deputy spokesman's actions, asserting that the issue concerned judicial independence. Despite this, disciplinary proceedings were initiated against Judge Lutostańska, under the assertion that the "Constitution" inscriptions were linked to a political movement.

However, on October 2, 2020, the Disciplinary Court at the Court of Appeal in Łódź halted the proceedings, determining that Deputy Disciplinary Spokesman Michał Lasota lacked the legal standing to initiate them. During the hearing, judges from Łódź appeared in T-shirts with the inscription "KonsTYtucJA" (Jałoszewski 2019).

It is notable that two weeks after her ruling, Judge Dorota Lutostańska, along with other judges from Olsztyn, posed for a photo wearing KonsTYtucJA T-shirts on Poland's 100th anniversary, in clear defiance of the government intimidation tactics.

### 2.2 Hanging up posters in the courts

Despite prohibitions based on court rules, independent judges took a bold step by hanging up posters in the courts. In December 2020, Kraków judges placed 70 posters within the Kraków court premises. These posters conveyed five demands outlined by judges'

**FIGURE 11.** Poster action in courts and the city
(freedom for Polish judges, crowned eagle with the judge's chain, with judicial oath).

associations, including Iustitia, Themis, Association of Family Law Judges in Poland, and Association of Family Law Judges Pro Familia:

1. Immediate reinstatement of Judge Paweł Juszczyszyn.

2. Appointment of a non-political NCJ.

3. Dissolution of the Disciplinary Chamber of the Supreme Court and removal of disciplinary spokesmen Piotr Schab, Michał Lasota, and Przemysław Radzik.

4. Guaranteeing citizens' right to an independent court in cases involving neo-NCJ participation in nomination procedures.

5. Upholding and enforcing judgments from Polish and European courts, including the CJEU's ruling from November 19, 2019.

FIGURE 12. Poster: Stop the persecution of judges with images of the three suspended judges. A 7x1.5m banner was created from this poster.

As Judge 5 emphasized, "Posters are our specialty. The first resolution, which we adopted on December 4, 2017, was published on the files. We have printed 10,000 of them. There was also an English version."

### 2.3 Decorating symbolic Christmas Tree in the courthouses

Since 2018, judges in Krakow have been adorning the court building's Christmas tree with symbolic ornaments, each year featuring a distinct theme such as the constitution, the European Union, and equality. This unconventional action aims to test the boundaries of court authorities' reactions. Judge 17 explained, "It must be a little provocative. The point is to spoil the well-being of the representatives of 'good change' by letting them know that it is not as good as they think it is."

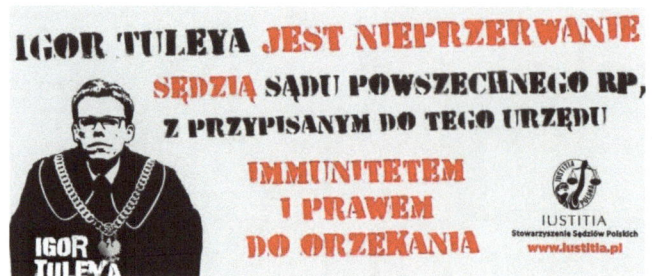

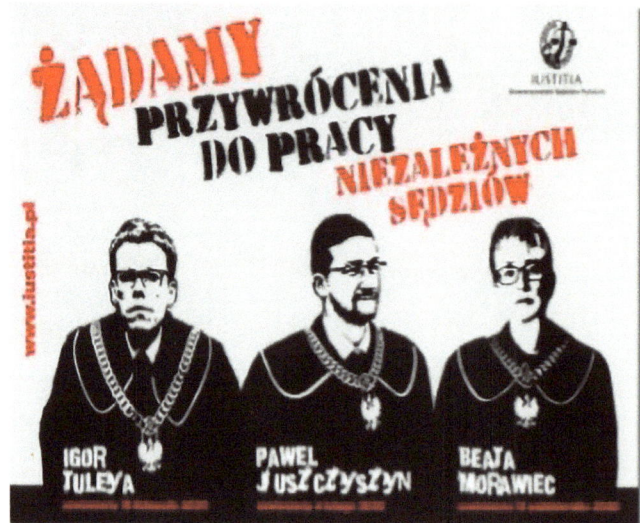

## 2.4 Distributing and placing stickers and nametags

Distributing and placing stickers (with faces of repressed judges like Igor Tuleya, Paweł Juszczyszyn, Beata Morawiec, free courts, firmly behind Tuleyą, firmly behind Zurek).

## 2.5 Placing stickers on court windows

Judges stuck these letters on the windows of the courts. For example, for two days in December 2020, Krakow judges, in solidarity with repressed Igor Tuleya hung up posters in

FIGURE 13. Demonstrators hold signs reading "Igor Tulema, will never walk alone" in Polish.

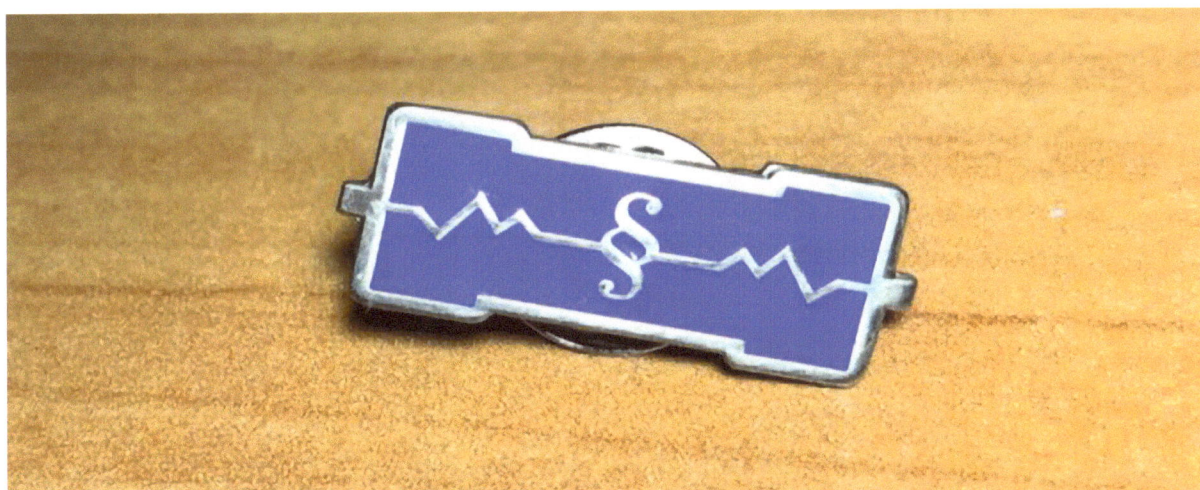

FIGURE 14. The Resister Judge badge references the solidarity traditions. The color matches the edge of the judge's gown while the symbol signifies "the law is still alive." There were also versions for lawyers and prosecutors.

the court in his defense. Posters appeared in the corridor, in judges' offices and in the court-house windows. The court authorities, on behalf of Minister Ziobro, ordered the posters to be removed, but the judges immediately hung new ones. They were also hung in the court's windows—the slogan "Wall behind Igor" could be seen from the street—and even on the door in the corridor in front of the office of the president of the District Court in Krakow, Dagmara Pawełczyk-Woicka, a nominee of Minister Ziobro and a member of the new National Council of the Judiciary (Jałoszewski 2020).

Resisting judges placed their name tags on their bench during official proceedings with a resistance sticker—for example, "Murem za Tuleją" "We stand (like a wall) behind Tuleya."

### 2.6 Shaming candidates to NCJ

The candidates for the National Council of the Judiciary (NCJ) were publicly exposed by AD on billboards, a move financed through crowdfunding. This strategy aimed to publicly shame the candidates participating in an illegitimate judicial body captured by the ruling party.

## 3. Acts of Expression Using the Medium of Digital Technology

### 3.1 Resistance through writings: Anonymous Judge's blog

Beginning in 2017, an anonymous judge blogger began publishing posts on the site: **judge2017.home.blog/**. The blogger introduced themselves as a judge "with more than a dozen years of experience, a member of a privileged caste according to some, and a living communist fossil according to others." They expressed a sincere belief in the profound significance of the separation of powers, the crucial nature of judicial independence, and the supremacy of the Constitution of the Republic of Poland (Judge 2017).

On the blog, the author critically and satirically examines the role of disciplinary spokesmen who act as prosecutors in the disciplinary court. In one blog post, the author outlined various methods employed by the Department of Internal Affairs of the National Public Prosecutor's Office against judges who resist, including:

1. **Spokesman Method:** This involves requesting files or their copies just before a session crucial for the prosecutor's office.

2. **Suspension Deterrence Method:** Suspending judges under the pretext that they lack the ability to issue appropriate rulings.

3. **Questioning Method:** Conducting extensive interrogations of all judges who have issued decisions inconsistent with certain views or expectations.

The article concluded with a humorous anthem in the Russian language, comparing the prosecutors to their Russian counterparts serving an anti-democratic state at the behest of the autocrat (Judge 2020).

The anonymous judge has written about specific resistance actions like the Chain of Lights, the prosecutor's actions, judges working for the Ministry of Justice, the resistance by and solidarity with the Krakow judges, educational meetings with high school pupils at the court, kamikaze actions, actions in defense of the Supreme Court, ostracism in the courts, and refusal to give opinions on candidates for competitions conducted by the neo-NCJ.

Invoking Winston Churchill's famous speech, the judge wrote: "We shall defend the Constitution. We shall defend the independence of courts. We shall defend our own independence. We shall defend our common right to free judiciary, fair and independent from politicians. We shall defend these values each day, in the courtrooms, during peaceful demonstrations, in public debate, in resolutions and appeals. Not only shall we defend these values in our work—we will defend them far beyond. We shall defend the Constitution and its enshrined values despite the threat of further repressions and harassment. We shall defend the Constitution notwithstanding the price" (2018d).

### 3.2 Podcasts

Iustitia established the Foundation of Legal Education, which operates a website and maintains a Facebook profile. The website serves as a platform offering educational resources for conducting classes. Notably, the foundation's members were invited to Reset Obywatelski, an internet radio station, to host a broadcast titled "Prawoteka" (a portmanteau of the Polish words for "law" and "library"), focusing on legal education and the engagement of young people online, coinciding with the Legal Education Day. The broadcast's success led to a weekly one-hour program hosted by judges from the foundation. The program covers a wide range of topics, including hate speech, domestic violence, the coup anniversary in Turkey, the PolAndRock festival, and insights into judges' lives beyond the courtroom.

### 3.3 "The Rule of Law—a Common Cause" YouTube videos

On Justice Day, May 23, 2022, Iustitia introduced a nationwide initiative titled "The Rule of Law: A Common Cause" ("Rządy Prawa Wspólna Sprawa"). Notably, Judge Anna Maria Wesołowska, known for her involvement in a popular Polish TV show centered on criminal hearings, played a prominent role. Through periodic YouTube videos and podcasts, Judge Wesołowska discussed common court cases that pique the interest of the Polish populace, such as loans in Swiss francs, payday loans, crafting last wills, and the legal implications of drinking and driving. The overarching objective was to simplify and explain how legal mechanisms function in everyday life. Five videos were released on Iustitia's YouTube channel, with view counts for these videos ranged from 115 to 600 (SSP YouTube). "The aim of the project is to promote the idea that the rule of law is everyone's business," said Judge 2.

> *We especially want this belief to grow among people who are less active in this field—young people, people from small and medium-sized towns in Eastern Poland. It will be important to listen to them and to develop a model of the Polish judiciary in the future. We want to hear the Poles.*

In addition to the video podcasts with Judge Wesołowska, the program includes national competitions with prizes, workshops and debates during major festivals, local picnics, and meetings, and emerging local clubs bearing the project name (SSP Facebook 2022). It was financed through a grant awarded to Iustitia by the Active Citizens' Fund by Iceland, Liechtenstein and Norway under the EEA and Norwegian funds.

### 3.4 Social media and messaging apps

Social media platforms are a common avenue for the judges to communicate with the public and each other. Certain judges manage Iustitia's social media efforts by writing or selecting posts, sharing reports, and designing graphics. Iustitia's Facebook page has over 50,000 likes and is worth more than one million zlotys (Judge 23). Judge 18 shared, "Our strength lies in the fact that we are credible, that we will not release any information if we are not 100 percent sure of the fact."

On Facebook, there are several pages in support of or led by resisting judges—including "Krakowscy sędziowie" ("Krakow Judges"), "Sędziowie łódzcy" ("Lodz Judges")—where one can find reports and announcements of their events. Another page, "Co w prawie piszczy?" (wordplay meaning "What is Happening in Law?"), which is led by the Toruń-Włocławek Branch of Iustitia, promotes legal education and organizes free and open meetings regarding the state of the judiciary. Yet another page, "Ślepym okiem Temidy" ("The Blind Eye of the Themis"), was launched because of the blindness of the Themis as stated by its author, Judge Arkadiusz Krupa from the Łobez District Court. He uses satirical cartoons posted on that page to criticize not only "good change" implemented by the ruling regime in the judiciary but also the judicial environment.

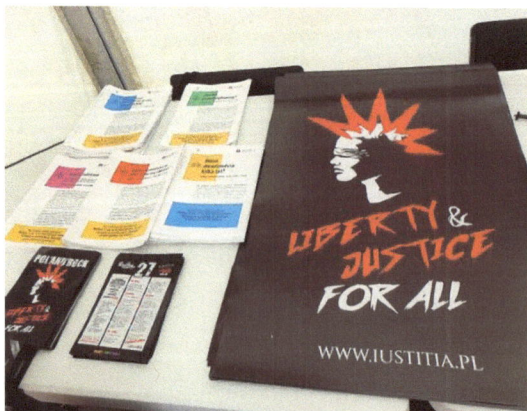

FIGURE 15. Iustitia posters at the PolAndRock Festival.

Judge 4 runs a popular personal blog "Okiem sędziego" ("With the Judge's Eye"). They shared, "I used to write a blog for people about the courts. Now I'm targeting the disciplinary spokesmen. These entries reach a wide audience."

Judges also use Twitter to bring attention to the rule-of-law crisis. Judge 11 shared:

*I am active on Twitter under my real name. I found out that I needed to speak. I am very active. I post videos of the sessions of the National Council of the Judiciary, revealing pathologies when grossly incompetent people enter and successful pass competition for judicial posts. Lots of people use this information.*

The independent judges also use social media messaging to communicate quickly with one another. As stressed by Judge 1, "Our communication network is huge. We have several dozen groups on different social medial platforms." These channels help judges and their allies organize resistance, prepare solidarity actions, and share experiences and ideas. Judges remain concerned about government surveillance of their communication. They communicate through Viber, Messenger, WhatsApp, Protonmail, and Signal. Judges also use ordinary email to coordinate. "We send each other photos, scans of decisions, letters from the prosecutor's office," said Judge 1. They also share newspapers, posters, promotional items, pens, conference invitations, and news about casual gatherings (Judge 16).

The judges appreciate the speed of communication these messaging apps offer. "Earlier, we met at the District Court in Warsaw to discuss a common position before the assembly. Now, we have groups on WhatsApp," said Judge 4. "One group has 90 people and there is always something going on. Thanks to this, a document issued by the president of the court can cover the whole of Poland in a few minutes."

### 3.5   *Using the government's centralized email system*
Since new authorities centralized the email system, each judge can write to any judge in Poland. The administrator is not able to delete an email from the mailbox by themselves—only the recipient can delete it. This allowed judges to communicate with any other judge, as Judge 17 shared: "I wrote an email to one repressed judge with support thanking me for her courageous attitude in the face of hatred." Though it is not possible to express all opinions in such communication, the judges use the "send to everyone" button to communicate with every other judge in the country at once.

### 4.   Acts of Expression Using the Medium of Human Language
In addition to expressing their concerns through actions and the use of their bodies and symbols, resisting judges have effectively used language against the populist overreach of the executive branch. Through writing and public speaking at festivals or lectures in

classrooms, they have helped raise the popular understanding of the rule-of-law crisis in Poland. As Judge 27 shared:

*We must not avoid public outreach. The essence of the crisis is the lack of information. The crisis around judiciary must be explained to the public. I feel it is my duty to explain. You need to reach people who do not have a well-established view. Explain what the law looks like and what are our reservations.*

"I take the floor very often, writing short texts for the newspaper *Gazeta Prawna*," said Judge 11, adding, "I also appear on TVN24 and directly in the CJEU. I use all possible forms to express myself." Judge 21 added, "I do not consider it appropriate to remain silent, and in public I try to speak in the language of arguments, not judgments."

## 4.1 Resistance through writing

In addition to social media and the internet, resisting judges began using established newspapers and open letters to express their opposition to what was happening to the judiciary.

## 4.2 Open protest letters

In October 2020, Warsaw Regional Court Judge Piotr Gąciarek penned an open letter to Przemysław Radzik, the Deputy Disciplinary Spokesman of the Common Courts, who was nominated by the ruling party. As Deputy Disciplinary Spokesman, Radzik is the one that initiates disciplinary proceedings against the resisting judges. Gąciarek's extraordinary act of public defiance challenged the government's bid to control the independent judiciary. Radzik and fellow spokesman Michał Lasota, with full approval of their boss, Piotr Schab, summoned judges for hearings while depriving them of the right to a lawyer. The judge criticized Radzik's actions against repressed colleagues, referring to those like him as having "lost their judicial ethos in their career and whose service to politicians has been mistaken for serving the state and the law." It was unprecedented that a judge would write under their own name to the newspaper in such a sarcastic way.

The letter defended judges under pressure, asserting that history would remember them for defending the rule of law against political interference. "They will write about those who today have the courage, strength and steadfastness to defend the rule of law, democratic principles, courts and judges against politicians, including the politician who appointed you as the deputy disciplinary officer." He concluded his piece by taking full responsibility for what he wrote including possible disciplinary measures: "I am counting on the fact that after this publication your colleague Michał Lasota or your supervisor Piotr Schab will take harmful actions against me, but I cannot remain silent when the public interest and the safety of all of us are at risk" (Gąciarek 2020).

After the president of the Warsaw Regional Court let Judge Igor Tuleya return to work after suspension, neo-judges Schab and Radzik quashed the decision and again suspended Tuleya. Judge Dariusz Mazur from Themis commented for the Polish daily *Rzeczpospolita* (2022):

> *Piotr Schab and Przemysław Radzik were appointed both as presidents of the Court of Appeal in Warsaw and central disciplinary spokesmen by Minister Ziobro, so it is clear that they use repressions against independent judges on the orders of this politician—it is hard to find a more emphatic example of fallen, politically corrupt and servile judges. To be precise, they no longer act like judges, but like political "triggers", people who walk on the short leash of the power camp.*

Piotr Gąciarek wrote another letter to the press where he demanded Schab execute the Warsaw Praga Regional Court's decision of March 21, 2022, that rejected his early suspension by the disciplinary court and ordered the return of the judge Igor Tuleya back to work. In his public letter, he appealed: "I am writing all this because despite unfavorable circumstances, despite the gradual destruction of the independence of the Polish judiciary, I still hope that Igor Tuleya, a painfully principled and honest judge, courageous and independent in adjudication, will be able to return to work." In post scriptum he underlined that he was assuming responsibility for writing publicly the critical letter against his superiors and concluded: "My name is Piotr Gąciarek and I am responsible for what I do" (SSP Iustitia 2024).

*They will write about those who today have the courage, strength and steadfastness to defend the rule of law.*

Gąciarek also wrote letters in defense of other repressed judges. For example, Judge Maciej Rutkiewicz was suspended by the president of the Elbląg District Court Anna Walkowiak, although according to the interim measure issued by the ECHR he should have been allowed to adjudicate. In his letter, he (2022) stated:

> *By removing Judge Maciej Rutkiewicz from his official duties, with the order of November 9, 2021, you clearly showed that Minister Ziobro was right in his appointments. You acted as befits someone who owes his position to Mr. Zbyszek. That's nice of you. And now, it has all been challenged, criticized, stripped of its majesty of sacrifice and loyalty. It's unfair. I know that you and I, as judges, must stay away from politics, but one thought is bothering me. Can you imagine a world in which Zbigniew Ziobro is no longer the omnipotent minister of justice and the prosecutor general, and those who rule do not rule anymore? Judges should not care about such things, but it seems to me that the*

*minister is an important figure in your professional life and his departure (from the function) could be a source of your sadness or even anxiety.*

Judge Tuleya also wrote a public letter in which he disagreed with the refusal of his motion concerning giving lectures at the Koźmiński University in Warsaw. In his letter dated September 21, 2021, to the deputy president of the Regional Court of Warsaw, Igor Tuleya wrote that he would not respect his decision that "constitutes a further unlawful violation of my fundamental rights and freedoms. You have already forbidden me from publishing columns in the media, thus restricting my right to freedom of speech. You are currently trying to interfere with my rights related to academic research and teaching." He also criticized that so far his academic activity was approved. "Today you claim that my research and teaching activity 'may adversely affect the further work of future graduates of the School of Procedural Law and Kozminski University, who are exposed to ethically unclear behavior already at the training stage.' I can assure you that the young lawyers I have dealt with know how to distinguish right from wrong and are aware that values such as honor and honesty are not for sale.

### 4.3   Letters to an international organization

The Polish judges wrote a letter to OSCE[1] requesting the organization to monitor the Polish presidential election in April 2020. The letter was prepared by judges from Szczecin. Its 612 signatories—all judges—addressed Ambassador Ingibjörg Sólrún Gísladóttir, the head of the OSCE Office for Democratic Institutions and Human Rights in Warsaw (Jałoszewski 2020). The judges called for "an in-depth monitoring of the ongoing electoral process in Poland." The letter was a reaction to the law adopted that month under which the presidential election would be held entirely through mail-in ballots on May 10 (eventually the election did not take place). On May 11, 2020, PiS MPs submitted a draft of a new law restoring the possibility of voting in polling stations, and those willing and quarantined to use the possibility of voting by correspondence. It was amended because Deputy Prime Minister Jarosław Gowin refused to take responsibility for all the irregularities connected with the unconstitutional voting on May 10. "As judges of Polish courts at all levels, we are concerned about changes in the electoral law. We are concerned about the threat of such basic standards as the principle of universality of elections and secrecy of voting. We shall never abandon the independence of courts and judges. And we shall never leave our Colleagues without help, support and solidarity" (Woźnicki 2020). The election finally took place on June 28, 2020.

---

1    ODIHR carries out election observation in OSCE-participating states to assess the extent to which elections respect fundamental freedoms and are characterized by equality, universality, political pluralism, confidence, transparency and accountability. A long-term, comprehensive, consistent, and systematic election observation methodology has become the bedrock of ODIHR's credibility in this field. The Office also supports authorities in their efforts to improve electoral processes and to follow up on recommendations by ODIHR election observation missions, by reviewing election-related legislation, providing technical expertise, and supporting the activities of citizen observer groups.

In the letter dated April 29, 2020, the judges requested the OSCE/ODIHR send observers to monitor the presidential election by mail. They emphasized that many Poles would not be able to take part in such elections due to the COVID-19 epidemic. A total of 1,278 judges from all over Poland signed the letter, including a group of 31 judges from the Regional Court in Piotrków Trybunalski and its subordinate district courts (17 such judges of district courts signed the letter to the OSCE). Of all the judges who signed the petition, only the district judges from Piotrków Trybunalski received the letters from the disciplinary commissioner with the demand to provide explanations in terms of eventual disciplinary proceedings (Judge 2019d).

## 4.4 Press articles

Resisting judges also wrote press articles specifically concerning and criticizing the Muzzle law, or they have been quoted in articles (such as Igor Tuleya and Krystian Markiewicz) (Mazur 2020; Gazeta.pl 2020). As Judge 27 shared:

> *The judges have a duty to communicate with the public. If it is absent, if the courts inspire fear rather than trust, it is easier for politicians to manipulate the judiciary. The ruling party is breaking the law, but majority of the population does not care. Judges must understand that it is in our interest to hold press conferences on important issues and to patiently justify judgments. We cannot issue harsh messages and take offense at journalists who misrepresent something. Since our community has been forced to fight for the good name of the judiciary, it no longer considers media spotlight or striving for social understanding to be unneeded.* (Kryszkiewicz 2020)

## 4.5 Judge wrote an article encouraging people to join action of 18th of month

When Judge Ewa Maciejewska wrote an article encouraging people join the pause in hearings on the 18th of each month, the authorities began the process of dismissing her from the role of deputy chairman of the Civil Department in the District Court in Łódź. At her department, all hearings for the 18th were postponed a couple days earlier. Gazeta Wyborcza wrote about the president of the court wanting to dismiss her (Rogowska 2021). The case was publicized in the media, on Facebook, and on the judges' blog. The judges also collected signatures against revoking her.

## 4.6 Awareness raising and resistance education during festivals

Iustitia organized festivals and joined other public events where it put up its tent and presented the situation in the judiciary. "We do it on our own, with our private money. We organize our travel and accommodation," said Judge 16. Assisted by grassroots civic organizations, judges embarked on tours across Poland, engaging with ordinary citizens. A shared realization among independent judges emerged that they had become vulnerable to the ruling regime's actions in 2015 due to inadequate communication with the public. Opponents had an array of media tools at their disposal to target the independent judiciary. Consequently, judges took the initiative to step out of the courtrooms and involve themselves in social initiatives, aiming to construct an identity of committed, responsive judges who comprehend and address the needs of the citizens (Judge 12). Judges traveled to festivals such as the Woodstock festival, PolAndRock Festival, and Opener Festival, and organized plays of public trials for attendees.

At the 2018 PolAndRock Festival, Iustitia judges built social trust. At a workshop, they held a debate concerning free courts with human rights defender Adam Bodnar, Judge Tuleya, Judge Bartłomiej Przymusiński, Judge Olimpia Barańska-Małuszek, and Ombudsman's Office attorney Zuzanna Rudzińska-Bluszcz.They packed the tent. Some audience members alleged the judges had not done anything productive in years, but many others supported the judges and asked about the rule-of-law crisis. They also held a meeting with Tuleya and Markiewicz concerning the limits of law and civil liberties. The audience chanted "Free Courts!" and asked a lot of questions, while the talks were held in a relaxed, open atmosphere. According to Iustitia, "The interest in the issue of civil liberties and free courts was enormous, the judges held a lot of valuable talks with festival goers. As the entire community, we received evidence of support and cordiality from people" (Iustitia 2018b).

Over four days at the 2022 Open'er Festival, Iustitia judges held competitions. They prepared quizzes for the festival participants, testing their knowledge of the constitution and the European Union. They also simulated a criminal and civil trial, including the Trial of the Wolf and Little Red Riding Hood (FEPI 2019).

At the 2022 Cieszfanów Festival, they organized the Rule of Law: A Common Cause workshops with one of the repressed judges, Paweł Juszczyszyn. There was also screening of the film *Judges Under Pressure* and a meeting with the filmmakers and subjects: producer Iwona Harris, director Kacper Lisowski, and Judges Tuleya, Juszczyszyn, and Waldemar Żurek (Iustitia FB 2022).

According to Adam Bodnar (2022), former Ombudsman, "festivals during the holiday season became a place of debate. Conference rooms and universities are closed, and festival tents are open. Thanks to social media, the message can reach everyone." He remarked that this "is a great trend."

*Because even if we manage to get out of the crisis of democracy, the massive participation of civil society in festivals will remain with us. Activities in the public sphere should mean an active search for a citizen, and not assuming that he will come to us and be interested in postulates, programs or values.*

Festivals are also an example of what real citizenship education can look like.

*It certainly cannot be static and textbook. I suspect that in a few years' time—as Polish schools will implement educational programs on the constitution, climate change, anti-discrimination, or sexual education—we will use models developed during the festivals. Workshops organized in sand, heat and dust become mini-laboratories for social change.*

FIGURE 16. Posters from the festivals

### 4.7 Using the academic pulpit as professor

Judges are often academics and professors at local universities. They used that academic pulpit to express their opposition to the changes in the judiciary. Judge 4 noted, "When I teach, I tell the students about the situation in the courts." As another judge explained:

*I want to show students that the thoughtless application of the law sometimes leads to an unfair sentence. I hope that when they become judges one day, it will sound in their minds and a red lamp will light up. These young lawyers need to be sensitized to the dangers we have not dealt with so far, the limits of compromise. Talk about human rights, show instruments useful in confrontation with people who do not want to obey the law. In the country in which we operate today, violations of the law by other lawyers cannot be formally assessed. There is only one thing known from history that remains—a social sanction.* (Subbotko 2021)

### 4.8 Judges in school

Judges intensified their educational activities and held courses in schools on human rights and constitutional law. They handed out copies of the constitution during these classes. The public schools volunteered to take part in the legal activities offered by independent judges.

### 4.9 Resolution of Assembly of Justices of the Supreme Court on dismissal of the President of the Supreme Court

The general assemblies were the first for a where judges could discuss and made decisions. Adopting unanimous resolutions in general assemblies of the courts led to growing solidarity and unity among resisting judges. It was important for the judges. It also helped create leaders.

On June 28, 2018, the General Assembly of the Justices of the Supreme Court issued a resolution that stated:

*We, the justices of the Supreme Court, attending the General Assembly of the Justices of the Supreme Court held on 28 June 2018, mindful of the oaths of office we made an allegiant to the Constitution of Republic of Poland, which is the supreme law of the Republic of Poland, state that Justice of the Supreme Court, Professor Małgorzata Gersdorf, PhD, D.Sc., shall remain—according to Article 183 section 3 of the Constitution of the Republic of Poland directly applied under Article 8 section 2 of the Constitution of the Republic of Poland—the First President of the Supreme Court, heading the institution in which we perform our service to the public, by 30 April 2020.*

They continued:

*Being inconsistent with Article 180 of the Constitution of the Republic of Poland, regulation provided in Article 111 paragraph 1 of the Act on the Supreme Court, removes, on 4 July 2018, a large number of justices from the Supreme Court. It constitutes an obvious violation by the legislature of one of the fundamental guarantees of independence of the judiciary and will soon significantly disrupt normal functioning of the Supreme Court. Justices who had begun their service on the Supreme Court before the Act on the Supreme Court of 8 December 2017 came into force, should continue such service until the age of 70 without any additional conditions.*

### 4.10   Constant reminder of injustice by Iustisia and support writings by judges

Iustitia provided information on their website tracking the repressive measures against Judges Juszczyszyn and Tuleya by disclosing their non-adjudication days due to the regime's actions. This highlighted the severity of the government's repressive actions, advocated for their reinstatement, challenged the legitimacy of the Disciplinary Chamber, and presented postulates to rectify the problem. As of February 9, 2023, Iustitia also reported that Judge Maciej Ferek had already been suspended for 475 days, shedding light on the extent of targeting independent judges.

### 4.11   Outreach to domestic mainstream media

Resisting judges operate in media at domestic and international levels. On the domestic level, the judges act in their district courts where they organize their media actions or take interviews. Judge 5 shared: "The media contacts me and asks for a comment. There were times when I gave interviews almost every day. TVN [the Polish independent media] knows that from Monday to Friday, if they come to court, they will be able to talk to me." Lawyer 2 commented: "We want to establish contact with each media. We have to go beyond our bubble.

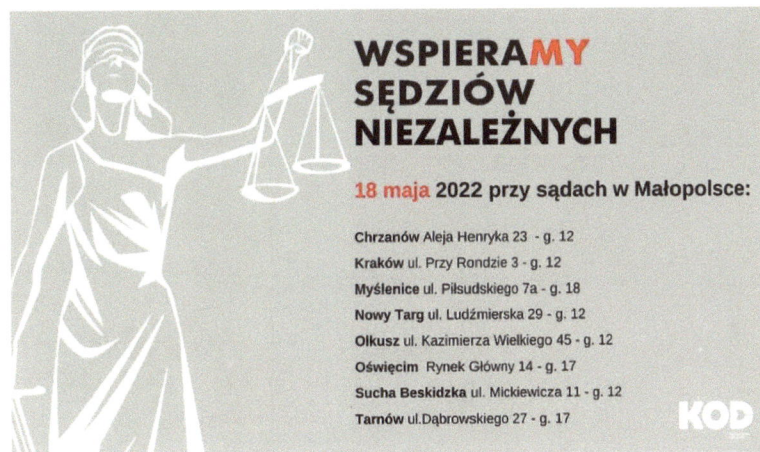

**FIGURE 17.** Protest poster that lists the cities, location and time of the expected protests in support of the independent judges.

I'm talking to radio stations, popular magazines. We create the TV leads by presenting our own material."

One judge has a weekly broadcast on local radio with students from the student legal clinic. In an interview with the author, they shared, "These are 3-minute programs that are very important. People listen and they like it."

Getting in the media controlled by the government or that are pro-government has been a challenge. Judge 4 said that "The only thing missing in our media campaign is greater participation in pro-government media." Judge 16 shared, "They stopped inviting us to TVP. The lack of participation in the state media makes it more difficult for us to break through." This limited access places resisting judges in a disadvantage as "TVP is often the only source of information for many, especially older, people" (Lawyer 2). Still, their growing presence and activism in social media of independent judges provides them with opportunity for unfiltered access to and reaching out directly to the public and younger audience.

"We managed to get the media interested in the issue of the rule of law," said Activist 2.

*We are grateful for the very detailed coverage. We had 28 press conferences in front of the Supreme Court when we said for the thousandth time that the Disciplinary Chamber is not a court. TVN 24 broadcasts it live. Thanks to this, our message reaches 5 million recipients.*

In contrast to public media captured by the ruling regime, some key private media outlets in Poland helped counter the slander campaign against resisting judges—including Onet, TVN, TVN 24, Gazeta Wyborcza, Oko Press, TOK FM (Judge 7, second interview).

91

**FIGURE 18.** The same protests were held in front of the Myślenice District Court and Gliwice Regional Court.

Independent judges also receive media awards. For example, Judge Jakub Kościerzyński received the award for the most media-savvy judge in Bydgoszcz, or Dorota Zabłudowska who received the award from the late president of the city of Gdańsk, Paweł Adamowicz.

Internet is yet another space of resistance through the media. Iustitia has had very active media team with expanding presence in the social media. Judge 16, one of the members on the team, said, "We have multiplied our recipients in a short time from 5-7,000 to 60,000 followers on the Iustitia's fan page on Facebook. Now the media broadcasters take the post from our fan page, copies it, and releases it as news."

### 4.12 Foreign media outreach

Independent judges and their associations Iustitia and Temis speak and write in English and have maintained extensive international contacts since 2016. Iustitia judges tasked with representing the cause in the foreign press have contacts with *Reuters*, *Bloomberg*, the *New York Times*, *BCC*, and *Al Jazeera* (Judge 13). Iustitia conducts regular media workshops for independent judges who speak English. As Judge 16 shared, foreign media "knows that we are a reliable source of information.

> *When foreign media comes they contact us by email. They don't want to talk to politicians but to us and the Free Courts. We have contacts with Denmark, Great Britain, Germany, and France. They ask to refer to them 2 or more judges for interview and we decide who will go. Credibility and the degree of commitment make them turn to us and not to domestic press agencies.*

Judges responsible for foreign media in Themis prepares analysis concerning the situation in the Polish courts. They are written in English and are cited by foreign media.

**FIGURE 19.** Poster: Demand they return to work (list of prosecuted judges that were suspended from adjudicating)—protest on the 18th at 18:00

Consequently, this information is the passed to national judges in other EU countries. As a result, they are well informed about the regime's attacks on the independence of judiciary in Poland.

### 4.13 Pro bono support for translations into English, French, and German

At the initiative of KOS, many public documents—such as the Prime Minister's and Prosecutor General's motions to the Constitutional Tribunal—were translated into English and published online. This has led to a quick response from foreign organizations like the EU institutions, academics, and civil society organizations.

## Acts of Omission

Judges have also employed various tactical choices classified as "acts of omission." These are the actions that require "not doing or saying" and can understood as confrontational acts in the form of political or judicial noncooperation or social noncooperation.

### TABLE 2. Judges' Tactics Using Actions of Omission

| Resistance Behavior | NATURE OF TACTIC INDUCEMENTS | |
|---|---|---|
| | CONFRONTATIONAL (COERCIVE) | CONSTRUCTIVE (PERSUASIVE) |
| Acts of Omission (Not Doing) | **Noncooperation** Refusal to engage in expected behavior through boycotts and strikes in order to penalize or increase costs on the opponent | **Refraining** Halting or calling off a planned or ongoing action to reward or persuade the opponent |

*Source: Beer 2021*

## 5. Acts of Omission as Political/Judicial Noncooperation

### 5.1 No court hearing day, every 18th of the month

On December 18, 2020, Iustitia announced the 18th day of each month as the Day of Solidarity with the Repressed Judges. The judges demand that the suspended judges—primarily Tuleya, Morawiec and Juszczyszyn—be reinstated. In solidarity, Iustitia asked all judges to refrain from scheduling hearings on this day each month (Iustitia 2020c). Every 18th day, beginning January 2021, judges gather in front of courts all over Poland to protest at noon. Joined by citizens, they do this to remind the public why the judges were unlawfully suspended, and they demand their return to judicial service. Judge 2 shared, "We don't expect judges to take these cases down. We said listen, have time, do it so that it is harmless for people, so that they do not suffer any harm from what the state is doing."

On May 18, 2022, in the Małopolska region alone, the protests were organized in front of the court buildings in Chrzanów, Kraków, Myślenice, Nowy Targ, Olkusz, Oświęcim, Sucha Beskidzka, and Tarnów (see the poster in Figure 19).

The protests were an opportunity to comment on current events. For example, at the event in June 2022, judges met at the stairs of the Kraków Court of Appeal building for the demonstration (the protest had been rescheduled to Monday as the courts were closed on Saturday, June 18). Judge Dariusz Mazur recalled the great symbolic victory of Waldemar Żurek before the ECHR and made it clear that the bill on the liquidation of the Disciplinary Chamber approved by the Sejm had little to do with the implementation of CJEU case-law.

In July 2022, the list of judges suspended by the Disciplinary Chamber of the Supreme Court was broader: Piotr Gąciarek Maciej Ferek, Maciej Rutkiewicz, and Krzysztof Chmielewski had now also been suspended.

### 5.2 Refusal to adjudicate with politicized judges sitting on the same bench

Judges also resisted by refusing to adjudicate alongside the politicized judges. Judge Anna Bator-Ciesielska was the first to refuse to adjudicate with Przemysław Radzik, the Deputy Disciplinary Spokesman who was connected to a smear campaign by a troll farm against the independent judges. The judge decided that she could not adjudicate a case of robbery with with Radzik because there were doubts about his independence and impeccable character, which a judge must have.

Though already being prosecuted for this, in an interview with OKO.press, she said that "the judge must have a conscience. And that she is not afraid, because the judge cannot be afraid." According to *Gazeta Wyborcza*, Radzik and the second deputy disciplinary spokesman, Michał Lasota were to be in the Kasta group on one of the communicators (Jałoszewski 2019). The Kasta group led a coordinated trolling effort against the resisting judges and was organized over WhatsApp.

Other judges followed the example of Judge Bator-Ciesielska by refusing to adjudicate with Radzik. "Schab and Radzik combine with adjudication the role of disciplinary spokesmen, who are to guard this new order, pursue and harass honest judges. But their political careers have nothing to do with judicial independence, so I cannot adjudicate with them," said Judge Marzanna Piekarska-Drążek (Grochal 2022).

Radzik threatened disciplinary proceedings against judges for delayed judgment justifications, which has been met with amusement, given his own record of lateness. Radzik himself has been tardy in providing justifications, with five out of six cases exceeding three months without valid reasons or consent for extension. Despite this, he faced no consequences due to his position as a disciplinary deputy spokesman (Grochal 2022).

### 5.3 Boycotting putting forward candidates to NCJ and judicial promotion

In March 2018, civil society organizations (such as AD and ORP) and judicial associations called for boycotting the elections to the neo-NCJ. It was a huge success as only 18 of 10,000 judges applied for the positions, and not even all of them gathered required number of signed endorsements from their peers (Iustitia 2020a).

Judges' boycotts of the new competitions to higher courts led to situations in which there was only one candidate for a post, and thus no genuine competition to speak of. Nevertheless, as of February 7, 2023, there were 2,465 neo-judges and assessors appointed by the neo-NCJ found in the courts of 283 cities. To monitor this problem, KOD prepared a free search engine to check whether a judge presiding over a case was appointed by the neo-NCJ (KOD nd).

### 5.4 Boycotting promotion process

Conscious that this is not the time for promotion, judges have also boycotted the promotion process. "I talked to some judges who took part in the promotion procedure," said Judge 3. "As a result, some people quit the promotion process." Judge 20 reflected:

> *In 2013, I was on a delegation to the Regional Court. I adjudicated in the criminal appeal department once or twice a month, taking into account the promotion. Eight years have passed, and I am still adjudicating in the District Court. We all found ourselves in such a situation that we would not take part in promotion procedures.*

### 5.5 Refusing to give opinion on candidates to the NCJ

Judges' assemblies are no longer giving their opinions about the candidates to the new NCJ, convinced, as stated by Iustitia's president in an interview with the author, that "Participation of judges in such competitions is against the law."

### 5.6 Refusing added duties

Judges refused to accept new duties in the courts that they were tasked with (Judge 17). If one was already a president of the court or a department, they would continue their function unless they could not do it in a proper manner. It was a way of preserving positions before judges appointed by the Minister of Justice took over.

For example, the District Court in Sulęcin, with a shortage of only seven judges, faced a challenging situation. Sebastian Petlik, a neo-judge linked to the new regime, opted to take a delegation to another court while simultaneously retaining his role as the district court's president. This decision resulted in Judge Starosta assuming Petlik's responsibilities and becoming a department head against his wishes. With only two judges in the civil department (Starosta and the delegated Petlik), the court's functionality was significantly impacted. As Judge Starosta shared in an interview with the author:

> *I am currently on sick leave, because last year the president of the District Court in Sulęcin (where 7 judges work) informed me that he was going on a delegation to the Regional Court in Gorzów Wielkopolski. At the meeting with him, I gave an ultimatum that either he or a colleague would take over as department chairman, or we would tell them that we would not take on additional duties. This cannot be done without the judge's approval. I refused and submitted a notification to the prosecutor's office about*

*the suspicion of a violation of powers—an illegal act that led to such situations when judges instead of taking responsibilities for their duties preferred the promotions. I also wrote to the Minister of Justice so that those responsible would know the consequences of posting. Delegating my duties increased my duties by 50%, which meant that I heard 2 times more cases than judges in similar courts in Janów Lubelski or Rzeszów. I did not want to be chairman of the department and I am treated as if I was—the files are returned to my shelf. There was a lot of pressure and the threat of disciplinary proceedings. I had trouble sleeping, I couldn't concentrate on my work, so I went to the doctor and got a sick leave. Then they tried to do the same with my friend, which resulted in the fact that for six months no one performed their duties in the civil department. Therefore, the president delegated a court officer there and asked other judges in the district whether they would like to be the president of the court in Sulęcin.*

### 5.7 Judicial disobedience of unjust law

A sequence of court rulings, aligned with the Polish Constitution, challenged the legal basis of COVID-19 restrictions imposed by the Polish government in 2020 and 2021.[2] These judgments contended that only an official "state of natural disaster" permitted more stringent restrictions on movement, business operations, and work (Wachowiec 2021). The courts refused to enforce regulations challenged by citizens who were fined for violating mask-wearing, social distancing, and public gathering limits.

The courts' interpretation emphasized that compulsory face coverings were only permissible for those already infected or suspected of infection, and that spontaneous gatherings were lawful. The distinction between organizing assemblies and participating in them was underscored. Additionally, the courts ruled that regulations allowing the government to limit movement or enforce quarantine were applicable only to individuals displaying COVID-19 symptoms. Notably, the courts acquitted a hairdresser fined for working during lockdown, contending that the regulations contradicted the Constitution, which permits freedom of economic activity restrictions solely through statutes and not regulations. As a result, citizens prevailed in most cases against fines imposed under pandemic regulations deemed "faulty legal measures to combat the outbreak" (Wachowiec 2021). Judge Adam Synakiewicz said:

*The words of the judge's oath and the ethos of the judicial service are not empty phrases for me, but signposts setting the only way to proceed. I have a duty to respect the*

---

2   The government introduced almost 50 regulations providing i.e. compulsory face coverings, strict limits on public gatherings, quarantine for those traveling from abroad or the closure of certain businesses and venues. The parliament authorized sanitary authorities to impose administrative fines of up to 30,000 zloty (€6,650) for violating the said measures and limited effective judicial review by making them immediately enforceable. Fines that can be imposed on the spot by police under the petty offenses code have also been increased to 5,000 zloty (€1,100).

*European convention and the judgments of the tribunal, which indicates how to proceed to ensure that every human being respects his fundamental rights. In the present situation, my private concerns are relegated to the background. I did not decide to become a judge only for good times.* (Szymaniak and Kryszkiewicz 2021)

## 5.8 Disobedience of the requirement to reveal association or memberships

Independent judges made public statements in which they declared they would not disclose information about their associational membership as required by the Muzzle law. This action was coordinated by Iustitia that prepared for judges a template of the statement with refusal to reveal (Iustitia 2020b). The judges' association explained on its webpage why this requirement to disclose associations contradicts the constitution and violates judges' right to private life. According to Judge 19:

*It interferes too much with my right to privacy and personal sphere for me to present such information. I informed the president of the Court of Appeal that, in my opinion, these provisions infringe the law and that I will not provide such information. The values given to me by the constitution are more important than the obligation to inform the president of the Court of Appeal about the associations in which I operate. If there are any attempts to interfere with my freedom, I will resist such attempts.*

Judge 4 said:

*This violates our right to privacy. So we told the judges that if you want, do not provide this information. I have never concealed that I am a member of Iustitia. According to the authorities, no matter how stupid the law is, I should obey. But it may happen that a judge is a member of an association that defends the rights of LGBT people, families with Alzheimer's, families of alcoholics or supporting ostomy patients.*

## 5.9 Strikes

It should be noted that according to Polish law, judges cannot go on strike. A legal strike by judges in Poland is not possible—only trade unions can do so. Judges cannot be a member of a trade union and thus cannot participate in a strike in any way. Nevertheless, strikes can take various forms, such as an Italian strike or a strike of overzealousness. Any judge who went on strike today would face disciplinary action. Therefore, judges do not consider the possibility. However, "when an emergency situation comes to solutions that will be unacceptable to us, the strike action will be subject to discussion. A sit-in strike or a refusal to perform our duties," said Judge 24.

The debate among concerning the feasibility of a strike centered on the absence of a constitutional right to strike within the judicial system. The primary concern was maintaining citizens' access to justice, with judges cautious not to compromise this fundamental right (Lawyer 1). While acknowledging the importance of voicing concerns, judges were wary of actions that could hinder citizens' legal recourse. Lawyer 3 shared, "A strike would be a disastrous move because the citizens are hostage to the strike. A judge, a lawyer, and a doctor cannot do this. Taking part in a demonstration is something else."

*Judges who opposed striking argued that it could disrupt citizens' cases, contradicting the fundamental duty to administer justice promptly.*

The distinction between striking and other forms of protesting became a focal point. Judges who opposed striking argued that it could disrupt citizens' cases, contradicting the fundamental duty to administer justice promptly. Suggestions emerged for alternative forms of resistance that safeguard citizen interests, such as refusing certain administrative tasks or noncooperation with government authorities. The question of solidarity arose, as judges considered the extent of participation required for a strike to be effective.

Differing perspectives also emerged regarding hypothetical scenarios, where extreme measures might push judges toward strike action. The potential arrests of fellow judges or severe threats to the independence of the judiciary were seen as potential triggers. Judge 1 said, "If Krystian Markiewicz was arrested, if Igor Tuleya was handcuffed and led to the prosecutor's office, when the colleagues were detained and the case was faked, we do not rule out any element of resistance that a citizen would have. Then we hang the gown on a peg."

However, most judges believed in finding ways to protect the judiciary without resorting to strikes, emphasizing their role as a shield for citizens against injustice. The consensus was that any form of resistance should prioritize citizens' rights while advocating for a strong and independent judiciary.

## 6. Acts of Omission as Social Noncooperation

Judges also resisted through acts of omission in the form of social noncooperation. These are instances of refusing to do those actions that they were not necessarily required to do yet were socially expected to do. Omissions included not participating in judicial disciplinary proceedings, resignation, ostracism, withholding signs of respect for the neo-judges, or refusing to address neo-judges as "president."

### 6.1 Not participating in judicial disciplinary proceedings

During the first disciplinary proceedings, the judiciary community faced a dilemma regarding the participation of defenders for the accused judges in hearings before the Disciplinary Chamber. On the one hand, judges claimed that one should not legitimize the actions of the chamber and would not appear during the hearing. Unjustified failure to appear at the hearing shall not stay the examination of the case, as appearance is not mandatory. But it does demonstrate that they do not respect the chamber. On the other hand, someone had to defend them. As Lawyer 7 shared:

*I was opposed to this position because it would mean giving up the field. In this situation, there is no reason to appoint a defense lawyer if they do everything to defend their client. [Defenders have to go to the court, participate in a hearing and perform their tasks] which does not mean legitimizing the activity of the Disciplinary Chamber, because we all emphasized in our actions its defectiveness and the defectiveness of the judicial nominations of people who adjudicate in these proceedings. We have to do everything based on the evidence, even to convince those persons sitting in the Disciplinary Chamber that the prosecution is unfounded. For me, it is a matter of pride that none of my judges ultimately faced disciplinary liability or was not held criminally responsible. Resistance makes sense.*

Consequently, independent judges would not respond to disciplinary spokespersons, even when summoned for interrogation. Repressed judges against whom the disciplinary proceedings were initiated did not attend the hearings against them. They would secure pro bono defense attorneys to represent them during the proceedings. This was a deliberate strategy. Their conspicuous absence from their own hearings would question the status of the Disciplinary Chamber, demonstrating that for them, this is not a court. At the same time, despite being absent, their rights were defended by the defenders who came on their behalf.

## 6.2 Resignation

Some judges also resisted by retiring. Judge Wojciech Łączewski, who resigned in November 2019, wrote in letter: "I am observing the changes in the judiciary introduced by the ruling party with great concern. As a result, the Republic of Poland, as a democratic state ruled by law, is on the verge of collapse." The NCJ had become "a caricature body that does not care for the independence of judges and the independence of courts" by using judges and people from the minister of justice's entourage in a hybrid war. The aim was to discredit judges who oppose the dependence of the courts on politicians from the ruling party.

*The conditions of the judicial service are constantly deteriorating, seasoned court offi-cials are leaving their jobs, and citizens whose cases cannot be heard without undue delay are suffering. In order to remain faithful to the oath taken in the presence of the President of the Republic of Poland, I must express my opposition to the destruction of the justice system in the name of the party's interest. (Ivanova 2019)*

Judge Jarosław Gwizdak, former president of the Katowice Wschód District Court, resigned in February 2019. This is how he described the reasons for his resignation:

*In 2015, after the change of governments, I naively believed that perhaps this time something could be changed in the judiciary. It seemed to me that my colleagues with whom I had previously worked in Iustitia had an idea for an efficient and independent judiciary. However, four years have passed and little has changed when it comes to the organization and improvement of work. I see judges who again have several hundred cases in their papers, I observe assessors who come to learn this profession and have no support. The courts are on the verge of collapse again, and the ministry is screeching the public as judges, describing them as an "extraordinary caste." Under such conditions, you don't want to. In addition, there were staff changes in Silesian courts, where people were often elected to managerial positions without qualifications for management. These nominations show that Silesia is not lucky or is under special supervision of the Ministry of Justice. And over all this is the unfortunate National Council of the Judiciary, whose members appreciate the opportunity to meet with MP Krystyna Pawłowicz or talk with MP Stanisław Piotrowicz. I do not know what Teresa Kurcyusz-Furmanik from Gliwice, a judge and lawyer with a fantastic past and professional achievements, is doing in this strange group.* (Pietraszewski 2019)

He also said:

*I stopped being a judge on June 3, 2019, after several years of beating my head against the wall. I wanted courts that were open to people, efficient and modern. I called for the computerization of courts on a large scale, because in the 21st century I do not want to continue using the fax machine. This was not the case. More important in this great "reform" of the judiciary is temporary political affiliation, and judges are to be "loyal to the state." I am gone. I've had enough.* (Gwizdak 2019)

Speaking to the author, he said, "My resignation was an act of resistance. You gotta have the balls to quit this."

Some judges resigned from other duties they held in protest. "I resigned from the position of international affairs coordinator as a sign of protest after the implementation of the Muzzle law," said one judge in an interview with the author.

However, judges generally do not see resignation as an effective strategic option. "Resignation would be like throwing the baby out with the bathwater. I will keep fighting for the independence of judges," said Judge 24. This is echoed by Justice Michał Laskowski from the Supreme Court: "I see no reason to quit the service. But I expect that I will be removed from this service. Any old judges of the Supreme Court could have peace of mind if retired, but remain in the service. We cannot give up" (Ivanova 2021).

To quit in the time of crisis is not perceived well by other judges. Judge 2 said, "It is not our duty to resign from the profession honorably. This is not what we are expected. Instead, we stay and fight for the court and the rule of law. Judges who are strong enough should fight." Judges do not see the possibility to resign. As Judge 22 shared, "I told myself that when my contact with the justice system was to end, it would only be by force [used by the other side]." Judge 4 agreed: "I'll be a judge until I get kicked out. I will fight to the very end. This is much better. When the judge resigns it is weak." This is because judges are more effective inside the system than outside it. "Maybe I thought about quitting before, but in being inside I'll do more than when I am out," said Judge 14. "The question of leaving as a form of protest would be such an ineffective and pointless solution," confirmed Judge 19. "In fact, someone else would come to take my place. I do not think it could be a form of protest under these conditions." The solidarity of the judicial community helps in remaining on the post. As Judge 16 shared, "Even though I feel tired, I believe in our case. I believe that as long as I am a judge and immunity protects me that I can do more when I stay. It is my duty to remain in this office."

### 6.3 Ostracism
As stated by Łukasz Bojarski (2019), "Disapproval of unworthy behavior or social ostracism has two dimensions."

> First is letting a specific person understand that we do not accept their choices. We want him or her to feel the importance of responsibility for his or her actions, we want to make him or her conscious, guilty, and willingful to repair. But the second, equally important dimension is the question about the assessment of behavior and deeds by history. You cannot ignore the attack on independent courts and the use of this situation by specific people. What lesson would there be for future generations? It must be clear that certain things are not appropriate.

Ostracism means no hands shaking with pseudo-judges; causing irritation, shaming. Shaming those who went to collaborate with politicians. "Naming and shaming: we name things, publicize them. We do it on a broad front," says Lawyer 3. Judge 1 said that "ostracism is indicated for a group that has been tempted by promotions or are ideologically conditioned (those who believe that the ruling party will realize the religious expectations—honest people that believe in the party)." In close relationships, contact breaks off, changing office rooms. "It works a lot for these people on the other side," said Judge 23.

"Ostracism and solidarity are of key importance," shared Judge 17.

*If consistently both elements existed and applied, it would be one of the best forms of influencing the attitudes of all judges, but assertiveness must be learned all your life. Judges are reluctant to show negative feelings towards other people because it is going beyond the comfort zone—it is more difficult to show, because it concerns former colleagues. Solidarity is easier. That is why it takes so long for the well-being of the advocates of the so-called "good change."*

Judge 1 said:

*There are people who have been severely affected by environmental ostracism—mainly those who signed letters of support for candidates for members of the neo-NCJ or who entered the National Council of the Judiciary themselves. I have known Paweł Styrna for many years. He reached out to me in the elevator and said hello, but I did not shake his hand, because I would not give it to anyone who breaks the Constitution. This causes a lot of irritation. It was my duty to manifest it.*

"For 6 months I did not shake hands with the president of the court," said Judge 9.

*On the one hand, I was driven mad by the narrative that the judges were at war, that they were like Home Army soldiers. But on the other hand, this judgment is important, the functioning of the judiciary is important. I tried to understand the motivations of these people, but I did not shake my hand to the president. I don't know if it was ok or not.*

Ostracism means naming and shaming.

*I had a friend (we studied together), who was promoted in court by the neo-NCJ and was sent to work in my department. We stated before each hearing, that there is a seat in the court of Mrs. E. who was appointed on such and such a day and for which there is a fear that she was not nominated in accordance with the Constitution, on which the Supreme Court spoke in a resolution of three joint chambers and that she is not qualified to be a judge of the Regional Court. This was to give the opportunity to submit applications for the exclusion of a judge. During this session—in 9-10 cases (20 lawyers and attorneys-at-law) not a single motion to dismiss a judge was filed, but this judge withstood only one session with us. Eventually, she changed the department where she could rule as a single judge. (Judge 2)*

"Ostracism comes down to not maintaining social relationships with such people," said Judge 22. "Even in some business relationships, contacts are avoided. I don't know how it works for the boycotted people. There are no real successes. How do they feel?"

Ostracism includes not talking to those who benefited from the rule of law backsliding. As Judge 5 said, "I will never talk to the president of the court. I will never ask about the weather. Our relationship is very business-like and very reluctant.... Apart from the clashes at the general meeting, we pass each other on a daily basis."

"You have to show these people at every step that they are doing wrong," said Judge 14.

*Everyone has more or less of this shame. I hope they will come to their senses. I asked them why they do it, why they take full advantage of it. They told me that I was exaggerating, that you had to function. These people avoid me, they know I'm right. I will shake hands with them, but avoid contact. One of the judges was promoted very quickly with such results and he is not coping with the district court and he asks why I do not talk to him. He also asked my chairman about it. He was only promoted because of his political connections. We were close to each other, now we just say hi.*

According to neo-judge Antoni Bojańczyk who complained in his letter to the First President of the Supreme Court, "Being much younger in my age and experience, I immediately extended my hand to welcome Mr. President. Mr. President's reaction was a demonstrative 'hold' of the hand extended to him. I had to wait a long moment with his hand suspended in the air before Mr. Zabłocki (clearly reluctant) decided, finally, to give me a hand." He also said that: "No institutional steps have ever been taken to ensure the creation of an atmosphere of inclusiveness and friendly treatment of new judges of the Supreme Court in the highest instance by a large group of 'older' judges of this Court" (Kryszkiewicz 2019).

Judge 19 expressed the discernment needed when ostracizing:

*I am also careful not to exaggerate too much—it is not the best tool in the fight for positive changes. Showing someone a certain contempt or a feeling of disapproval of being superior to me that I am on the good bright side and you definitely are not, and that is why I condemn you. This can lead to the deepening of the dispute. You have to fight the problem and the effects of these changes, and not the people who benefit from it. However, people who have become harmful because of their activities should face consequences.*

Other judges do not participate in the ostracism campaign. As Judge 11 shared, "It is blatant and unworthy of the judges to take advantage of this moment to get promotions. I do not ostracize, but I don't feel like talking to such people. And I do not criticize those who do not shake hands with such people."

Ostracism is intended to discourage potential followers and to provide a consistent message (Judge 6). As Judge 2 said, "What is the point of going out before the courts and protesting when you go out later for coffee with neo-judges or going to nomination events? It doesn't have a clear message."

*6.4 Withholding common signs of respect for the neo-judges*

One of the resistance actions was withdrawing common signs of respect for the new judges sitting in the panel of the Disciplinary Chamber appointed by the compromised NCJ. Lawyer 7 said, "I came up with an idea how not to have to get up when the members of the Disciplinary Chamber entered the room—I didn't sit down, so I didn't have to get up." Some spoke impersonally to avoid the use of the phrase "your honor," while others did not address them at all (Judge 4; Lawyer 7). As lawyer Michał Wawrykiewicz shared online, "As a defender of an unlawfully suspended judge Juszczyszyn, I have no obligation to stand before a body that is not a court within the meaning of Polish and European law" (Iustitia 2022).

*6.5 Refusing to call neo-judges "President"*

From 2017 to 2018, 158 court presidents were replaced by the neo-NCJ. In response, judges refused to use the customary title "president" when addressing those nominated by the Minister of Justice. Instead, they referred to them as "mister" or "missus." This meant that they did not want to stay in the familiar relationship with the neo-judges anymore. The relationship became very formal.

## Acts of Commission

Judges have also employed various tactical choices classified as "acts of comission." These are the actions that require "doing or creating" and can understood as confrontational acts in the form of disruptive intervention (most often in a political or judicial capacity) or creative intervention (either political/judicial, economic, social, or psychological).

### TABLE 3. Judges' Tactics Using Actions of Commission

| Resistance behavior | NATURE OF TACTIC INDUCEMENTS | |
| --- | --- | --- |
| | CONFRONTATIONAL (COERCIVE) | CONSTRUCTIVE (PERSUASIVE) |
| Acts of Commission (Doing or Creating Something) | **Disruptive Intervention** Direct action that confronts another party to stop, disrupt, or change their behavior | **Creative Intervention** Direct action that models or constructs alternative (competing) behaviors and institutions or takes over existing institutions |

*Source: Beer 2021*

## 7. Political/Judicial Disruptive Intervention

*7.1 Kamikaze strategy: derailing the system from within*

Resisting judges, in coordination with Iustitia, embraced the kamikaze strategy that aimed to question the legitimacy of the government-controlled National Council of the Judiciary (neo-NCJ) and the whole nomination process for judges that it exercised control over (**see Appendix III**). Essentially a kamikaze judge was a sort of a trojan horse that would enter the government-controlled judiciary system from inside and join or use established processes in order to stymie or derail them. This strategy came, however, with a risk to professional reputation.

Iustitia from the beginning of the first competition, already on July 14, 2018, declared that the competition was invalid as the successive changes to the constitutional laws practically did not allow for substantive assessment of candidates for the Supreme Court, and the competition procedure itself was deemed unconstitutional.

On July 22, 2018, Iustitia revealed how the competition could be questioned: by way of an appeal against the resolution of the NCJ to the still-independent Supreme Administrative Court. In the Resolution of the Management Board, Iustitia declared, "We will support those competition participants who appeal to the Supreme Administrative Court (SAC), questioning the validity of the competition mode." At the same time Iustitia shared the position that "lawyers actively involved in the dismantling of the principles of a democratic state ruled by law and the guarantee of proper protection of citizens by independent courts should take into account a serious threat to their professional and civic reputation."

*Themis called on all lawyers to boycott the recruitment to the new Supreme Court.*

. On July 23, 2018, Themis, the second association of judges, issued a statement in which it called participation in the competition procedure to the Supreme Court a violation of the constitution. Themis called on all lawyers to boycott the recruitment to the new Supreme Court announced by President Andrzej Duda. It called for "refraining from participating in these procedures, and for those who have already submitted their candidacies to withdraw them" and added that "the names of people aspiring to the Supreme Court in the conditions of the currently created lawlessness will become a synonym of servility to the system destroying the state of law and taking away citizens' freedom in pieces" (Jałoszewski 2018).

Judges responded to the appeal of the Iustitia and some of them took part in the ongoing competition becoming Kamikaze judges. In order to understand the two contradictory appeals it has to be noted that in general both judicial associations were against the participation of the ongoing competitions for judicial posts. At the same time Iustitia saw the possibility of challenging the unconstitutional changes in the judiciary by questioning the conformity of the new regulation with the EU law and European Convention on Human Rights. Iustitia promised support for those who would accept a risk of ostracism and take part in the competition to raise the question of the validity of the whole process. This was because only the official candidates to the judiciary positions of the Supreme Court could appeal to SAC to question the validity of the competition procedure for the appointment of judges set up and controlled by the government-dominated NCJ. Iustitia also promised it would support those independent candidates who would appeal to the SAC. With their appeals lodged the kamikaze judges also asked and thus gave SAC a legal avenue to refer the case regarding the validity of the NCJ status and that of the new chambers of the supreme court to the CJEU.

While reflecting on the kamikaze strategy, Judge 1 observed:

> *The kamikaze judge is a clandestine independent judge who puts forward his candidature in a competition to a judicial post and ideally the government-controlled National Council of the Judiciary would accept that candidature and does not discover the true nature of this subversive candidature which could in turn lead to its rejection and likely prosecution of such a judge. At the same time, I had to explain to my colleagues that this person is not really a candidate, but indeed a kamikaze judge.*

Another judge noted that Kamikaze judges "don't really think that about themselves as kamikaze. They do not look at their action as a suicidal mission aimed at inflicting as much damage on the enemy as possible through a surprised and unexpected attack" (Zawiślak 2019). Kamikaze judges knew that they would not win the competition and that their mission had professional risks.

The goal of the kamikaze judge was not to win but to question the whole procedure. They lost before the neo-NCJ, they questioned its decision to the Supreme Administrative Court and asked the last one to refer the question of the status of the neo-NCJ and the new chambers of the Supreme Court to the Court of Justice of EU.

The first candidates who took part in this coordinated 'kamikaze' action and applied for the position of the Supreme Court judge in the Disciplinary Chamber of the Supreme Court were judges: Jacek Barcik, a legal scholar from the University of Silesia, judge Sławomir Forenc from the Bełchatów District Court and judge Arkadiusz Tomczak from the Warsaw Administrative Court. There were others, like judge Piotr Borowiecki from the Warsaw Administrative Court and judge Rafał Zawalski from the Warsaw Praga-Południe District Court that applied to the ERPA. Similarly to the disciplinary chamber, the ERPA chamber is a newly constituted entity, composed of neo-judges, loyal to the ruling party.

Judge Piotr Gąciarek from the Warsaw Regional Court and judge Rafał Skrzecz from the Warsaw-Wola District Court applied as kamikaze judges to the Criminal Chamber of the Supreme Court while Judges Katarzyna Wróbel-Zumbrzycka and Marta Kożuchowska-Warywoda took part in the competition for a judge respectively in the new Chamber of Extraordinary Review and Public Affairs and in the Criminal Chamber (Zawiślak 2019). The purposes of these independent judges joining the rigged competition process was to question the whole competition process supervised and executed by politicized and unconstitutionally elected NCJ.

Jacek Barcik, one of the kamikaze judges, explained (2018) why he was applying for the post of the Supreme Court judge in the Disciplinary Chamber in the following manner:

*I believe that every person submitting his candidacy to the Supreme Court should use this opportunity to challenge the legality of the current procedure for the appointment of judges. The ethical duty of each candidate is to appeal against the decision of the National Council of the Judiciary concerning the judiciary appointment to the Supreme Administrative Court. And this is only possible when one takes part in the staged by NCJ competition. As part of the procedures before this SAC, we must seek to refer questions for a preliminary ruling to the Court of Justice of the European Union. In my opinion, the procedure of appointing judges of the Supreme Court does not guarantee that in the future this highest judicial body in Poland will indeed independently and impartially, without political influence, decide on cases submitted to it.... Therefore, our court, which is the Court of Justice of the European Union, should decide on the matter. However, this court cannot do it itself, because it must be given an opportunity to do so. This position is shared by me and a group of committed and informed candidates to Poland's Supreme Court. They risk their names so that the ruling political group cannot barbarously take over the Supreme Court, ultimately strangling the independent third power in Poland. We hope that other candidates will join us. Illegal procedures must be vigorously stigmatized.*

According to Judge 2, "Kamikaze strategy was the first action that was not merely reactive to what the authorities did, but was active and planned in advance by our side to reach certain results." Judges could appeal only if they participated in the competition. It was not about to win but to question the whole procedure. So when judges lost before the neo-NCJ, they questioned its decision to the Supreme Administrative Court and asked the last one to refer the question of the status of the neo-NCJ and the new chambers of the Supreme Court to the Court of Justice of EU. Judges make a reference to the resistance against the German occupation:

*Kamikaze judges is about us trying to make changes from inside or at least prevent bad changes/deterioration of the situation for as long as possible. Even during the German occupation there were two organizations—the Polish Red Cross (PCK) and Rada Glowna Opiekuncza (Main Welfare Council)—that were legal and had to work with Germans trying to mitigate the horrific impact of the occupation. Here, we want to stop illegal capture of the judiciary. Kamikaze strategy aims not only to delay but to derail the negative changes. Despite initial hesitation by judges, it was eventually embraced by many. We decided to take part in the competitions, challenge the process to the SAC with the goal of having the proceedings suspended and having SAC refer a question regarding the whole process and the status of NCJ to the CJEU for a preliminary ruling.* (Barcik 2018)

By resolutions of 24 and 28 August 2018, the NCJ rejected the appointment of two kamikaze judges for the purpose of assigning a position as judge at the Criminal Chamber of the Supreme Court, and of three other kamikaze judges for the purpose of assigning seven positions as judges at the Civil Chamber of that court. Those resolutions moreover contained proposals for the appointment of other candidates to the above positions. All five judges appealed to the SAC and asked, as a precautionary measure, for the suspension of the resolutions. The SAC ordered that the implementation of those resolutions be suspended, stayed the proceedings and referred the case to the CJEU for a preliminary ruling. In its referral, SAC asked CJEU to consider the composition of the body (NCJ) whose key function is to safeguard the independence of the judiciary while their representatives are now being elected by the legislature and whether such format in fact undermines the principle of institutional balance.

Judge 25 shared:

*We received cases brought by independent Kamikaze judges who took part in the competitions for higher judicial positions set up by the neo-NCJ. Their appeals, instead of going to the Extraordinary Review and Public Affairs Chamber according to the standard rules were first kept at the Supreme Court's administration office and then referred to the Labor Chamber—the complainant addressed our chamber, this was sent to us despite the fact that according to the division of duties, it should be referred to the Extraordinary Review and Public Affairs Chamber.*

Judge Monika Frąckowiak was the first to challenge the legality of the neo-judge of the Supreme Court. In 2019, she sued the neo-judge of the Disciplinary Chamber Jan Majchrowski to Chamber of Labor and Social Security of the Supreme Court and challenged his status as a judge. On the basis of this case, the adjudication panel of the Chamber of Labor and Social Security of the Supreme Court referred questions for a preliminary ruling to the CJEU aimed at assessing the status of neo-judges of the Supreme Court.

The CJEU has already dealt with the questions related to the Frąckowiak case. In the second half of March 2022, the Court ruled that the questions were inadmissible. The Tribunal found that under Polish law Judge Frąckowiak had no right to appeal against Majchrowski's appointment to the Disciplinary Chamber. At the same time, the CJEU recalled that it had already ruled on the status of persons adjudicating in the Disciplinary Chamber of the Supreme Court on July 15, 2021. The Court then ruled that its members did not meet the criteria of independent judges. That is why the European Commission demanded the liquidation of the Chamber (Jałoszewski 2022).

Judge 11 reflected on their role in implementing the kamikaze strategy as it was the only way to be able to question the status of the neo-judges. Being a part of the competition allowed the candidates to legally question the procedure at the national courts making them refer the case for preliminary ruling to the CJEU and, after exhaustion of domestic remedies, to the ECHR.

*I applied for a competition for a judge in the Disciplinary Chamber of the Supreme Court, despite the fact that the NCJ is an illegal and politicized body.... If I hadn't officially joined the judicial competition, I wouldn't have been able to submit the lawsuit, not having a legal interest in it. As a result of my lawsuit, the Chamber of Labor and Social Security of the Supreme Court referred a question on the legal status of the newly constituted and controlled by the government NCJ for a preliminary ruling to the CJEU.*

### 7.2 Disclosing recording of the NCJ competition

The sessions led by the state controlled NCJ were recorded and showed the way NCJ members were questioning the candidates for judges. The recordings were posted on the Twitter account of Judge Bartłomiej Starosta (@Bartek_Star), who regularly analyzes such hearings and points to the irregularities of the competition proceedings led by the neo-NCJ.

Judge Piotr Gąciarek, who was a candidate for the Supreme Court, was questioned in August 2018 by the NCJ. He recorded his own hearing on his phone, even though permission had not been granted to make his hearing public. He disobeyed it, and the recording was published on Iustitia's website (Hearing of the Vice-President 2018). According to Judge Gąciarek, the weight of the procedure concerning appointment of the Supreme Court judge is too important and must be available for the public to hear (TVN 24 2018).

### 7.3 Brief work stoppage during case hearings

Judges engaged work stoppages in the form of 30-minute adjournments during hearings, protesting the authorities and changes that undermined judiciary independence. The first one took place at noon on April 20, 2017. Judges of appeal and regional courts across Poland had adopted a resolution in which they asked judicial associations to "establish a forum for cooperation between representatives of the judicial self-government" (Forum FWS). The amendment to the act on the NCJ was about to liquidate the existing judges' assemblies. The work stoppage allowed each district, regional, and appeals court to select representatives of the new forum. 120 judges from Katowice Regional Court stopped their work for at least 30 minutes. At the beginning of the meetings, they listened to the appeal of the former president of the Supreme Court, Professor Adam Strzembosz. During the meeting, the judges chose the representatives of the Judges Cooperation Forum.

### 7.4 Halting a hearing to explain resistance

Judges have also used work stoppages for educational purposes. They have adjourned hearings to explain to the parties why the judicial protest was taking place. As Judge 4 shared, "I am ordering a 5-minute break in each case, indicating to the minutes that the break is to show solidarity with the unlawfully suspended judge Igor Tuleya."

### 7.5 Self-Denunciation

In a novel show of solidarity, Krakow judges introduced a fresh approach to support their persecuted counterparts. In December 2019, around 70 judges from Krakow participated in a poster campaign within the Krakow Regional Court premises, advocating for the demands of judges' associations. The Regional Court's president responded by initiating disciplinary proceedings against Judges Dariusz Mazur and Mariusz Czajka. In response, the 70 judges collectively signed letters of self-denunciation, admitting their involvement in putting up the posters. They acknowledged their guilt, emphasizing that fairness demanded consequences for all involved. They also attached photographic evidence of their participation. This event was documented on the Themis website, highlighting their proactive stance in defending repressed judges (Themis 2020). One judge explained to the author, "I am trying to defend the repressed people. I speak only..., I'm in a fight.... I wrote to Lasota's disciplinary spokesman that I had done a lesson with the classes about the Constitution and the independence of judges."

### 7.6 Asking for repressive order in writing

Judges also changed their attitude toward authorities. Thus far, they had not questioned the legal basis of the requests of the Ministry of Justice addressed to the courts. After 2017, it all changed. They realized that most of the actions lack any legal ground. One judge shared in an interview with the author: "When Dariusz Pawłyszcze from the Ministry of Justice demanded that all cases where judges question the status of a judge be reported, I wrote back to him to indicate the legal basis for the request."

## 8. Political/Judicial Creative Intervention

### 8.1 Dismissal of a court decision on the grounds of the illegitimacy of a judge appointed by the neo-NCJ

The "neo-judge" label refers to those nominated by the neo-NCJ to any judgeship on any court level. In 2020 there were about 1,000 neo-judges, and in 2023, about 2,600 (KOD nd).

Judge Adam Synakiewicz from the Częstochowa Regional Court dismissed the Zawiercie District Court's ruling because it was issued by the judge in the court of first instance that was nominated to his position as a result of the recommendation by the neo-NCJ seen as illegitimate by resisting judges.

The judge from Częstochowa referred to the judgments of the European Court of Human Rights in the case of *Reczkowicz v. Poland* and, that of the CJEU from 14 and 15 July 2021 to ignore the provisions of the Muzzle law that forbade common court judges to examine judicial appointments, including the legal status of people appointed to judicial posts. Earlier he wrote six dissenting opinions to the judgments claiming that neo-judge Monika Maciążek had no status as a judge because she was recommended to her position by neo-NCJ. And he emphasized that his goal was to send a clear message that there is no consent to what the ruling party was doing to the judiciary. Moreover, the judge argued he wanted to protect the Polish state from a flood of complaints filed by citizens against Poland with the European Court of Human Rights (Mamoń 2021).

On 24 August 2021 the Częstochowa Regional Court, sitting in a single-judge formation, issued a judgment (case no. VII Ka 651/21) in a criminal case, that dismissed the ruling of the lower court on the ground that. Due to the participation of the neo-judge on the bench, the court had been serving unlawfully within the meaning of Article 439 § 1 of the Code of Criminal Procedure which states "the appellate court at the session quashes the contested decision, if an unauthorized or incapable person participated in the issuance of the decision."

## 8.2 Challenging constitutionality of the regime

Judges have adopted the practice of dispersed judicial review of constitutionality as an alternative to the Constitutional Tribunal. This approach involves assessing the constitutionality of new provisions, particularly those enacted by the ruling party, within common courts. Lawyer 7 highlighted that between 2017 and 2020, the courts increasingly utilized this method to evaluate new enactments that seemed to conflict with the Polish Constitution. Unlike the traditional approach of referring to newly passed statutes, this dispersed review involves the direct application of the Polish Constitution by common courts, effectively bypassing the compromised Constitutional Tribunal.

According to Tomasz Tadeusz Koncewicz (2016), "All those who oppose it must now concentrate on finding ways to make sure that Polish constitutional system is able to defend itself from within." Lawyer 7 shared:

> Today, they reach for functional, systemic, pro-constitutional, pro-convention, pro treaty interpretations—taking the position of the multicentricity of the legal system, which allows, in cases of archaic regulations, to derive the applicable norm in a specific case under examination—enshrined in the constitutional axiology, human rights, so that the decisions issued in these cases could be finally based on the provision of the Code of Offenses interpreted in such a way that, by definition, a simple technical provision would not be rashly applied as a means to suppress rights and freedom.

As Lawyer 7 underlined: "I consider it to be the greatest achievement of those times."

Judge 19 said:

> I have no problem with the direct application of the constitution and it is not about omitting the provisions of statutes, but about the pro-constitutional interpretation of these provisions. If we are talking about the freedom of assembly and the provisions specifying the acts intended to infringe this freedom of assembly, then when interpreting these provisions—these provisions cannot be applied in isolation from the Constitution. Disturbing another assembly [that is statutory prohibited by the ruling party]—it should also be interpreted in accordance with the Constitution—if someone says that this assembly is opposed, he or she has the right to do so.

Judges became people's judges when they started using dispersed judicial review of constitutionality in petty offense proceedings during a pandemic with regard to restricting the freedom of movement or ordering healthy people to wear masks. "I used the dispersed judicial review of constitutionality in pandemic offenses, ban on economic activity, ban on entering the forest," said Judge 7. Various provisions of the Code of Criminal Procedure, such as the judge's obligation to prepare a justification of the judgment on a form, also turned out to be unconstitutional. Therefore, the only way to oppose to the provisions was for the citizens to appeal to the courts and invoke the constitution directly. "A lot of good happened during the pandemic because people started citing the constitution during the trial," said Judge 14. "When they understood that there was no air without a constitution, they understood why the courts were so important."

Other judges resist against the new procedural they consider contrary to the international law. "I do not provide justifications on the form," said Judge 12. "I argued this with the judgments of the ECHR (fair trial and justification understandable for the participants). We are restoring the constitutional standard to unlawful regulations." As Judge 16 shared:

*While adjudicating in the courtroom, I did not apply some of the provisions of the Code of Civil Procedure resulting from the changes of the last 2 years—they do not meet the standards of protection of the rights of a party in the proceedings or even limited these rights. Recently, I have been designating matters for closed meetings instead of closed doors. I issue judgments in camera only if the parties consent to it. This is a guarantee of the right to a fair trial. I issued a justification for the judgment when I omitted the judgment of the Constitutional Tribunal, where the so-called "quasi-judge" adjudicated.*

"My task is not only to directly apply the law and its interpretation within a given field, but also to interpret the system. I refer to the Constitution and acts of international European law. Before, I had not noticed these areas of law," said Judge 7. Judges also refused to write reasonings of the judgments on the ministerial forms, as they considered them impractical and contrary to the requirements of the fair trial.

## 8.3 *Submitting preliminary questions to the european court*

Judges also resisted by submitting preliminary questions to the Court of Justice of European Union. For example, Judge Gąciarek posed the question to the CJEU in the context of Judge Tuleya's case, whose immunity had been lifted by the Disciplinary Chamber and who was suspended from performing his judicial duties. Among other things, Gąciarek asked whether Court President Piotr Schab had to implement the decision of the illegal Disciplinary Chamber. Judges received the support of KOS before submitting a preliminary ruling.

Referring cases to the CJEU is not always easy and requires the judge to consider many opposing interests. For example, Judge 24 did not use this opportunity in one of the last cases before she was suspended, but she could not because it would have led to the suspension of criminal proceedings in which the accused person was about to be acquitted. "It would be inhuman. For me, it was not exactly a good solution, but the welfare of this person was more important than mine."

Judge 25 commented on how they prepared to address the question of the rule-of-law crisis:

> *In the Supreme Court we have an outstanding specialist in European law, who was able to prepare technical questions for a preliminary ruling: what to pay attention to, what things to refer to, plus a group of judges who are courageous in a good sense. The first question on TVN—December 5, 2019, issued by dr hab Piotr Prusinowski, dr hab. Dawid Mięsik, Bogdan Wilk—it started. The organization of the judiciary is an internal matter under the autonomy of the Member States—but the question is not whether the Supreme Court is to be divided, but it touches on the essence of the matter: the independence of the judge, the independence, the impartiality of the court—the foundation of everything.*

### 8.4 Use of legal opinions

The natural remedy for judges to resist are legal remedies. As stated by Judge 27, "Judges only have legal instruments at their disposal—they are based on the supposition that they are effective." Therefore they make use of legal opinions of the recognized experts in certain fields to support their stance against the authorities, and also to show to the public, including the international community, that they are right. Judge 2 shared, "We make extensive use of legal opinions. It is natural to use legal means. Complaining a decision even when the legal action is not available, finding someone who would like to submit such a legal remedy."

### 8.5 Lawsuits and complaints by resisting judges

As experts in court proceedings, judges know how to fight using legal means, including filing lawsuits and legal complaints in domestic and European courts. There are several examples of judges using this tactic. In one case, judges filed lawsuits to establish that neo-judges in the Supreme Court are not judges according to law. There were also lawsuits brought to establish that members of the neo-NCJ are not actual members of this institution.

In another example, Judge Żurek filed a lawsuit against National Public Television (TVP) for defamation. He also issued a lawsuit against deputy minister of Justice Patryk Jaki, stating "Patryk Jaki slandered me on the television by saying that Judge Żurek is in the group of people who do not pay alimony" (Jałoszewski 2021). Additionally, Judge Żurek brought a lawsuit concerning mobbing against the president of the regional court in Krakow, newly elected by the Minister of Justice. The judge claimed that he was harassed by the president of the court and challenged the president transferring him from one division to another without his consent, which was in violation of the law.

Judges also filed complaints to the European Court of Human Rights.[3] At the time of this writing, their complaints have already resulted in eight judgments by the ECHR.[4] Judge Łukasz Biliński, after having been transferred to another division in the court, decided to submit a complaint to the ECHR. As he claimed in an interview with the author:

> *The restriction of the right to a court violated my rights as a citizen whose legal sphere has changed. In this way, my activity may help other judges being in a different situation and they will not be able to appeal—example of the case of judge Gąciarek, who was transferred to another department after having expressed a dissenting opinion. Similarly, Judge Żurek. These are my actions that are meant to serve others.*

### 8.6 Gathering information and archiving

The resistance collected cases of repression and categorized them into disciplinary proceedings, investigations, transfers to another position, and many types of soft repression (Lawyer 2). The judges try document everything: all resolutions, voting results, who took part in judge competitions (Judge 3). Judicial associations in cooperation with civil society organizations monitor and archive cases of pressure exerted on judges, prosecutors, and attorneys. There were several reports concerning repression against judges published as part of the Archive of Repression by KOS and Iustitia.[5] There is also The Wiktor Osiatyński Archive and portal in English, ruleoflaw.pl.

## 9. Economic Creative Intervention

### 9.1 Creating an option for financial resources and legal aids for the repressed judges and prosecutors

Since suspending judges meant a significant decrease in their salary, the Senior Judge's Home Foundation has created a special aid fund, from which non-refundable financial aid is

---

3    These include pending cases of *Brodowiak and Dżus v. Poland* (nos. 28122/20 and 48599/20), *Biliński v. Poland* (no. 13278/20), *Pionka v. Poland* (no. 26004/20), and *Tuleya v. Poland* (no. 21181/19).

4    *Xero Flor w Polsce sp. z o.o. v. Poland*, 4907/18, 7 May 2021; *Broda and Bojara v. Poland*, 26691/18 and 27367/18, 29 June 2021; *Reczkowicz v. Poland*, 43447/19, 22 July 2021; *Dolińska-Ficek and Ozimek v. Poland*, 49868/19 and 57511/19, 8 November 2021; *Advance Pharma sp. z o.o v. Poland*, 1469/20, 3 February 2022; *Grzęda v. Poland* [GC], 43572/18, 15 March 2022; *Żurek v. Poland*, no. 39650/18, 16 June 2022; *Juszczyszyn v. Poland*, 35599/20, 6 October 2022.

5    See **https://komitetobronysprawiedliwosci.pl/archiwum-represji/**.

allocated to support the judges. For example, Judge Paweł Juszczyszyn has been getting 40 percent less income for 1.5 years. The fund covers the missing salary. It is based on the contributions of individual persons, mostly other judges, who regularly contribute each month (Judge 7). Judge 2 said:

> *We could afford each judge who had his remuneration cut so that he would not lose one zloty. Judges are in different life situations, not everyone can afford to survive. We didn't get into it. We contacted them ourselves—we often spoke to them that it is not their private fight, and we have an obligation toward them. We say, "You will get the money back and you will return it to the fund."*

In their 2020 Statement of the National Board, Iustitia declared:

> *We shall ensure that Judge Paweł Juszczyszyn will not be left on his own. No judge will be left alone if he is subjected to repression by taking advantage of a politically appointed ministerial disciplinary commissioner for judges, his deputies or members of the Disciplinary Chamber because of the observance of the fundamental principles of the rule of law.*

Judge 24, who received financial assistance, said:

> *I was supported financially by the senior judge's house foundation, which helped me during the suspension period and covered the part of my salary that was suspended. Once I recovered my salary, I made a donation as a way to pay back the money. I received support from people on the streets who reacted in a very nice way. I have never been accosted by someone with a negative attitude. There are a lot of such people who support me until today.*

Judge 14 stressed: "If I was alone, the government steamroller would run over me. I had a lot of support from Żurek, Morawiec, and my Themis association."

Judge 27 highlighted what he received in terms of solidarity support:

> *Assistance in collecting documents, providing information, legal advice, but also gestures very important in the mental sense that colleagues from the Supreme Court took part in the press conference, objected, their presence in the courtroom, specific letters, no problem with finding a lawyer. And my case was tiny.*

## 10. Legal Aid to Prosecuted Judges

### 10.1 Pro bono attorneys

The resistance also supports the judges with legal aid. Judge 16 reflected, "There are lawyers from Poland who say that they will be happy to represent me pro bono. I received dozens of offers in one day."

This is a flagship activity of KOS, which organizes a platform for legal assistance once a judge faces disciplinary charges. It is possible thanks to numerous attorneys volunteering their time and skills. They represent judges in disciplinary cases and prepare all the tactics for defense. It also concerns criminal cases, labor cases, and defamation cases. But it is not only attorneys. The idea is that a judge is represented by another judge, prosecutor, and attorney in the disciplinary proceedings.

### 10.2 Pro bono judges

Judges defend other judges in disciplinary cases. For example, Judge Maciej Czajka defended Judges Żurek and Morawiec. Judge 16 recollected:

> I got involved in the case of Judge Alina Czubieniak, who was convicted first in the disciplinary proceedings without lawyers. I get involved in social media right away to clarify the matter so that this person is protected, because she could not speak on her own behalf. I was in the media, speaking about the prosecuted judge. I also referred her case to Iustitia's disciplinary team and KOS. Immediately a team of many people started working, developing the strategy, and wrote the pleadings. She was ultimately convicted but received full legal assistance. Attorney Radosław Baszuk was a defense attorney. We shared internationally the information about the prosecution of this judge. The American Bar Association got involved.

## 11. Social Creative Intervention

### 11.1 Establishment of Foundation of Legal Education

Iustitia started the Foundation of Legal Education, first known as the Judges Training Center and responsible for judges' training. At some point, Judge Krystian Markiewicz suggested that judges should not necessarily concentrate on training themselves as judges but more on important activities outside the judiciary such as the legal education of young people. The center changed their name to the Legal Education Foundation. Every year since 2016, the foundation organizes the Day of Legal Education that has a nationwide character. It has a special theme that changes each year, such as hate speech or the protection of the environment. It includes simulations of hearings, tours of the District Court in Warsaw and other courts, and meetings with judges and prosecutors.

The foundation also organizes the Day of Justice every May 23—the anniversary of the death of Judge Falcone. They announce the event on its website and in cooperation with the press. They also invented other initiatives, like competitions for best essay, poster, and photo concerning the court. In 2019, together with the European Commission, the foundation announced a poster competition themed as 15 years of Poland in the European Union. The prize of a study visit to Brussels was awarded to the seven winners.

Before the COVID-19 pandemic, the foundation also organized training for judges in cooperation with the European Commission representative.

## 11.2 Raise awareness events

Iustitia and KOD organized legal cafes open to all citizens and lawyers to have discussions about the rule of law, democratic values, local government, the independence of judges, and human and civil rights (such as abortion). This has helped build an ethos within the legal community and the citizens who joined the sessions. As the initiative grew, the idea was for people to get first-hand information while giving judges the energy to keep fighting (Judge 1).

At the October 8, 2018, legal café in Opole, Judge Tuleya talked about the independence of courts (Opole Legal Café 2018). At the November 21, 2018, legal cafe in Warsaw, Judge Gąciarek participated in the "Judges After Hours" event (Judges After Hours 2018). Another legal cafe took place on May 25, 2022, with Judge Paweł Juszczyszyn in Bielsko-Biała. The judge talked about whether the restoration of the rule of law in Poland was possible and what impact lawyers could have on it, as well as whether Europe understood the struggle of Polish judges for courts free from political influence (Silesian Legal Café 2022).

## 11.3 Tour de Konstytucja

Another Awareness Raising event was the "Tour de Konstytucja," which ran from June 4 to August 8, 2021. The aim was to use dialogue to educate citizens about freedoms and rights enshrined in the constitution. As Lawyer 2 said, "It was about uniting the community—we are together, we have common values, we can win." Judge 7 said in their second interview:

*It was necessary to awaken the feeling that there are more of us and to want to act again, to feel good energy, to give a hope to active and conscious people. To make noise in this area, so that those who live in the "TVPiS"[6] bubble think about why we need to talk about breaking the constitution and what we can do about it. There were also those in the crowd who tried to interrupt or were skeptical, but we always had someone who politely spoke to them.*

---

6    The name is a portmanteau of TVP (the state-controlled public television) and PiS.

All suspended judges like Igor Tuleya or Paweł Juszczyszyn were engaged in this educational campaign. Iustitia covered train tickets or gas for the judges to participate in the tours. Coordination of the Tour de Constitution is based on cooperation and contacts with citizens from civic, and local networks and organizations such as local KOD. As part of the Tour de Constitution, trial scenarios and questions for constitutional quizzes are prepared. There was also a "Rule of Law" relay race. "It is about walking a few kilometers for the rule of law," according to Judge 7, who was one of the organizers.

Judge 27 reflected:

*I really liked the fact that it is an activity with promotion and social celebration of the constitution—the foundation of our common living in small towns. There were over 70 of these meetings and many people watching events later.... The formula is very interesting—reading the preamble—taking the constitution seriously. It is known that it is building a secular community.*

## 12. Psychological Creative Intervention

### 12.1 Expression of solidarity and psychological aid

For resisting judges, solidarity is essential. It has both a symbolic and strategic purpose. Beyond its symbolic importance, it serves as a means of coordinated defense against repressive actions. KOS proposed that the defender of the judge should be a judge, lawyer, and prosecutor, thus reflecting the unity of the legal professions in the face of repression. According to Judge 12, solidarity is "the fule that drives us to act."

*The essence of humanity is helping someone in a difficult situation, making a phone call, looking for a defender. This is why intervention groups were created so that people in the cogs of the repressive machine are not left alone. This tradition of solidarity allowed judges to resist.*

Judge 2 commented:

*We decided that no judge could be left alone. If the state machine collapses on someone's head, we do not look if someone is from Iustitia or not. If a judge is subjected to repression, we help him—someone comes, calls—man, you can count on our help. I very often personally assure them of my support.... We can provide resisting judges with legal, economic, media and psychological aid. Any other aid. We have a disciplinary and immunity team that gives us its recommendations on whether or not we are in—we offer aid or not. If there is a common struggle for which people give the most—such a person has every possible help. We guarantee everything. This is how we react. One*

120

*for all, all for one. It works. If the state is trying to introduce a chilling effect, we want to unchill it and show that no one will be left alone.*

"Prosecuted judges feel the solidarity. When they had a case in court, they would come to our presidents for coffee showing solidarity," said Judge 25, while Judge 23 echoed, "Solidarity is essential—it gives us strength." They continued:

*The solidarity of judges is of enormous importance.... This is good for the psyche. You don't feel like you are fighting alone. What we can do are assemblies in defense of judges, support pickets, protest letters, and solidarity actions.*

### 12.2 Small gestures of kindness

Judges also offered small gestures of kindness to show their solidarity. As Judge 4 shared:

*I wrote an email to the judge who had the disciplinary proceedings saying that I fully sympathize with her, that she was right. She cried. After Paweł Juszczyszyn was suspended, I bought a postcard, wrote words of support for Paweł and traveled from Warsaw to Olsztyn. This is how I got to know him. For Beata Morawiec, I bought a biographical book about a strong, indomitable woman who won. She was very happy.*

### 12.3 Signature drive

When the CJEU ordered the end of the Disciplinary Chamber's activities, judges collected signatures under the statement. In July 2021, more than 4,000 judges signed an appeal to the government and the president of the Supreme Court demanding that "all obliged authorities... fully implement the order of the Court of Justice of the European Union of 14 July 2021 (C-204/21) and the judgment of this Court of 15 July 2021 (C-791/19), including the immediate cessation of the action of the Disciplinary Chamber of the Supreme Court" (Jałoszewski 2021). Judges also collected signatures under a petition that prosecution of Judge Tuleya was unlawful.

### 12.4 Psychological support

Every persecuted judge is offered psychological aid pro bono. "We did not succeed on a larger scale, because of the nature of a judge—we think we have to be strong. I'm afraid to go to a psychologist for fear of falling apart", said Judge 16. Still, such aid has been offered and available to the prosecuted judges and their families.

## 12.5  Solidarity with repressed prosecutors

Solidarity extends to repressed prosecutors as well, evident in the significant support they received when they were relocated to new offices 300 km away. The backing came not only from fellow prosecutors but also citizens and judges. KOD members led initiatives of support, like finding apartments in new locations and sending postcards. Flowers and warm greetings greeted them upon arrival. This solidarity takes a professional dimension too, as prosecutors share defense strategies against charges and offer assistance during disciplinary proceedings. A list of pro bono lawyers, as well as representation by judges and lawyers, exemplifies the robust professional solidarity extended to repressed prosecutors. As Prosecutor 1 shared:

> These are connected vessels. We are mobilized by the resistance of judges. Some judges impress me very much—they are role models in the fight for an independent prosecutor's office. We receive a lot of support from judges and lawyers. This is very important for the prosecutors who were alone at the beginning. We live in a time where community and support are very important. I received a lot of postcards from judges, lawyers, prosecutors, and ordinary citizens. It touched me very much. I received a credit of trust. We are decent people so we should be trusted. If you don't know how to behave, it's worth being decent.

Commenting on the reciprocity between the professions, Prosecutor 2 shared:

> We try to support the judges and they try to support us. There is an agreement at board level via associations. Judges take part in prosecutors' actions and vice versa. We came out together with more general civic initiatives—Tour de Konstytucja, PolAndRock Festival, where we dealt with the issues of the Istanbul Convention and the history of violence on our initiative.... We received a lot of kind words. Action: send the postcard to the prosecutor—in Jarosław, where I was relegated, several thousand cards were waiting for me. My colleagues went to individual prosecutor's offices—there they showed that you can be an independent prosecutor. A lot of support from judges from those areas who joined the search for apartments because the prosecutor's office did not provide accommodation. If it was necessary, the judges offered me an apartment in and around Rzeszów.

> Human solidarity exists in the prosecution because I have experienced it myself. Like those kids in the District Prosecutor's Office—they behaved very nicely when I faced disciplinary charges. There is no ostracism about unethical behavior and buying prosecutors through upward delegation, awards. There is rather tacit consent. I guess it's also such a slight envy why he did it and I didn't. The worst: there is no such legal backbone in the prosecutor's office. We have, for example, an assessor who gets nominated

*after 2 years and does everything to get a delegation to the PO within a month. It also proves the lack of criticism of one's own imperfections. For 20 years of work for me—I approach my skills and gaps with more and more humility, because I am not alpha and omega. However, these young people are convinced of their own righteousness and there is no ostracism in this respect.*

*Judge 13 shared:*

*Together with representatives of other legal professions, we design and provide opinions on legal acts. We maintain day-to-day contacts with the bar and attorney-at-law council, with prosecutors from Lex Super Omnia.*

*Judge 16 recounted:*

*I was on a canoe trip where the prosecutors from Lex Super Omnia were—it turned out that we started to share values in the environment, world view. This is not a political view, but a world view, and on universal issues—loyalty, faithfulness to principles, inadequacy. Here we are talking about some foundations. When it comes to values, they know what's important and that you cannot sell yourself.*

*When Prosecutor Krasoń was removed, Krakow judges protested in front of the prosecutor's office demanding their reinstatement.*

**FIGURE 20.** Individual photos of judges supporting
Igor Tuleya—We stand for Igor Tuleya

*12.6  Solidarity selfies*

Another act of resistance were the solidarity selfies (individual and group) in support of repressive judges done by judges. Through it, they demonstrated their support, with everybody standing with a judge facing repressions. In the instance pictured, it was about waiving Igor Tuleya immunity. It was posted on Facebook. "The case of Igor Tuleya is intended to show other judges what will happen to them when they issue judgments that, for some reason, may not suit the ruling party. Every judge must fear that in a moment he will be like Igor Tuleya, who is tried by the Disciplinary Chamber. This would be a politician's dream, we will not allow it, we will defend persecuted judges," said the president of Iustitia, Prof. Krystian Markiewicz.

# TABLE 4. Mapping the Judges' Civil Resistance Tactics

| Resistance Behavior | NATURE OF TACTIC INDUCEMENTS CONFRONTATIONAL OR CONSTRUCTIVE | | | |
|---|---|---|---|---|
| **Acts of Expression (Saying)** | **Protest or Appeal** Communicative action to criticize, coerce, inform, or persuade | | | |
| | HUMAN BODY | MATERIAL ARTS | DIGITAL TECHNOLOGY | HUMAN LANGUAGE |
| | 1. March of 1000 Gowns 2. Standing with letters 3. Black Friday protest 4. Attending disciplinary proceedings 5. Running in solidarity 6. Gathering of judges in front Supreme Court | 1. KonsTYtucJA T-shirts 2. Hanging posters in Courts 3. Decorating Christmas trees 4. Distributing stickers and nametags 5. Placing stickers on court windows Shaming NCJ candidates | 1. Anonymous blogging 2. Podcasts 3. YouTube videos 4. Social media and messaging apps 5. Government's centralized email system | 1. Resistance through writing 2. Open protest letters 3. Letters to international organizations 4. Press articles 5. Articles encouraging popular mobilization 6. Awareness raising and education during festivals 7. Academic pulpit 8. School courses 9. Legal resolutions 10. Constant update on websites 11. Outreach to local media 12. Outreach to foreign media 13. Translating public documents |

| | Noncooperation Refusal to engage in expected behavior through boycotts and strikes in order to penalize or increase costs on the opponent | |
|---|---|---|
| **Acts of Omission (Not Doing)** | POLITICAL | SOCIAL |
| | 1. No court hearting days 2. Refusing to adjudicate with politicized judges 3. Boycotting candidate submissions 4. Boycotting promotion process 5. Refusing to give candidate opinions 6. Refusing added duties 7. Disobeying unjust laws 8. Disobeying requirement to reveal associations 9. Strikes | 1. Not participating in disciplinary proceedings 2. Resignation 3. Ostracism 4. Withholding respect 5. Refusing to call neo-judges "President" |

| | Disruptive or Creative Intervention Direct action that confronts another party to stop, disrupt, or change their behavior, or that models or constructs alternative (competing) behaviors and institutions or takes over existing institutions | | | | |
|---|---|---|---|---|---|
| **Acts of Commission (Doing or Creating Something)** | POLITICAL/JUDICIAL DISRUPTION | POLITICAL/JUDICIAL CREATIVE INTERVENTION | ECONOMIC CREATIVE INTERVENTION | LEGAL | SOCIAL CREATIVE INTERVENTION | PSYCHOLOGICAL CREATIVE INTERVENTION |
| | 1. Kamikaze strategy 2. Disclosing recordings 3. Brief work stoppages 4. Using hearings to explain resistance 5. Self-denunciation 6. Asking for repressive orders in writing | 1. Dismissing court decisions by illegitimate judges 2. Challenging regime's constitutionality 3. Submitting preliminary questions to European Court 4. Use of legal options 5. Lawsuits and complaints 6. Gathering and archiving information | 1. Creating financial resources for repressed judges and prosecutors | 1. Pro bono attorneys 2. Pro bono judges | 1. Establishing the Foundation of Legal Education 2. Events to raise awareness 3. Tour de Konstytucja | 1. Expression of solidarity and psychological aid 2. Small gestures of kindness 3. Signature drive 4. Psychological support 5. Solidarity with repressed prosecutors 6. Solidarity selfies |

*Adapted from Beer 2021*

# Key Findings and Takeaways for Stakeholders

When faced with the assault on their independence, Polish judges chose not to remain silent. They responded forcefully and publicly, which was unprecedented in their profession. They not only used all available legal remedies from the bench to counter the attack on their autonomy, but also mobilized outside the courtrooms in cooperation with civil society organizations. This led to the creation of an extraordinary resistance movement comprised of judges, lawyers, prosecutors, academics, and regular citizens.

The Polish judges have been extremely creative and comprehensive in their resistance actions. They organized numerous demonstrations and assemblies, such as the "March of a Thousand Gowns," the "Chain of Lights," and protests in solidarity with repressed judges, which drew hundreds of thousands of participants. They reached out to the media to publicize the oppression they faced and to comment on the current situation of the administration of justice. Judges also engaged in social media campaigns, organized press conferences and legal cafes, signed petitions and appeals, attended conferences and rock music festivals to promote the rule of law, and wore T-shirts with the inscription "Constitution."

As part of their ongoing non-cooperation, they held 30-minute work stoppages every 18th day of the month to protest in solidarity with oppressed judges. They refused to communicate with those who benefited from the new system, to adjudicate with neo-judges, to respond to disciplinary spokesmen or attend disciplinary hearings, and to recognize rulings given by neo-judges. They used the Constitution and EU law against unconstitutional provisions and boycotted elections to the neo-NCJ.

Judges' other acts of resistance included solidarity actions such as providing pro bono legal aid, organizing a fund for suspended judges subjected to salary cuts, attending disciplinary proceedings of fellow judges, offering psychological support, providing pro bono support for translations, and archiving all forms of repression and violations of the rule of law.

Judges creative intervention include multifaceted forms of resistance such as coordinated kamikaze strategy, preliminary reference rulings, application for interim measures to the ECHR, actions of self-denunciation and legal education campaigns.

Judges demonstrated remarkable adaptability and innovation in their resistance tactics during the crisis, effectively collaborating with allies at both national and international levels. The impact of their resistance was far more significant than anticipated, characterized by its ongoing and evolving nature, continually gaining new supporters and forms of expression.

Their efforts led to President Andrzej Duda's 2017 vetoes of controversial judicial reform bills, reinstatement of judges forced into early retirement, and challenges to the status of the National Council of the Judiciary and new Supreme Court chambers by the CJEU and ECHR. The CJEU's interim measures resulted in financial penalties against Poland, and the ECHR's measures halted disciplinary proceedings against repressed judges. Unconstitutional changes in the judiciary were highlighted internationally, increasing global awareness and prompting action. The resistance movement significantly raised awareness of constitutional rights, with judges exercising their right to speak out and protest, directly applying the Constitution, ECHR, and EU law in their rulings. Combining legal expertise with strategic activism, Polish judges protected judicial independence and set a powerful example of resisting authoritarianism and upholding the rule of law.

Finally, judicial resistance was one of the factors that led to the fall of the populist government and the takeover of power by the democratic opposition in the fall of 2023. One of the key tasks of the new government will be to restore the rule of law and the independence of the judiciary.

## Takeaways for Judges

**1. Judges must transform into "people's judges" to connect more effectively with ordinary citizens.** They need to shift from being confined to the courtroom to becoming active participants in society. A silent, unseen judge benefits the ruling authorities, but during times of crisis, judges cannot remain passive. The primary strategy involves gaining an audience, finding channels to garner support, and persuading skeptics. Public confidence in the judiciary, undermined by ruling party attacks, can only be restored if judges take risks and publicly defend their independence. Judges must engage with ordinary citizens, who may not fully understand democratic institutions and their interconnections. By doing so, judges can counter the false narratives spread against them and reinforce the judiciary's role as a protector of democratic values.

**2. Judges must change their attitude in the courtroom.** In order to win over the society, judges must behave differently in the courtroom, opening themselves up and changing habits. Judges should remember that apologizing or explaining the reason for delaying the start of a hearing is not only an expression of respect for the participants, but also relieves tension and builds the authority of the court, which results in the correct course of the hearing. Judges should pay more attention to the correct and comprehensible instruction of witnesses and parties giving evidence or being interrogated. Judges should also pay due attention to announcing judgments in an accessible manner that leaves no doubt as to their content.

**3. Judges have a duty to uphold their judicial oath and engage in judicial disobedience when necessary.** A judge must act with conscience and without fear, as fear has no place in the judiciary. Judicial disobedience entails the obligation to fulfill their judicial mission regardless of enacted legal acts, rejecting any actions that violate basic human and civil rights. This commitment to justice must be maintained even at the risk of facing disciplinary proceedings.

**4. Independent judges can resist populist changes in the judiciary by adhering strictly to the Constitution and international law.** When expected to interpret a statute literally, they opt for a pro-constitutional interpretation or choose not to implement executive acts and ordinances that conflict with constitutional principles. This approach signifies judicial obedience to the Constitution itself. Consequently, courts have started applying a dispersed judicial review of constitutionality, effectively replacing the politicized Constitutional Tribunal. Additionally, courts should consistently apply EU law, the ECHR, and other relevant international laws to ensure justice and uphold judicial independence.

**5. Judges should utilize all procedural opportunities, ensuring no case is overlooked.** Every situation should be used to challenge decisions, aiming for resolutions in the CJEU, the ECHR, or earlier in the Supreme Court or Supreme Administrative Court. This persistent approach will help rebuild the legal system in the future, aligning it with the standards established by the CJEU and the ECHR.

**6. Judges should prioritize legal education to cultivate the belief that the rule of law is a collective responsibility.** This effort should focus on engaging young people and individuals from smaller communities who may be less involved in legal matters. By listening to their perspectives and involving them in shaping the future of the judiciary, a stronger commitment to upholding the rule of law can be fostered across society.

**7. Judges should leverage social media platforms such as Facebook and Twitter for their resistance efforts.** Social media provides a direct means of communication with the public and facilitates organizing local actions that can quickly gain national attention. Judges should also engage with the media to ensure accurate representation and understanding of their actions, recognizing that they may be targeted by attacks.

**8. Judicial resistance entails a strategic use of media and communication channels.** Judges engage with media at local, national, and international levels, providing them with crucial information regarding actions taken to defend judicial independence. It's essential to inform the public about the motivations behind these actions and establish contacts with various media outlets to ensure broader coverage. Cooperation between court spokespersons and the media is vital to ensure society comprehends the events transpiring within the judiciary.

**9. Judges should utilize Internet communication platforms (such as Viber, Messenger, WhatsApp, Protonmail, and Signal) to maintain constant communication and plan their strategies effectively.** This real-time communication is vital for organizing resistance, sharing experiences, and exchanging ideas on how to resist. Through these channels, judges can connect with a wide network of individuals within judges' associations, enabling swift information exchange and coordination of efforts, akin to a well-oiled machine.

**10. Resistance means staying in office rather than resigning,** as judges are duty-bound to fight for the court and uphold the rule of law. Resigning as a form of protest would be ineffective, as someone else would simply take the position. Judges must persist within the system to effect change and fulfill their duty to uphold justice.

**11. Judges should initiate informal dialogues with international entities,** including representatives from organizations like the European Commission, United Nations, European Commissioner for Human Rights, European Parliament, Parliamentary Assembly of the Council of Europe, the Venice Commission of the Council of Europe, Norwegian Funds, and American lawyers' associations. Additionally, they should actively partake in study visits abroad, leveraging these occasions to advocate for the prioritization of judicial independence within their respective countries.

**12. Judges should uphold their right to critique judicial amendments, leveraging their deep understanding of institutional functioning to safeguard integrity.** Preserving the freedom to protest and engage in public discourse is crucial, as judges' responsibilities transcend the courtroom, necessitating the sharing of expertise when societal integrity is at stake.

**13. Judicial associations should emulate the operational structure of trade unions,** recognizing the significant time commitment required from judges who balance association responsibilities with judicial duties. To incentivize increased participation from already engaged members, certain guarantees or privileges should accompany union involvement, acknowledging the additional workload undertaken.

**14. Preparation for the post-crisis period is paramount,** requiring strategic planning to rebuild and reinforce the rule of law and fundamental principles. The complexity of the situation necessitates innovative approaches to effectively address the challenges that lie ahead.

## Takeaways for Lawyers

**1. Establishing a central platform is essential for coordinating strategies among judges, prosecutors, attorneys, and civil society representatives.** This platform should serve as a hub for various organizations dedicated to upholding the rule of law and supporting individuals facing harassment from authorities. Institutional foundations should be established to provide legal professionals with assistance, including groups of lawyers ready to offer support. The platform's responsibilities include monitoring cases of pressure on legal professionals, informing the public about such cases, providing legal support to those affected, and taking action to uphold judicial independence and the rule of law.

**2. It is natural that all legal professions should become active.** There should be a team of attorneys established to represent *pro bono* judges in explanatory and disciplinary proceedings. It is a grassroots movement to help the oppressed judges and prosecutors to survive.

**3. Involving judges and lawyers from other EU Member States is crucial.** Resisting judges should maintain strong relationships with judges' associations across Europe and globally. This approach will transform the defense of the rule of law from a national to a European issue, raising awareness that protecting the rule of law in one country safeguards it in others. It's vital to recognize that national judges are also European judges, requiring independence to uphold European law effectively. This perspective fosters solidarity and underscores the interconnectedness of judicial independence across Europe.

**4. Law academics shall do more for resistance of judges.** Scholars have practical duty to protect rule of law. They could offer their expertise. They should put pressure by signing the appeals in defense of oppressed judges or those who are engaged in the resistance. Participating in protests, informing others what is going on in their country, explaining the difficulties of law to explain the current situation, writing to the newspapers, being present in media.

**5. Reaction to the attack on the rule of law / independence of courts should be immediate.** When the first institution is in risk of losing its autonomy / independence judges, prosecutors, lawyers, civil society organizations should not wait for another attack but should react immediately. If it was the Constitutional Tribunal attack it should involve solidarity of all legal professions despite the former conflicts. It is proven that once the first institution is taken over the populist authorities won't stop and will continue with others.

### Takeaways for other Domesic and International Allies

**1. The mainstream media (private media) can and should be used in resistance strategies due to their greater reach than social media.** It should be used to counter the slander campaign. The state media strongly influenced the formation of the negative image of judges and the negative attitude of many people towards fighting judges.

**2. The resistance actions and the threat to judicial independence should be publicized abroad.** English is a universal language, making it imperative to disseminate information about these events in English to reach a global audience. Foreign media often lack insight into the complexities of legal systems, necessitating clear explanations and updates. Establishing a blog and Twitter account can serve as rapid information sources in English. Reports detailing developments should be prepared to inform international audiences, including foreign media outlets, major newspapers, policymakers in Brussels, and popular media platforms. By raising awareness internationally, pressure can be exerted on international bodies to address these issues and uphold judicial independence.

**3. There is a need of political pressure from the EU bodies.** The EU bodies should act without delay and using all possible procedures to tackle all potential and real rule of law infringements.

## Takeaways for Activists

**1. Solidarity is indispensable for judges facing repression, providing them with vital support and resilience.** This solidarity encompasses various actions, such as attending disciplinary hearings, providing legal aid, offering media assistance, psychological support, pro bono translations, financial aid, organizing assemblies and pickets, writing protest letters, and engaging in other forms of collective action. When repressed judges have a strong support network, they are better equipped to withstand challenges. People's backing empowers them and amplifies their voice, emphasizing the broader significance of judicial independence and justice beyond individual cases. Creating support groups and fostering connections across different sectors are key strategies to bolster solidarity and advocate effectively. Operating within an organization based on friendship rather than hierarchy fosters a sense of community and shared purpose among supporters.

**2. Ostracism is of great importance.** This involves actions such as refusing handshakes with pseudo-judges, causing irritation, and public shaming of those who collaborate with politicians. Naming and shaming are effective tactics to expose unethical behavior, especially among judges tempted by promotions or influenced by ideology. Ostracism entails avoiding social and professional interactions with such individuals, including conferences, joint research, and sitting on the same bench. By discouraging potential followers and making individuals on the other side feel alienated, ostracism serves as a powerful tool to uphold ethical standards and maintain integrity within the judiciary.

**3. The involvement of civil society organizations is crucial in supporting judicial resistance and defending judicial independence.** The success of the resistance rests in the collective—"it is impossible to fight alone." Collaboration with advocates, legal advisers, NGOs, and civic movements on the local level helps garner citizen support across cities. Civil society organizations also play a vital role in engaging with political forces to reverse attacks on the rule of law, informing the public about the situation, and highlighting the jeopardy to the rule of law. Additionally, they contribute to the legislative process as experts or critics and can organize demonstrations and protests in defense of the rule of law and repressed judges.

## Takeaways for Scholars

The research for this monograph was conducted in the context of an ongoing judicial resistance where the resisting judges are still being repressed and the international courts' judgments still are not enforced. This monograph has explored how judges resisted using all accessible resources to help them wage sustained and successful campaigns against unprecedented attack on their independence, and it encourages scholars to think deeply and comprehensively about several issues:

**1. There is still a lack of research concerning the common characteristics of judicial resistance around the world.** As discussed in Appendix I, there were cases of resistance in Romania, France, Spain, Tunisia, South Sudan, Pakistan, Egypt, and elsewhere, but no one has yet examined what is common in judicial resistance, what are the common measures judges are undertaking. This would help to understand the specific character of judicial resistance as a form of nonviolent protest.

**2. More research is needed to focus on the character of prosecutors' resistance.** Attention should be given to the common points between judicial and prosecutorial resistance but also to the differences. For example, prosecutors could be easily removed, transferred, or repressed. Therefore, the risk a prosecutor takes in resistance is much higher.

**3. There is also a need to assess why Polish judges refrain from going on strike.** At the same time their colleagues from France, Tunisia, Spain, and other countries go on strike when they protest. This research requires a comparative and socio-legal perspective.

# Appendix I. Resistance by Judges in Global Perspective

To shed light on the matter of judicial resistance around the world, we present several examples of judges' resistance from different countries. These cases demonstrate that judges and their allies, including lawyers, are not simply passive enforcers of existing laws but can actively engage as activists with a clear political agenda aimed at safeguarding democratic rule of law.

## Pakistan

On March 9, 2007, then-President General Pervez Musharraf dismissed Supreme Court Chief Justice Iftikhar Muhammad Chaudhry, alleging "misuse of office." The dismissal was largely influenced by the Chief Justice's actions since 2005, including questioning Musharraf's dual role as president and army chief. Musharraf also felt that the court was too independent from the executive branch.

A standoff arose between Justice Chaudhry and Musharraf when the former refused to resign. Amid that standoff, a powerful movement emerged called the Lawyers' Movement for Judicial Independence (Phelps 2009). Led by lawyers, the movement aimed to support the chief justice and defend the judiciary's independence from the Musharraf-controlled executive.

The movement's goal extended beyond the restoration of the chief justice, encompassing the defense of constitutional rule and, implicitly, the removal of Musharraf from power for undermining the rule of law. Extensive media coverage shed light on the movement's activities and the police violence encountered, generating sympathy and motivating others to join, including the previously disinterested or apathetic urban class. The movement achieved what political parties had failed to do: sparking a robust discourse on the lack of government accountability and galvanizing ordinary people to defend the rule of law. The most important actions organized by the movement included the Long March of a half million demonstrators calling for Musharraf's resignation and the reinstatement of the deposed judges and a mass sit-in that persisted until the government agreed to reinstate Chief Justice Chaudhry (Rafiq 2008).

To exert international pressure on the Musharraf regime, the movement engaged in international outreach efforts, including writing letters and holding meetings with officials from the United States and the United Kingdom, asking them to demand that Musharraf repeal the emergency rule.

Despite the government's use of violent repression, the mass protests across the country persisted for several months (HRW 2007). Through sustained pressure and mobilization, Musharraf was forced to back down. In July 2007, he restored the chief justice to office (Khan 2007). This victory, achieved through the organized force of legal professionals, fundamentally transformed the judiciary in Pakistan.

According to a Pakistani Supreme Court advocate, the movement's formation was "the first time in Pakistan's history that lawyers have dropped their conflicting political affiliations and forged an unprecedented professional unity to restore the rule of law" (Khan 2007). A Human Rights Watch report added: "For the first time in Pakistan's history, the country's senior judiciary as a group saw itself not as an ally and enforcer of the executive but beholden to the rule of law and the constitution" (HRW 2007).

Musharraf's later attempt to seize power by declaring a state of emergency on November 3, 2007, backfired and led quickly to a renewed mass resistance. Approximately two-thirds of Pakistan's 97 senior judges refused to recognize the imposition of the emergency rule. The judges were dismissed and detained, including Chaudhry (HRW 2007).

However, this repression backfired. Instead of quelling the resistance, it galvanized lawyers nationwide who defied Musharraf's suspension of the constitution. The civil resistance led by the lawyers garnered international support. Unable to assert control over the defiant judiciary and its allies and confronted with mounting pressure both domestically and internationally, Musharraf resigned as the head of the military in late November 2007, and the emergency rule ended the following month (Phelps 2009). Within a year, Musharraf lost the presidency, resigning in summer 2008 to avoid potential impeachment from the newly elected parliament.

The struggle for a free judiciary and the reinstatement of Chaudhry continued even after Musharraf's resignation. The election of Asif Ali Zardari, the widower of Benazir Bhutto, as president in late 2008 did not resolve the standoff with the legal profession despite election promises. Yet again, the lawyers' movement mobilized across the country. They organized a mass march on Islamabad joined by many supporters from civil society. Pressured by the movement, Zardari finally reinstated Chaudhry as chief justice in March 2009.

The leaders of the resistance were primarily lawyers and local bar associations, including the Supreme Court Bar Association. Pakistan's legal society provided a well-structured framework for effectively communicating messages to the movement's activists. The Lawyers National Action Committee, in collaboration with the Pakistan Bar Association, did all the central decision-making for the movement. Messages were disseminated through local bar councils throughout the country (Ahmed 2009). Notably, although they allowed political parties to participate in a supportive capacity. they organized and acted independently of the parties.

## Egypt

Despite the significant control exerted by the executive in Egypt over the judiciary, particularly in terms of judicial appointments through the Supreme Judicial Council, the judges have been neither toothless nor passive in their apparent subordination to authoritarian rulers. The Judges' Club, an influential association established in 1939, has over decades persistently challenged the executive control of the judiciary, including through various amendments to the Law on Judicial Authority.

Despite operating within constraints imposed by different Egyptian presidents, the judges have managed to uphold a level of credibility in the eyes of the public, positioning themselves as an independent and authoritative body. Judges were also helped by determined lawyers, who challenged various legislation before the Supreme Constitutional Court during the 1990s and early 2000s. The court's rulings, which sometimes favored the government but also ruled against it, helped expose the hypocrisy in the regime's rhetoric of rule of law and the workings of the judicial system (Brown 2016).

The struggle for greater judicial autonomy in Egypt intensified during the 2000s under Mubarak's regime, reaching its peak in 2005. During this time, judges sought greater autonomy to supervise the first multi-party elections which were scheduled for that year. In early 2006, they released a report exposing corruption and vote rigging in the 2005 parliamentary elections. In response, the regime began prosecuting the judges and summoned the report's authors to appear before the disciplinary court. In protest, the Judges' Club organized a sit-in, which drew public attention (Mekki and Bastawisi 2006). This sparked a civic coalition led by Youth for Change and Kefaya, who demonstrated in support of the prosecuted judges. They organized week-long sit-ins with tents outside the Judges Club office and in Tahrir Square, showing solidarity with the judges and protesting the government's decision to prosecute them.[1]

In Egypt, the courts have played a dual role, serving both the regime and its opponents. The regime has used the courts to curtail opposition and tighten control over the country's political life. Opponents have used the courts to challenge the state. According to Noha Aboueldahab (2017), this use of the courts in Egypt "meant that authoritarianism, as well as resistance to it, took on a heavily legalistic form."

This struggle has continued under President Abdel Fattah El-Sisi, who imposed severe measures against Egyptian civil society, including against the right to protest and the freedom of assembly. However, the courts have challenged some executive decisions. One example is the Supreme Administrative Court's ruling in January 2017, which upheld Egyptian sovereignty over the Tiran and Sanafir islands, countering Sisi's decision to transfer their control

---

1    See forthcoming ICNC Press memoir by anonymous Egyptian activist.

to Saudi Arabia (Reuters in Cairo 2016). The ruling reflected a popular opposition to ceding the islands' sovereignty. While the court system may not want or be able to threaten the core of the regime, these cases highlight that the judiciary can exhibit surprising levels of independence when it aligns with public sentiment or the mobilized resistance on the streets, despite the executive's apparent dominance (Aziz 2016).

## Romania

When the Romanian government attacked judicial independence by creating the Section for Investigation of Offenses within the Judiciary (SIOJ), it faced strong opposition from judicial associations. These associations not only organized mass protests but also requested a preliminary opinion from the Court of Justice of the European Union (CJEU) in a series of cases challenging the establishment of the SIOJ. In its judgment on May 18, 2021, the CJEU found that the special tribunal for judges violates the Cooperation and Verification Mechanism (CVM) and the institutional safeguards of judicial independence (Hogic 2022).

In 2017, the Romanian Parliament enacted the "justice laws," which entailed substantial changes to the three main laws governing the organization and the statute of the judiciary. These were enacted without taking into consideration the firm opposition of more than half of the judiciary (Călin and Pîrlog 2021). That December, more than a thousand Romanian judges, prosecutors, and trainee magistrates silently protested in front of courts and prosecutor's offices. Some held their robes or the constitution, but most displayed printed copies of the common oath of office they had taken at the start of their careers. The protests were held in the main cities where the courts are located.[2] The judges also protested changes in the criminal code which would drastically limit the investigative powers of police and prosecutors.

On 4 April 2019, approximately 30 Romanian judges and prosecutors protested at the Brussels Palace of Justice in Belgium for the rule of law. It lasted for about an hour, during which the protesters were applauded and encouraged by dozens of Belgian and German judges, as well as Belgian lawyers (Călin and Pîrlog 2021).

That same year, the Romanian Judges' Forum Association sought the opinion of the Bureau of the Consultative Council of European Judges (CCJE) regarding the independence of the judiciary in Romania. According to the opinion: "Judges certainly have the right to stand against any other policies or actions affecting their independence resulting from new legislation or amendments to the existing one or in the case of discriminatory or selective

---

2    In order of population from greatest to least: Bucharest, Cluj, Timișoara, Iași, Constanța, Craiova, Galați, Brașov, Pitești, Bacău, Oradea, Brăila, Târgu Mureș, Botoșani, Suceava, Baia Mare, Satu Mare, Piatra Neamț, Târgoviște, Tulcea, Slatina, Călărași, Zalău, Miercurea Ciuc.

approaches during the selection or appointment of judges, or political engineering to provide for a decisive role of the dominant political force, for example, during elections/appointment by Parliament, or interference into the judicial administration through executive bodies, for example by the Ministries of Justice, as well as in other cases" (Călin and Pîrlog 2021).

In their struggle for independence, Romanian associations of judges and prosecutors have actively engaged in continuous dialogue with relevant European and international entities, including the European Commission, European Parliament, Venice Commission, Consultative Council of European Judges, Consultative Council of European Prosecutors; European Network of Councils for the Judiciary, GRECO, and MONEYVAL. Among their actions was a flash mob organized by Romanian and Belgian magistrates in Brussels. Additionally, Romanian courts have referred to the CJEU regarding the interpretation of the EU law in the context of legislative amendments aimed at safeguarding an independent disciplinary procedure for Romanian judges, thereby removing any risk related to political influence on disciplinary procedures.

According to Nedim Hogic, the mobilization of judges serves not only to elicit CJEU engagement but also to prevent the capture of the judiciary, making it resilient against external constraints. Similar to the resistance in Poland, the Romanian judges demonstrated allegiance to both their national order and the CJEU. This strategic behavior is aimed at preserving their reputation while upholding their independence. Moreover, it is a natural outgrowth of the model of judicial dialogue between the national and European courts that is now being uprooted after being successfully entrenched across European jurisdictions (Hogic 2022).

## France

France has "a history of political arrogance towards the judiciary which, in turn, has fostered political activism among its members." In 1968, judges supported student protesters demanding radical social reforms by releasing them from custody. Subsequently, a judges' syndicate was established which organized conferences on human rights, legislation, prison reform, class justice, and even judicial strikes. In 1976, a judicial strike was organized to protest unfavorable working conditions. In 1979, around 1,300 judges participated in a strike opposing changes to the policy of judicial recruitment. Two years later, judges organized another strike against direct and indirect political interference with the judiciary (De Haan, Silves and Thomas 1989).

In December 2021, most French judges staged a walkout to demand better working conditions. Across the country, judges, lawyers, magistrates, clerks, and staff gathered outside courthouses. They protested excruciating work hours, understaffed courts, and accelerated legal proceedings. They held signs declaring "Sick justice," "The justice we render no longer makes sense," and "Statistics everywhere, justice nowhere." This was the first time France's largest trade union of judges, the conservative Union Syndicale des Magistrats, approved a strike (Burdeau 2021).

## Other Examples of Judicial Resistance

There are further examples of judicial resistance from around the world. To show the complexity of this phenomenon, we summarize actions undertaken by judges in various countries.

In 2003, Burundian judges went on a 50-day strike, demanding better working conditions, increased independence, and higher salaries. Although the government did not meet most of their demands and the judges eventually resumed work, a joint government–magistrate committee was established to review judicial independence and propose measures for implementing magistrate statutes (Judges Resume 2003).

In 2009, Spanish judges staged an unprecedented one-day strike to demand more resources for the courts. In their opinion, they work "under an intolerable workload using outdated technology." Around 63 percent of the country's 3,500 serving judges joined the protest. Demonstrations took place outside courtrooms in several Spanish cities, calling for the hiring of more judges, setting workload limitations, and the full computerization of the legal system. However, judges continued minimum service for critical cases such as arrests and marriages (Spanish Judges 2009).

In 2012 alone, judges in Benin, Colombia, Ghana, Greece, Malawi, Morocco, Spain, Sri Lanka, Tunisia, and Yemen went on strike demanding greater judicial autonomy (Trochev and Ellett 2014).

In 2016, judicial officers in Telangana, India, went on strike, protesting alleged arbitrary decision in posting judicial officers in the newly created state by the high court. This was not their first strike. In April 2004, all but one of the 27 judges of Punjab and Haryana High Court took mass leave to protest their treatment by the then-chief justice (Mahapatra 2016).

On June 7, 2016, Belgian judges staged a demonstration highlighting their concerns regarding insufficient financial resources, risks of losing judicial independence under executive supervision, staff shortages, and changes to their pension system. The judges gathered at 8:45 a.m. in front of court buildings nationwide to protest the government's budget plan. In an open letter endorsed by 60 percent of the judges, they expressed their grievances (Les Mesures 2016).

In May 2017, judges in South Sudan organized a strike to demand better pay, improved working conditions, and the removal of Chief Justice Chan Reec Madut from his position for disregarding their requests. The judges were shocked by President Salva Kiir's removal of the chief justice. In response, the president dismissed the 14 judges through a decree without following the proper procedure. In solidarity with the dismissed justices, the judges' general assembly decided to continue the general strike until all their demands were met (Biajo 2017).

In May 2019, Lebanese judges went on strike over allowance cuts. However, they made an exception to hold hearings for cases related to the release or trial of detainees. This marked the third strike in the history of the Lebanese judiciary. Similar movements had occurred in 2017 and 2018 in response to government decisions, such as the elimination of the cooperation fund for judges and judicial assistants. The strikes ceased only after the government rescinded its decisions (Diab 2019).

In February 2022, Tunisian judges orchestrated a two-day strike against the dissolution of the Supreme Judicial Council—the constitutional institution that safeguarded judicial independence and oversaw the conduct, accountability, promotions, and demotions of judges. On the first day of the strike, the judges took to the streets, while on the second day, they organized a sit-in in front of the court (Marsi 2022). A few days later, administrative judges in Tunisia carried out a one-day strike in response to President Kais Saied's order granting himself authority to appoint, dismiss, promote, and punish judges (Tunisia 2022).

# Appendix II. Structure of the Judiciary of Poland

This section provides an overview of the judiciary structure in Poland. This will elucidate the government's attempts to gut the independent judiciary in Poland, how and where the resistance within the judiciary began, its growth and spread, and where the choking points are that either prevent resistance from metastasizing or make it challenging for the government to quash it.

The judiciary of Poland is organized into a four-tier court system, comprising the Supreme Court, the common courts, administrative courts (including the Supreme Administrative Court of Poland), and military courts, as enshrined in Article 175(1) of the constitution. The common courts—which include appellate courts, regional courts, and district courts—have competency in criminal, civil, economic, labor, and family law. Common court judges are nominated by the National Council of the Judiciary and are appointed for life by the president. The appointment of the new judges and court assessors happens in five stages. First, there is a call for competition for a judicial post published by the Minister of Justice in the Official Journal. Second, the candidates apply for a post to the president of the court in which the post is held. Third, the candidates are opinionated by the boards of judges and then voted by the court's general assembly. Fourth, the NCJ chooses the candidate for the judicial post based on such a procedure. It makes its decision through a resolution. The list of candidates chosen by the NCJ is sent to the President for approval. Refusal by the NCJ to include a candidate on the nomination list may in general be contested in the Supreme Court, but according to current law (which in that respect was found by the CJEU to be likely in violation of European Union law), there is no legal recourse in the case when the NCJ denies the Supreme Court nomination. Last, according to the current constitutional and statutory regulations, the President appoints new judges and court assessors among those nominated by the NCJ upon receiving their oath. The President's decision is published in the Official Journal. All judges must retire by age 65 or, if declaring an extension on turning 64 and presenting a certificate of good health, age 70.

Outside of these four tiers, there are two tribunals: the Constitutional Tribunal, responsible for ensuring that the state complies with the constitution, and the State Tribunal, responsible for trying the highest state officials for crimes specified in the constitution. The judges of these tribunals are nominated by the parliament for a fixed term of nine years, which cannot be renewed. They are selected through a simple majority vote, and their term begins upon taking an oath administered by the president.

In Poland, at the end of 2018, there were a total of 9,776 judges, including 9,240 in the courts of first instance, or the regional and district courts (Evaluation n.d., 19).

## The Court Bodies

According to Article 21 of the Common Courts' System Act, the court's bodies are comprised of the following, for each type of court:

1. **For district courts:** the president of the court and the director of the court;

2. **For regional courts:** the president of the court, the board of the court, and the director of the court;

3. **For courts of appeal:** the president of the court, the board of the court, and the director of the court.

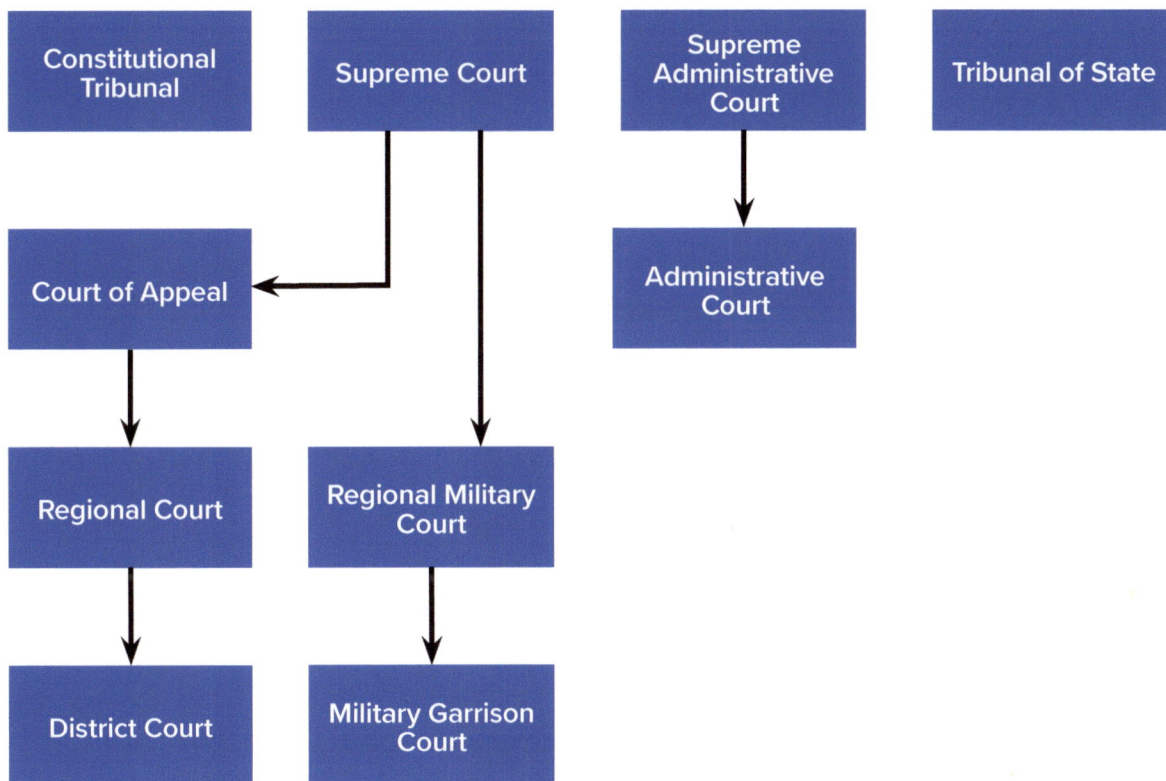

**FIGURE 21.** Structure of the Judiciary in Poland

*Source: Author*

## The Board of the Court

Before the Muzzle law entered into force on February 14, 2020, the board of the court of appeal consisted of five members elected by the general assembly of the court of appeal (comprised of judges of that court) and the president of the court of appeal. The elections would be held by secret ballot. For the election to be valid, at least half of all meeting members were required to vote. The Muzzle law changed the process so that the minister of justice would now appoint the positions of the president of the court of appeal and the presidents of regional courts from the area of jurisdiction of the court of appeal.

## Judicial Self-Government: General Assemblies of the Courts

According to Article 3 of the Common Courts' System Act, the judges form the judges' self-government, and the bodies of the judges' self-government are:

1. The general assembly of judges of the court of appeal;

2. The general assembly of judges of the regional court;

3. The general assembly of judges of the district court.

The tasks of the general assembly of judges were mainly opinion-making in nature. However, the implementation of the Muzzle law stripped the general assemblies of their rights, including the ability to express opinions on judicial promotions before the new National Council of the Judiciary. Due to concerns about its legality and impartiality, the judges refused to participate in the procedure before the neo-NCJ. Additionally, the ruling party introduced a law that prohibited both assemblies and boards of judges from adopting resolutions on "political matters" and undermining the legality of the functioning of the authorities and "constitutional organs." Furthermore, a provision requiring roll call voting during assemblies was introduced, eliminating the anonymity and secrecy of votes. This deliberate procedure aimed to identify and potentially prosecute judges who passed critical resolutions against Minister of Justice and Prosecutor General Zbigniew Ziobro, President Andrzej Duda, or the new National Council of the Judiciary. It was designed to help the disciplinary spokesman catch rebellious judges and discourage the others from resisting (Pankowska and Jałoszewski 2020). As Judge Dariusz Mazur put it, "it is hard to avoid the impression that the purpose of this solution is to create 'proscription lists' of rebellious judges who will then be subjected to various types of administrative and disciplinary repressions" (Mazur 2020).

Before the change, the general assemblies also declined to provide opinions on candidates in judge competitions. For example, on December 12, 2019, the General Assembly of Representatives of Judges of the Regional Court in Warsaw adopted resolutions that refused

142

to give opinions on candidates for judges of district courts until judges who were members of the neo-NCJ and elected by politicians resigned. They also demanded the reinstatement of Judge Paweł Juszczyszyn, called for changes to the NCJ, requested the President of the Regional Court in Warsaw to suspend his activities in competition procedures, and assessed the actions of disciplinary spokesmen Piotr Schab, Przemysław Radzik and Michał Lasota as a consistently implemented action aimed at subordinating courts and judges to politicians (Sędziowie 2019).

The administrative division, as shown in Figure 1, appeared straightforward, but it concealed significant tensions and conflicts. The key conflict was between common judges and appointed judges to the highest courts, primarily the Constitutional Tribunal. While the Constitutional Tribunal served as a guardian of the Polish constitution and acted as a barrier between politicians, policymakers, and the judiciary, it created contention by issuing controversial rulings (especially pertaining to the church). As Judge 2 commented, the rest of the judiciary "never liked the Constitutional Tribunal."

## Conflict Between the Supreme Court and the Constitutional Tribunal

The conflict between the Constitutional Tribunal and the Supreme Court escalated into a dispute over powers, particularly concerning the fraudulent nature of issuing interpretative judgments. Moreover, it has gone so far, and its parties are so entrenched in their positions, that in practice it has become undecidable (Dąbrowski 2017).

The Supreme Court disagreed with the Constitutional Tribunal's authority to determine whether a particular interpretation of a provision is in line with the Constitution. In the opinion of the Supreme Court, introduce interpretative novelties into the legal system that would bind the courts' jurisprudence solely based on its own interpretation of the provisions. Such actions may lead to an unjustified omission of a sovereign legislator solely empowered to legislate and is burdened with the risk of enacting a law, which exceeds the constitutional and statutory powers of the Constitutional Tribunal. In this context, negative interpretative rulings contain an interpretation of provisions only in terms of form, while in the substantive legal aspect, they sometimes constitute lawmaking acts that go beyond the limits of the constitutional prerogatives of the tribunal. Nevertheless, the Constitutional Tribunal continued to issue such judgments (Kowalski 2010).

In its December 17, 2009, resolution, the Supreme Court declared, "A judgment of the Constitutional Tribunal stating in an operative part that a given interpretation of a normative act is inconsistent, which does not result in the loss of the binding force of the provision, shall not constitute grounds for reopening the proceedings pursuant to Art. 4011 of the Code of Civil Procedure." The resolution was given the force of a legal principle. In the justification, the Supreme Court presented the arguments raised in the literature against the interpretative judgments of the Constitutional Tribunal. It argued that such judgments fall outside the Constitutional Tribunal's jurisdiction as defined in Article 188 of the Basic Law. Furthermore, the Supreme Court emphasized that the Constitutional Tribunal, having lost the power to establish universally binding interpretations of statutes, should not issue decisions that have such legal effects.

The resisting judges perceived that the Constitutional Tribunal had a significant communication problem. As Judge 7 shared:

*The difference in the way my question referred for a preliminary ruling after a year was treated by the CJEU and the way my question of law was treated by the Constitutional Tribunal is heaven and earth. The Constitutional Tribunal has always seemed to be very detached from the entire judicial system. The person of the president—Professor Andrzej Rzepliński, who was not particularly liked by the legal community—judges, prosecutors, and lawyers in Poland. It also made it easier to get up and protest together. The human and emotional factor was missing, that we felt somewhere that this directly affects us. It wasn't what citizens feel all the time now.*

Moreover, according to the interviewed judges, Andrzej Rzepliński—then-president of the Constitutional Tribunal—was never well-liked by the judiciary. In 2012, the Tribunal issued a ruling that judges found difficult to welcome, declaring that the freezing of judges' remuneration in that year did not violate the constitution. When the tribunal was attacked by PiS, the lawyers' community did not mobilize in its defense. The judges' association, Iustitia, which spearheaded the resistance of judges after 2015, had been particularly aggrieved by Rzepliński's calling Iustitia "unreliable itself because it violates the constitution. It is a de facto trade union, and the constitution prohibits judges, inter alia, from creating and belonging to trade unions" (Siedlecka 2012).

In addition to this visible division there were others inside the judiciary. Judge 9 observed: "We have always been divided into so-called 'palaces,' that is, regional and appellate judges, and district judges, who are the most numerous. In addition, there was a division into big city judges and those from smaller centers."

# Appendix III. The Interviews

In considering judicial resistance in Poland, this study incorporated the voices and experiences of Polish judges, prosecutors, lawyers, activists and academics. Care was taken to ensure the inclusion of a range of resistance participants who could offer diverse insights into character of judicial resistance in Poland. A second key determinant of interviewee selection was the role of activists in judicial resistance in various courts from the district and regional courts to the Supreme Court. Gender was another crucial factor in the selection of interviewees. Women are playing an important role in the nonviolent campaign. The author interviewed 18 women from different geographical areas and professions. The author conducted 54 interviews with 43 interviewees from different backgrounds and geographical areas. The interviewees were drawn from different groups classified for the purpose of this study as: Group One: The judges, Group Two: Former judges, Group three: Prosecutors, Group Four: Lawyers, Group Five: Academics, Group Six: Activists. All of them have been engaged in resistance against the illiberal backsliding in Poland, defending judicial autonomy and the rule of law. Some of them faced disciplinary proceedings, others were defending or protesting on the streets. They are also involved in everyday resistance in many ways. We adopted a uniform set of confidentiality measures that protect the identities of all interviewed activists. The names of the interviewees were coded for confidentiality (see Table 5). All the interviews were conducted only after verbal consent had been obtained from the interviewees.

| TABLE 5. INTERVIEWEES FOR THIS STUDY | | | |
|---|---|---|---|
| JUDGES | | | |
| Interviewee | Gender | Interview Date | Profile |
| Judge 1 | M | 16, 22, 29 Jun, 7 Jul 2021 | Judge from the regional court in a big city |
| Judge 2 | M | 24 Jun, 9 Jul, 6–7 Sep 2021 | Judge from the regional court in a big city |
| Judge 3 | F | 24 Jun 2021 | Judge from the regional court in a big city |
| Judge 4 | M | 25 Jun 2021 | Judge from the regional court in a big city |
| Judge 5 | M | 1 Jul 2021 | Judge from the regional court in a big city |
| Judge 6 | M | 2-9 Jun 2021 | Former judge from the district court in a big city |
| Judge 7 | F | 5-22 Jul 2021 | Judge from the district court in a small city |
| Judge 8 | F | 6 Jul 2021 | Judge from the district court in a big city |
| Judge 9 | M | 7 Jul 2021 | Judge from the district court in Southern Poland |
| Judge 10 | F | 7 Jul 2021 | Judge from the district court in Northern Poland |
| Judge 11 | M | 27 Jul 2021 | Judge from the district court in Western Poland |
| Judge 12 | M | 27 Jul 2021 | Judge from the district court in Northern Poland |
| Judge 13 | M | 28 Jul 2021 | Judge from the district court in Western Poland |

| Judge 14 | M | 29 Jul 2021 | Judge from the district court in Eastern Poland |
| Judge 15 | F | 30 Jul 2021 | Judge from Northern Poland |
| Judge 16 | F | 2 Aug 2021 | Judge from the regional court in Western Poland |
| Judge 17 | M | 2 Aug 2021 | Judge from the regional court in Southern Poland |
| Judge 18 | F | 3 Aug 2021 | Judge from the district court in Southern Poland |
| Judge 19 | M | 4 Aug 2021 | Judge from the district court in Central Poland |
| Judge 20 | F | 5 Aug 2021 | Judge from the district court in Central Poland |
| Judge 21 | M | 5 Aug 2021 | Judge from the district court in Western Poland |
| Judge 22 | M | 10 Aug 2021 | Judge from the regional court in Central Poland |
| Judge 23 | F | 11 Aug 2021 | Judge from the regional court in Central Poland |
| Judge 24 | F | 11 Aug 2021 | Judge from the regional court in Southern Poland |
| Judge 25 | F | 13 Aug 2021 | Judge from the supreme court |
| Judge 26 | M | 13 Sep 2021 | Former judge of the Constitutional Tribunal and academic |
| Judge 27 | M | 2 Aug 2021 | Judge from the supreme court |

| LAWYERS | | | |
|---|---|---|---|
| Interviewee | Gender | Interview Date | Profile |
| Lawyer 1 | F | 17 Jun 2021 | Attorney from a big city |
| Lawyer 2 | F | 26 Jun 2021 | Lawyer and activist from NGO in a big city |
| Lawyer 3 | M | 2 Jul 2021 | Attorney from a big city |
| Lawyer 4 | M | 8 Jul 2021 | Attorney from Central Poland |
| Lawyer 5 | M | 28 Jul 2021 | Attorney from Central Poland |
| Lawyer 6 | M | 6 Aug 2021 | Attorney from Central Poland |
| Lawyer 7 | M | 10 Aug 2021 | Attorney from Central Poland |
| Lawyer 8 | M | 22 Jul 2021 | Lawyer and academic from Central Poland |

| ACTIVISTS | | | |
|---|---|---|---|
| Interviewee | Gender | Interview Date | Profile |
| Activist 1 | M | 23 Jun 2021 | Chairman of one of the biggest civil society organazations defending the rule of law |
| Activist 2 | F | 25 Jun- 6 Jul 2021 | Activist and lawyer from NGO in a big city |
| Activist 3 | F | 29 Jul 2021 | Lawyer from an NGO in Central Poland |
| Activist 4 | F | 9 Aug 2021 | Lawyer, academic and activist |

| PROSECUTORS | | | |
|---|---|---|---|
| Interviewee | Gender | Interview Date | Profile |
| Prosecutor 1 | F | 2 Jul 2021 | Prosecutor from the regional prosecutor's office |
| Prosecutor 2 | F | 3 Aug 2021 | Prosecutor from the district prosecutor's office in Central Poland |

| ACADEMICS | | | |
|---|---|---|---|
| Interviewee | Gender | Interview Date | Profile |
| Academic 1 | M | 8 Jul 2021 | Former judge of the Constitutional Tribunal and academic |
| Academic 2 | M | 4 Aug 2021 | Academic from France |

# Works Cited

## LEGAL DOCUMENTS AND RULINGS

**Commissioner** for Human Rights. "Commissioner for Human Rights." Office of the Commissioner for Human Rights, August 22, 2012. **https://bip .brpo.gov.pl/en/content/commissioner -human-rights**.

**Constitutional** Tribunal. "Judgment of 12 December 2012, K 1/12, OTK ZU 11A/2012/pos. 134."

————— "Judgment of 10 March 2022, K 7/21."

————— "Judgment of 24 November 2021, case no. K 6/21."

————— "Judgment of 7 October 2021, case no. K 3/21."

————— "Judgment of 14 July 2021, case no. P 7/20."

**Court** of Justice. "Judgment of 15 July 2021, Case C-791/19, *Commission v Poland*, EU:C:2021:596."

————— "Judgment of 6 October 2021, Case C-487/19, W.Ż., EU:C:2021:798."

————— "Order of 14 July 2021, Case C-204/21 R, *Commission v Poland*, EU:C:2021:593."

————— "Order of 6 October 2021, Case C-204/21 R-RAP, *Commission v Poland*, EU:C:2021:834."

**Court** of Justice of EU. "Judgment of 19 November 2019 in Joined Cases C-585/18, C-624/18 and C-625/18 *A.K. v Krajowa Rada Sądownictwa*, and *CP and DO v. Sąd Najwyższy*, EU:C:2019:982."

————— "Judgment of 5 November 2019, C-192/18, *Commission v. Poland*, ECLI:EU:C:2019:924."

————— "Order of 17 December 2018, C-619/18 R, *Commission v Poland*."

**European** Commission for Democracy Through Law (Venice Commission). "Opinion no. 683 / 2012." October 15, 2012. CDLAD (2012)0 20. **https://www.venice.coe.int /webforms/documents/default.aspx ?pdffile=CDL-AD(2012)020-e**.

————— "Opinion no. 977/2020." January 19, 2020. CDL-PI(2020)002 On Amendments To The Law On The Common Courts, The Law On The Supreme Court, And Some Other Laws. **https://www.venice.coe.int/webforms /documents/default.aspx?pdffile= CDL-PI(2020)002-e** (Accessed February 3, 2022).

**European** Commission for Democracy Through Law (Venice Commission) and OSCE/ODIHR. "Joint opinion on the draft amendments to the legal framework on the disciplinary responsibility of judges in the Kyrgyz Republic." CDLAD(2014)018.

**European** Commission for the Efficiency of Justice. "Evaluation of the judicial systems (2018–2020)." 2018, 19. **https://rm.coe.int /en-poland-2018/16809fe2e9**.

**European** Court of Human Rights. "Communication in the case of *Biliński v. Poland* (no. 13278/20)."

————— "Communication in the case of *Brodowiak and Dżus v. Poland* (nos. 28122/20 and 48599/20)."

————— "Communication in the case of *Pionka v. Poland* (no. 26004/20)."

————— "Communication in the case of *Tuleya v. Poland* (no. 21181/19)."

————— "Judgment of 26 April 1995, *Prager and Oberschlick v. Austria*, no. 15974/90."

————— "Judgment of 26 February 2009, *Kudeshkina v. Russia*, no. 29492/05."

————— "Judgment of 27 May 2014, *Baka v. Hungary*, no. 20261/12."

————— "Judgment of 28 October 1999, *Wille v. Liechtenstein*, no. 28396/95."

————— "Judgment of 29 June 2021, *Broda and Bojara v. Poland*, nos. 26691/18 and 27367/18."

————— "Judgment of 15 March 2022, *Grzęda v. Poland [GC]*, 43572/18."

————— "Judgment of 16 June 2022, *Żurek v. Poland*, no. 39650/18."

————— "Judgment of 22 July 2021, *Reczkowicz and Others v. Poland* nos. 43447/19, 49868/19 and 57511/19."

————— "Judgment of 3 February 2022, *Advance Pharma sp. z o.o v. Poland*, no. 1469/20."

————— "Judgment of 6 October 2022, *Juszczyszyn v. Poland*, no. 35599/20."

————— "Judgment of 7 May 2021, *Xero Flor w Polsce sp. z o.o. v. Poland*, no. 4907/18."

————— "Judgment of 8 November 2021, *Dolińska-Ficek and Ozimek v. Poland* (nos. 49868/19 and 57511/19)."

————— "Judgment of 6 July 2023, *Tuleya* v. Poland, nos. 21181/19 and 51751/20,

————— "Judgment of 24 October 2023, *Pająk and Others* v. Poland, no. 25226/18,

————— "Judgment of 23 November 2023, *Wałęsa* v. *Poland*, no. 50849/21.

**Extraordinary** Congress of Polish Judges. "Resolution No. 1." **https://krs.pl/pl/dzialalnosc/konferencje/199-nadzwyczajny-kongres-sedziow/271-uchwala-nadzwyczajnego-kongresu-sedziow-polskich-nr-1.html.**

————— "Resolution No. 2." **https://krs.pl/pl/dzialalnosc/konferencje/199-nadzwyczajny-kongres-sedziow/270-uchwala-nadzwyczajnego-kongresu-sedziow-polskich-nr-2.html.**

————— "Resolution No. 3." **https://krs.pl/pl/dzialalnosc/konferencje/199-nadzwyczajny-kongres-sedziow/269-uchwala-nadzwyczajnego-kongresu-sedziow-polskich-nr-3.html.**

**Iustitia.** "Course of the Hearing of the Vice-President of the Management Board of the Warsaw Branch of Iustitia—Judge Piotr Gąciarek by the Evaluation Team of the National Council of the Judiciary of August 22, 2018." Sound record. **https://www.iustitia.pl/nowa-krs-nowy-sn/2480-ujawniamy-przebieg-przesluchania-sedziego-piotra-gaciarka-przez-zespol-ds-oceny-krajowej-rady-sadownictwa-z-dnia-22-sierpnia-2018-r.**

**Law** of 20 December 2019. "Concerning the amendment of the Law on judiciary system, law on Supreme Court and some other laws (Dz. U. 2020, poz. 190)."

**Management** Board of the SSP IUSTITIA. "Resolution of 22 July 2018 on candidatures for the positions of judges of the Supreme Court (2018)." **https://www.iustitia.pl/83-komunikaty-i-oswiadczenia/2442-uchwala-zarzadu-stowarzyszenia-sedziow-polskich-iustitia-z-dnia-22-lipca-2018-r.**

**National** Board of the Polish Judges' Association "IUSTITIA." "Statement on the escalation of the repression against judges in Poland and the signature of the repressive act by the President of the Republic of Poland." February 4, 2020. **https://www.iustitia.pl/en/activity /informations/3670-the-polish-judges -association-iustitia-national-board-s -statement-over-the-escalation-of-repression -against-judges-in-poland-and-the-signing-of -the-repressive-act-by-the-president-of-the -republic-of-poland**.

**ODIHR.** "The final Opinion on the bill on the amendment to the Act on the National Council of the Judiciary and some other acts (2017)."

**Supreme** Court. "Judgment of 15 December 2017, SNO 51/17, LEX no 2429623."

————— "Resolution of 28 January 2014, BSA-I-4110-4/13."

————— "Resolution of 17 December 2009, III PZP 2/09."

————— "Resolution of 17 July 2013, III CZP 46/13, OSNC 2013, No. 12, item 135."

————— "Resolution of the Assembly of the Justices of the Supreme Court of 28 June 2018." **https://www.sn.pl/aktualnosci/SitePages /Wydarzenia.aspx?ItemSID=410-292d9931 -9fa5-4b04-8516-5c932ff6bdf2&ListName =Wydarzenia&rok=2018**.

**TVN** 24 Poland. "Sędzia Gąciarek nagrał przesłuchanie w KRS. 'Zbyt ważne, żeby to robić w trybie niejawnym' [Judge Gąciarek recorded the hearing in the National Court Register. 'Too important to do this secretly']." August 23, 2018. **https://tvn24.pl/polska/sedzia-piotr -gaciarek-nagral-przebieg-przesluchania -w-krs-ra863122-2380668**.

**United** Nations Office on Drugs and Crime. "Commentary on The Bangalore Principles of Judicial Conduct." September 2007. § 134. **https://www.unodc.org/documents/corruption /publications_unodc_commentary-e.pdf**.

**Venice** Commission. "Opinion on the Act on the Public Prosecutor's Office As Amended." Adopted by the Venice Commission at its 113th Plenary Session (Venice, December 8–9, 2017). **https://www.venice.coe.int/webforms /documents/default.aspx?pdffile=CDL -AD(2017)028-e**.

**Venice** Commission and OSCE/ODIHR. "Joint Opinion on a Proposal for a Constitutional Law on the Changes and Amendments to the Constitution of Georgia." CDLAD(2005)003.

**Vice-President** of the Court. "Order in Case C-204/21, *Commission v Poland*, 27 October 2021."

## FILM, VIDEO, AND AUDIO SOURCES

**FreeCourts.** "Nasz Raport 2000 dni bezprawie ma także wymiar przestrzenny [Our Report 2000 Days of Lawlessness also has a spatial dimension]." June 24, 2021. **https://www .facebook.com/watch/?v=439181923886507**.

**Iustitia.** "35 Irena Kamińska #KongresSędziów." Sep 8, 2016. **https://www.youtube.com/watch ?v=qAeQtznU16Q&t=1s**.

————— "Przesłanie prof. Adama Strzembosza z okazji Zebrań Sędziów 20 kwietnia 2017." Apr 13, 2017. **https://www.youtube.com /watch?v=px3GC1bhZG4**.

————— "Wolne wybory [Free elections]." October 6, 2021. **https://www.youtube.com /watch?v=U9ecSqABnpY**.

**Lisowski,** K. "Tysiąc tóg [Thousand gowns]." **https://vod.pl/filmy/tysiac-tog-caly-film -online/tgym6eh.**

**Okręgowa** Rada Adwokacka w Warszawie. "Konferencja Doświadczenie i zobowiązanie. 45-lecie powstania KOR." Sep 21, 2021. **https:// www.youtube.com/watch?v=Oedsz6DEWt0.**

**Oxford** Poland Constitutional Symposium 2017. "The second panel: Gizbert-Studnicki / Morawski / Endicott." May 9, 2017. **https:// www.youtube.com/watch?v=3p5egncsjm4.**

**Polsat** News. "W południe odbyły się zebrania sędziów. Przerwa w rozprawach na pół godziny [At noon, meetings of the judges were held. Half-hour intermission]." April 20, 2017. **https://www.polsatnews.pl/wiadomosc/2017 -04-20/w-poludnie-zebrania-sedziow-beda -przerwy-w-rozprawach/.**

**Radio** Katowice. "Kongres Prawników Polskich [Congress of Polish Lawyers]." May 20, 2017. **https://www.radio.katowice.pl/zobacz,29247 ,Kongres-Prawnikow-Polskich-.html.**

**Sukiennik,** W. "Kasta." TV series on: **https:// vod.tvp.pl/website/kasta,50162540.**

**SSP** Iustitia. "SSP Iustitia." *YouTube Channel*. Accessed May 24, 2024. **https://www.youtube .com/c/SSPIustitia.**

**TVN** 24 Poland. "Łamanie konstytucji to łamanie człowieka." Protesty w obronie sądów ["Breaking the constitution is breaking a person." Protests in defense of the courts]." **https:// tvn24.pl/polska/protest-przed-palacem -prezydenckim-w-obronie-sadow-krs-i-sn -ra793139-2574852.**

**TVN** Warsaw. "Gersdorf dziękuje w imieniu sędziów. „Takiego wsparcia nie widział świat" [Gersdorf thanks on behalf of the judges. "The world has never seen such support"]." **https://tvn24.pl/tvnwarszawa/najnowsze /gersdorf-dziekuje-w-imieniu-sedziow -takiego-wsparcia-nie-widzial-swiat-582728.**

## BIBLIOGRAPHY

**Aboueldahab,** N. "Transitional Justice Policy in Authoritarian Contexts: The Case of Egypt." **https://www.brookings.edu/research /transitional-justice-policy-in-authoritarian -contexts-the-case-of-egypt/.**

**Adamski,** M., and A. Łukaszewicz. "Marsz Tysiąca Tóg Przeszedł Ulicami Warszawy [The Thousand Gowns March Marched Through the Streets of Warsaw]." *Rzeczpospolita*, January 11, 2020. **https://www.rp.pl/sady-i-trybunaly /art9085521-marsz-tysiaca-tog-przeszedl -ulicami-warszawy.**

**Ahmed,** Z. S. *Lawyers-led Movement for the Freedom of Judiciary and Promotion of Democracy in Pakistan* (Draft). 2009.

**Akcja** Demokracja. "Judgment of the CJEU. Goodbye to the Disciplinary Chamber and the neoKRS!" https://www.akcjademokracja. pl/wyrok-tsue-zegnamy-izbe-dyscyplinar- na-i-neokrs/.

————— "Sąd Najwyższy: Zostańcie! [Supreme Court: Stay!]" **https://dzialaj.akcjademokracja .pl/campaigns/354.**

————— "Sądy Wolne od Polityków! [Courts Free from Politicians!]" **https://www .akcjademokracja.pl/kampania/bronmy-sadow/.**

**Allan,** J. "The Activist Judge—Vanity of Vanities." In *Judicial Activism: An Interdisciplinary Approach to the American and European Experiences*, edited by L. P. Coutinho, M. La Torre, S. D. Smith, New York: Springer, 2015.

**Anisin,** A. "Debunking the Myths Behind Nonviolent Civil Resistance." *Critical Sociology* 46, nos. 7/8 (2020): 1121–39.

**Applebaum,** A. "The Disturbing Campaign Against Poland's Judges." *The Atlantic*, January 28, 2020. **https://www.theatlantic.com/ideas/archive/2020/01/disturbing-campaign-against-polish-judges/605623/.**

**Archiwum** Osiatyńskiego. "Home." Accessed May 24, 2024. **https://archiwumosiatynskiego.pl/en/.**

**Aziz,** S. "Theater or Transitional Justice: Reforming the Judiciary in Egypt." In *Transitional Justice in the Middle East*, edited by Chandra Lekha Sriram. New York: Oxford University Press, 2016.

**Bachmann,** K. "The Tribunal's Shredder is Clogged [Trybunalska Niszczarka się Zatka]." *Tygodnik Powszechny*, September 19, 2021.

**Bakiner,** O. "Judges Discover Politics." *Journal of Law and Courts* 4, no. 1 (2016): 131–157.

**Barak,** A. *The Judge in a Democracy*. Princeton University Press, 2006.

**Barcik,** J. "Dlaczego Kandyduję do Sądu Najwyższego i Dlaczego Nie Zostanę Sędzią SN [Why I Am Running for the Supreme Court and Why I Will Not Become a Judge of the Supreme Court]." **https://www.iustitia.pl/dzialalnosc/informacje-oswiadczenia/informacje/2457-j-barcik-dlaczego-kandyduje-do-sadu-najwyzszego-i-dlaczego-nie-zostane-sedzia-sn.**

————— "Ochrona Praworządności w Radzie Europy i Unii Europejskiej ze Szczególnym Uwzględnieniem Niezależności Sądów i Niezawisłości Sędziów [Protection of the Rule of Law in the Council of Europe and the European Union, with Particular Emphasis on the Independence of the Courts and Judges]." *CH Beck*, Warsaw, 2019.

**Barcz,** J., A. Grzelak, and R. Szyndlauer. "Problem Praworządności w Polsce w Świetle Dokumentów Komisji Europejskiej. Okres 'Dialogu Politycznego' 2016–2017 [The Problem of the Rule of Law in Poland in the Light of the Documents of the European Commission. Period of 'Political Dialogue' 2016–2017]." *DW Elipsa*, Warsaw, 2020.

**Barcz,** J., and A. Zawidzka-Łojek (editors). "Sądowe Mechanizmy Ochrony Praworządności w Polsce w Świetle Najnowszego Orzecznictwa Trybunału Sprawiedliwości UE [Judicial Mechanisms for Protecting the Rule of Law in Poland in the Light of the Latest Jurisprudence of the Court of Justice of the EU]." *DW Elipsa*, Warsaw, 2018.

————— "Wniosek Komisji Europejskiej w Sprawie Wszczęcia w Stosunku do Polski Procedury Art. 7 TUE. Ramy Prawno-Polityczne [The European Commission's Proposal to Initiate the Procedure of Art. 7 TEU. Legal and Political Framework]." *DW Elipsa*, Warsaw, 2018.

**Bárd,** P. "Luxemburg as the Last Resort: The Kúria's Judgment on the Illegality of a Preliminary Reference to the ECJ." VerfBlog, September 23, 2019. **https://verfassungsblog.de/luxemburg-as-the-last-resort/. DOI: 10.17176/20190923-232735-0.**

**Bartkiewicz,** A. "Akcja Demokracja Demonstrowała Przed Pałacem Prezydenckim [Action Democracy Demonstrated in Front of the Presidential Palace]." *Rzeczpospolita*, September 22, 2017. **https://web.archive.org/web/20180211131146/http://www.rp.pl/Spoleczenstwo/170929601-Akcja-Demokracja-demonstrowala-przed-Palacem-Prezydenckim.html.**

**Bartkowski,** M. (editor). *Recovering Nonviolent History: Civil Resistance in Liberation Struggles*, Boulder: Lynne Rienner Publishers, 2013.

**Biajo,** N. "South Sudanese Judges' Strike Continues Despite Dismissals." *VOA News*, July 14, 2017; **https://www.voanews.com/a/south -sudan-judges-strike-continues-despite -dismissals/3944773.html**.

**Bień-Kacała,** A. "Illiberal Judicialisation of Politics in Poland." *Comparative Law Review* 22 (2019). **https://doi.org/10.12775/CLR.2019.006**.

**Biuletyn** Informacji Publicznej Rzecznika Praw Obywatelskich. „Solidarność z sędzią Igorem Tuleyą. RPO Adam Bodnar pod Sądem Najwyższym." April 22, 2021. **https://bip.brpo .gov.pl/pl/content/solidarnosc-sadzia-igore -tuleya-rpo-adam-bodnar-pod-SN**.

**Bodnar,** A. „Co Prawnik Robi na Festiwalu? [What does a lawyer do at the festival?]" *Polityka*, August 18, 2022, **https://www.polityka.pl /tygodnikpolityka/kraj/2177876,1,bodnar-dla -polityki-co-prawnik-robi-na-festiwalu.read**.

————— "Polish Road Toward an Illiberal State: Methods and Resistance," *Indiana Law Journal*: Vol. 96: Iss. 4, Article 3 (2021).

**Bogdanowicz,** P., and M. Taborowski. "Regulacje Dotyczące Stanu Spoczynku Jako Narzędzie Służące Odsunięciu Określonej Grupy Sędziów od Pełnienia Urzędu na Stanowisku Sędziego Sądu Najwyższego—Uwagi na Tle Wyroku Trybunału Sprawiedliwości z 24.06.2019 r., C-619/18, Komisja Europejska Przeciwko Rzeczypospolitej Polskiej [The Retirement Age Regulations as a Tool to Remove a Particular Group of the Supreme Court Judges: Some Remarks about Court of Justice Judgment of 24 June 2019, C-619/18, European Commission v. Poland]." *Europejski Przegląd Sądowy* 12 (2019):15–25.

**Bojarski,** Ł. «Bon Ton Sądowy i Trybunalski. Kilka Słów o Neosędziach [Bon court and tribunal tone. A few words about neo-judges]." *Dziennik Gazeta Prawna*, November 19, 2019; **https://prawo.gazetaprawna.pl/artykuly /1438152,neosedziowie-tk-sn-ostracyzm -zamach-na-niezaleznosc-sadow-wyrembak -bojanczyk.html**.

————— "Sędziowski Ruch Oporu [Judicial Resistance Movement]." *Dziennik Gazeta Prawna*, January 14, 2020.

————— "Civil Society Organizations for and with the Courts and Judges—Struggle for the Rule of Law and Judicial Independence: The Case of Poland 1976-2020." *German Law Journal* 22, no. 7 (2021): 1344–84. doi: 10.1017/ glj.2021.72.

**Bojarski,** Ł., Grajewski, K., Kremer, J., Ott, G., Żurek, W. eds. Konstytucja, Praworządność, Władza Sądownicza. Aktualne Problemy Trzeciej Władzy w Polsce [Constitution, Rule of Law, Judiciary. Current Problems of the Third Power in Poland]. Wolters Kluwer Polska, Warsaw, 2019.

**Bramsen,** I. "How Civil Resistance Succeeds (or Not): Micro-dynamics of Unity, Timing, and Escalatory Actions." *Peace & Change* 43 no. 1 (2018): 61–89.

**Brand-Ballard,** J. *Limits of Legality: The Ethics of Lawless Judging.* New York: Oxford, 2010. DOI: 10.1093/acprof:o- so/9780195342291.001.0001.

**Brown,** N. "Judicial Militancy Within Red Lines." *Carnegie Endowment for International Peace*, November 2, 2016, **http://carnegieendowment .org/publications/?fa=64999**.

**Burdeau,** C. "An Unusual Strike Even for France: Judges Walk Out." *Courthouse News Service*, December 15, 2021; **https://www .courthousenews.com/an-unusual-strike -even-for-france-judges-walk-out/**.

**Burrowes,** R. J. *The Strategy of Nonviolent Defense: A Gandhian Approach.* Albany: State University of New York Press, 1996.

**Burrows,** Mathew, and Maria J. Stephan (editors). *Is Authoritarianism Staging a Comeback?* Washington: The Atlantic Council, 2015.

**Byliśmy** na Open'er Festival [We were at the Open'er Festival] 2022; **https://www .edukacja.iustitia.prawo.pl/wiadomosci /bylismy-na-opener-festival-2022/**.

152

**Bździkot,** T. "Sędzia Beata Morawiec Wróciła do Pracy [Judge Beata Morawiec Returned to Work]." *Radio Kraków*, June 8, 2021; **http://www.radiokrakow.pl/aktualnosci/krakow/sedzia-beata-morawiec-wrocila-do-pracy/**.

**Călin,** D., and B. Pîrlog. "Romania. How Judges and Prosecutors Fight for European Values." 2021. **https://www.iee-ulb.eu/content/uploads/2021/08/Romania.-How-Judges-and-Prosecutors-Fight-for-European-Values-2.pdf**.

**Campbell,** T. *Separation of Powers in Practice*. Stanford, 2004.

**CBOS.** "Zaufanie społeczne. Komunikat z badań nr 43" [Social Trust Research Communication] (2020). **https://www.cbos.pl/SPISKOM.POL/2020/K_043_20.PDF**.

**CBOS.** "Oceny z działalności instytucji publicznych. Komunikat z badań nr 50" [Evaluation of the activities of public institutions] (2022). **https://www.cbos.pl/SPISKOM.POL/2022/K_050_22.PDF**.

**Chenoweth,** Erica. *Civil Resistance: What Everyone Needs to Know*. New York: Oxford University Press, 2021.

**Chenoweth,** Erica, and Maria J. Stephan. *Why Civil Resistance Works: The Strategic Logic of Nonviolent Conflict*. New York: Columbia University Press, 2011.

**Chrzczonowicz,** M. "Wielka Demonstracja w obronie niezależnych sądów." ["Great Demonstration in defense of independent courts], *Oko Press*, November 23, 2017. **https://oko.press/wielka-demonstracja-obronie-niezaleznych-sadow-konstytucja-byc-samo-szanowana-hymn-flaga-godlo/**.

**Cowen,** L. "The Lawyer's Role in Civil Disobedience." 47 N.C. L. Rev. 587 (1969). **http://scholarship.law.unc.edu/nclr/vol47/iss3/3**.

**Creswell,** J. W. and V.L.P. Clark. *Designing and Conducting Mixed Methods Research*, 3rd Edition. Los Angeles: Sage Publications, 2017.

**"Curia** has grossly interfered in elections." *Miniszeterelnok*, May 7, 2018. **https://miniszterelnok.hu/curia-has-grossly-interfered-in-elections/**.

**Czaja,** J. "Sądownictwo powszechne" [Common judiciary], in *Jak przywrócić państwo prawa* [How to restore the rule of law], edited by T. Zalasiński. Warsaw: Fundacja im. Stefana Batorego, 2019.

**Dąbrowski,** M. "Spór o wyroki interpretacyjne Trybunału Konstytucyjnego—głos w dyskusji" [Dispute over the Interpretative Verdicts of the Constitutional Tribunal—the Standpoint in the Discussion], Przegląd Prawa Konstytucyjnego 2 (2017): 29–54.

**Davies,** C. "Head of Polish supreme court defies ruling party's retirement law," *The Guardian*, July 4, 2018. **https://www.theguardian.com/world/2018/jul/04/poland-supreme-court-head-malgorzata-gersdorf-defies-retirement-law**.

**De Haan,** W., J. Silvis, and P. A. Thomas. "Radical French Judges: Syndicat de la Magistrature," *Journal of Law and Society* 16, no. 4 (1989): 477–82.

**Diab,** Y. "Lebanon: Judges Go on Strike over Allowances Cuts," *Asharq Al-Awsat*, May 8, 2019. **https://english.aawsat.com//home/article/1712941/lebanon-judges-go-strike-over-allowances-cuts**.

**Dudouet,** Veronique (editor). *Civil Resistance and Conflict Transformation: Transitions from Armed to Nonviolent Struggle*. London: Routledge, 2015.

**Elbląg:** Prezes sądu zabrała sędziom togi przed marszem [Elbląg: The president of the court took the gowns from the judges before the march]. *Interia*, January 11, 2020. **https://wydarzenia.interia.pl/kraj/news-elblag-prezes-sadu-zabrala-sedziom-togi-przed-marszem,nId,4255637**.

153

**Eötvös** Károly Policy Institute. "Judicial Independence and the Possibility of Judicial Resistance in Hungary." *EKINT*, 2021. **http://ekint .org/lib/documents/1612860445-EKINT _Judicial_Independence_and_the_Possibility _of_Judicial_Resistance_in_Hungary.pdf.**

**Eurobarometer** (2021). "Perceived independence of the national justice systems in the EU among the general public." **https://europa.eu /eurobarometer/surveys/detail/2272.**

**Feinberg,** M., R. Willer, and C. Kovacheff. "The activist's dilemma: extreme protest actions reduce popular support for social movements." *Journal of Personality and Social Psychology* 119, no. 5 (2017): 1086–111.

**Filipek,** P. "The New National Council Of The Judiciary And Its Impact On The Supreme Court In The Light Of The Principle Of Judicial Independence." Problemy Współczesnego Prawa Międzynarodowego, Europejskiego i Porównawczego 16 (2018): 177–96.

————— "Nieusuwalność sędziów i granice kompetencji państwa członkowskiego do regulowania krajowego wymiaru sprawiedliwości—uwagi w świetle wyroku Trybunału Sprawiedliwości z 24.06.2019 r., C-619/18, Komisja Europejska przeciwko Rzeczypospolitej Polskiej" [Irremovability of Judges and the Limits of a Member State's Competence to Regulate Domestic Judiciary]. *Zeszyty Naukowe Sądownictwa Administracyjnego* 6 (2019).

**Fleck,** Z. "Judges Under Attack in Hungary." *VerfBlog*, May 14, 2018. **https://verfassungsblog .de/judges-under-attack-in-hungary/.**

**Flückiger,** P. "Polish Civil Society Wakes Up." *Deutsche Welle*, September 8, 2017. **https:// www.dw.com/en/judicial-reform-polish-civil -society-rises-up/a-40030135.**

**Frank,** R. "Trust in Professions 2018: A GfK Verein Study from Firefighters to Politicians." **https://www.nim.org/sites/default/files/medien /135/dokumente/2018_-_trust_in _professions_-_englisch.pdf.**

**Fuller,** L. "Positivism and Fidelity to Law — A Reply to Professor Hart," *Harvard Law Review* 71, no. 4 (1958): 630–672, doi:10.2307/1338226.

**Fundacja** Edukacji Prawnej Iustitia [FEPI]. "Proces Wilka 2 z bajki o Czerwonym Kapturku [The Trial of the Wolf 2 from Little Red Riding Hood]." March 15, 2019. **https://www.edukacja .iustitia.prawo.pl/wiadomosci/proces-wilka-2 -premiera/.**

**Gąciarek,** P. "Sędzia Gąciarek do sędziego Radzika: Służba politykom pomyliła się Panu ze służbą państwu i prawu" [Judge Gąciarek to Judge Radzik: Serving politicians has confused you with serving the state and the law]. *Gazeta Wyborcza,* October 31, 2020. **https:// wyborcza.pl/7,162657,26466000,nikt-nie -chcialby-zeby-apelacje-od-wyroku-w-sprawie -o-zabojstwo.html.**

————— "List otwarty sędziego Gąciarka do Prezes Walkowiak" [Judge Gąciarek's open letter to President Walkowiak]. September 16, 2022. **https://forumfws.eu/galeria/okiem -obserwatora/gaciarek-walkowiak/.**

**Gajcy,** A. "Tribunal's ruling on abortion to be 'corrected'. PiS politicians to the judges: give us some leeway," *TVN 24*, June 26, 2019. **https://tvn24.pl/tvn24-news-in-english/polish -court-rules-in-favour-of-man-who-refused -print-lgbt-posters-ra947916-2290300.**

**Gajda-Roszczynialska,** K., and K. Markiewicz. "Disciplinary Proceedings as an Instrument for Breaking the Rule of Law in Poland." *Hague J Rule Law* 12 (2020): 451–48.

**Gałczyńska,** M. "Troll farm at the Ministry of Justice, or 'we do not lock up for doing good'." **https://www.iustitia.pl/en/activity/informations /3241-troll-farm-at-the-ministerstwie -sprawiedliwosci-co-juz-wiemy/168sb5e.**

**Gamson,** W.A. "Reflections on The Strategy of Social Protest." *Sociological Forum* 4, no. 3 (1989): 445–67.

**Garlicki,** L. "Die Ausschaltung des Verfassungsgerichtshofes in Polen?" [Disabling the Constitutional Court in Poland?], in: Transformation of law systems in Central, Eastern and Southwestern Europe in 1989–2015, eds. A. Szmyt, B. Banaszak, Gdańsk, 2016.

**Gazeta.pl.** "Sędzia Igor Tuleya o 'ustawie kagańcowej': To rozwód z Europą" [Judge Igor Tuleya on the "Muzzle law": It's a divorce from Europe]." January 24, 2020. **https://wiadomosci.gazeta.pl/wiadomosci/7,114884,25628865,sedzia-igor-tuleya-o-ustawie-kagancowej-to-rozwod-z-europa.html.**

**Gelderloos,** P. *How Nonviolence Protects the State.* Cambridge: South End Press, 2007.

**Gersdorf,** M. "List M. Gersdorf, Pierwszej Prezes Sądu Najwyższego do Zgromadzenia Ogólnego Sędziów TK" [Letter from M. Gersdorf, the First President of the Supreme Court, to the General Assembly of Constitutional Tribunal Judges]." April 21, 2016. **http://niezniknelo.pl/OK2//trybunal/list-m-gersdorf-pierwszej-prezes-sadu-najwyzszego-do-zgromadzenia-ogolnego-sedziow-tk/index.html.**

**Gersdorf,** M., and M. Pilich. "Judges and Representatives of the People: A Polish Perspective." *European Constitutional Law Review* 16, no. 3 (2020): 345–78.

**Gomułowicz,** A. "Sędziowski aktywizm" [Judicial Activism], *Zeszyty Naukowe Sądownictwa Administracyjnego* 6 (2019): 7–19.

**Górski,** A. "Triada cnót sędziowskich" [The Triad of Judicial Virtues]. *Krajowa Rada Sądownictwa* 3 (2010): 49–50.

**Górski,** A., and M. Klonowski. "Dozwolone granice krytyki władzy sądowniczej w świetle orzecznictwa Europejskiego Trybunału Praw Człowieka" [Permissible limits of criticism of the judiciary in the light of the jurisprudence of the European Court of Human Rights]. *Europejski Przegląd Sądowy* 1 (2018): 24–8.

**Grabowska-Moroz,** B. "Kryzys konstytucyjny z Trybunałem Konstytucyjnym w roli głównej. Cz. 1" [Constitutional crisis with the Constitutional Tribunal in the lead role. Part 1]. *Kwartalnik o Prawach Człowieka* 1 (2016).

————— "Żurek v Poland—when judges become rule of law actors. Challenges and achievements of judicial mobilisation in Poland". *ERA Forum* (2024). **https://doi.org/10.1007/s12027-023-00778-1.**

**Graver,** H.P. *Judges Against Justice: On Judges When the Rule of Law is Under Attack.* Berlin: Springer, 2015.

**Gregorczyk-Abram,** S., P. Kieszkowska-Knapik, M. Wawrykiewicz, M. Ejchart, and K. Michałowski. *2,000 Days of Lawlessness.* Warsaw: Free-Courts Initiative, June 2021. **https://wolnesady.org/files/2000_days_of_Lawlessness_FreeCourts_Report.pdf.**

**Grochal,** R. "Tak działają egzekutorzy Ziobry. 'Ten cytat najlepiej go charakteryzuje—nigdy nie wybacza'" [This is how Ziobro's enforcers work]. *Newsweek*, September 3, 2022. **https://www.newsweek.pl/polska/polityka/nowa-faza-czystek-w-sadach-kogo-wyrzucaja-egzekutorzy-zbigniewa-ziobry/3np00t0.**

**Grzelak,** A., and A. Sakowicz. "Wymóg niezależności sądu krajowego jako element skutecznej ochrony sądowej (uwagi na tle wyroku TS z 9.11.20191 r. dla polskiego wymiaru sprawiedliwości)" [Requirement of Independence of a National Court as an Element of Effective Judicial Protection]. *Europejski Przegląd Sądowy* 14 (2020): 79–84.

**Gutowski,** M., and P. Kardas. "Sądowa kontrola konstytucyjności prawa. Kilka uwag o kompetencjach sądów powszechnych do bezpośredniego stosowania konstytucji [Judicial review. The competence to review the constitutionality of statutory law by common and administrative courts in light of direct application of the Constitution]." *Palestra* 2016.

**Gwizdak,** J. Odszedłem. Miałem dość. [I left. I had enough.] TVN 24, 2019. **https://tvn24.pl /magazyn-tvn24/sedzia-odszedlem-mialem -dosc,233,4007**.

**Hart,** H.L.A. "Positivism and the Separation of Law and Morals." *Harvard Law Review* 71, no. 4 (1958): 593–629. doi:10.2307/1338225.

**Hogic,** N. Supremacy of EU law and judicial independence in Romania. *Diritti Comparati*, March 7, 2022. **https://www.diritticomparati .it/supremacy-of-eu-law-and-judicial -independence-in-romania/**.

**Human** Rights Watch. *Destroying Legality: Pakistan's Crackdown on Lawyers and Judges.* Report. December 2007. **https://www .hrw.org/sites/default/files/reports/pakistan 1207web.pdf**.

————— *Pakistan: Protesters in Judge's Case at Risk of Violence.* News Release. March 15, 2007. **https://www.hrw.org /news/2007/03/15/pakistan-protesters -judges-case-risk-violence**.

**Iustitia.** "18-ty dzień każdego miesiąca Dniem Solidarności z Represjonowanymi Sędziami [The 18th day of each month is the Day of Solidarity with Repressed Judges]." December 18, 2020c. **https://www.iustitia.pl/83-komunikaty -i-oswiadczenia/4061-18-ty-dzien-kazdego -miesiaca-dniem-solidarnosci-z -represjonowanymi-sedziami**.

————— "Apel do Koleżanek i Kolegów Sędziów—Łańcuch Światła [Appeal to Colleagues of Judges—Chain of Light]." *Iustitia.* November 23, 2017c. **https://www.iustitia .pl/79-informacje/1954-apel-do-kolezanek-i -kolegow-sedziow-lancuch-swiatla**.

————— "Decyzje kadrowe w sądach AD 2017/2018—ujawniamy pełne zestawienie [Personnel decisions in courts 2017/2018—we reveal the full list]." May 15, 2018a. **https://www .iustitia.pl/informacja-publiczna/2223-czystki -kadrowe-w-sadach-ad-2018-ujawniamy -pelne-zestawienie**.

————— "Judges' appeal to citizens to defend the constitutional legal order and the independence of the courts." December 12, 2017d. **https://www.iustitia.pl/79-informacje /1975-apel-do-obywateli**.

————— "Nowo powołany przez Min. Ziobro prezes rezygnuje z funkcji [The president newly appointed by Min. Ziobro resigns from his function]." November 15, 2017b. **https://www .iustitia.pl/79-informacje/1945-jeden-z -nowo-powolanych-w-ostatnich-dniach-przez -min-ziobro-prezesow-rezygnuje-z-funkcji**.

————— "Pol'and'Rock Festival 2018 i my." *Iustitia,* August 6, 2018b. **https://www.iustitia.pl /79-informacje/2460-pol-and-rock-festival -2018-i-my**.

————— "Position of the Association of Polish Judges IUSTITIA on the obligation of judges to disclose membership in associations, imposed by the 'Muzzle Act'." March 11, 2020b. **https://www.iustitia.pl/83-komunikaty-i -oswiadczenia/3727-stanowisko -stowarzyszenia-sedziow-polskich-iustitia -w-sprawie-obowiazku-ujawnienia-przez -sedziow-przynaleznosci-do-zrzeszen -nalozonego-ustawa-kagancowa**.

————— "Protest Sędziów Rzeczypospolitej Polskiej [Protest of the Judges of the Republic of Poland]." *Iustitia,* November 14, 2008. **https://www.iustitia.pl/83-komunikaty-i -oswiadczenia/196-protest-sedziow -rzeczypospolitej-polskiej**.

————— "Rządy Prawa Wspólna Sprawa na Open er Festival 2022 [Rule of Law Common Cause at Open er Festival 2022]." **https:// www.edukacja.iustitia.prawo.pl/wiadomosci /bylismy-na-opener-festival-2022/**.

————— "The National Council of the Judiciary is not valid anymore." February 16, 2020a. **https://www.iustitia.pl/en/activity/informations /3710-iustitia-the-national-council-of-the -judiciary-is-not-valid-anymore-oko-press**.

————— "Wawrykiewicz about the Disciplinary Chamber of the Supreme Court." *Facebook.* May 28, 2022. **https://www.facebook.com/sedziowie/photos/a.260887620624303/5228379587208390/.**

————— "Wiceprezesi Sądów Apelacyjnych w Lublinie i Wrocławiu odwołani faxem [Vice-presidents of the Courts of Appeal in Lublin and Wrocław dismissed by fax]." *Iustitia*, November 15, 2017a. **https://www.iustitia.pl/79-informacje/1944-wiceprezesi-sadow-apelacyjnych-w-lublinie-i-wroclawiu-odwolani-przez-min-ziobre-faxem.**

Iustitia on the Cieszfanów Festival [Iustitia FB]. *Facebook.* August 18, 2022b. **https://www.facebook.com/events/466365191972933/.**

**Ivanova,** E. "Sędzia Łączewski zrzeka się urzędu. I donosi do prokuratury na Ziobrę oraz hejterską grupę 'Kasta' [Judge Łączewski resigns from office. And he reports to the prosecutor's office on Ziobro and the hate group 'Kasta']." *Gazeta Wyborcza*, October 11, 2019. **https://wyborcza.pl/7,75398,25296178,sedzia-laczewski-zrzeka-sie-urzedu-i-donosi-do-prokuratury.html.**

————— "Prezes Izby Karnej SN: Czuję się sędzią europejskim [President of the Criminal Chamber of the Supreme Court: I feel like a European judge]." *Gazeta Wyborcza*, November 2, 2021. **https://wyborcza.pl/7,75398,27758820,prezes-izby-karnej-sn-czuje-sie-sedzia-europejskim.html?fbclid=IwAR0BowCLqo6PdiXw4vR55sM3q38ZhdRrqyY9HJ0yC8Zif81ISRBOvvWe6h0.**

**Jakubowski,** T. "Afera hejterska miała miejsce. Sędzia przyznaje w TVN 24, że zbierał informacje ['There was a hate scandal.' The judge admits on TVN 24 that he was collecting information]." *Gazeta Wyborcza*, January 24, 2022. **https://wyborcza.pl/7,75398,28035690,afera-hejterska-sedzia-przyznaje-ze-zbieral-informacje.html.**

**Jałoszewski,** M. "Dyscyplinarka dla sędzi za koszulkę z napisem 'Konstytucja' [Disciplinary for the judge for the T-shirt with the inscription 'Constitution']." *Oko Press*, March 27, 2019a. **https://oko.press/dyscyplinarka-dla-sedzi-za-koszulke-z-napisem-konstytucja/.**

————— "Legalny SN do Trybunału Sprawiedliwości UE: Zbadajcie status nowych sędziów SN, nie wycofamy pytań [Legal Supreme Court to the Court of Justice of the EU: Examine the status of new Supreme Court judges, we will not withdraw questions]." *Oko Press*, May 4, 2022. **https://oko.press/legalny-sn-do-tsue-nie-wycofamy-pytan/.**

————— "Ponad 600 sędziów apeluje do OBWE o monitoring wyborów i wysłanie swoich obserwatorów do komisji wyborczych [More than 600 judges call on the OSCE to monitor the elections]." *Oko Press*, April 28, 2020. **https://oko.press/ponad-600-sedziow-apeluje-do-obwe-o-monitoring-wyborow-i-wyslanie-swoich-obserwatorow-do-komisji-wyborczych/.**

————— "Powstał fundusz dla represjonowanych sędziów. M.in. dla Juszczyszyna, któremu zabrano połowę pensji [A fund for repressed judges was established]." *Oko Press*, February 2, 2020. **https://oko.press/powstal-fundusz-dla-represjonowanych-sedziow/.**

————— "Sędzia Bator-Ciesielska, która nie chce sądzić z Radzikiem: 'Nie boję się. Ślubowałam Rzeczpospolitej' [Judge Bator-Ciesielska, who does not want to judge with Radzik]." *Oko Press*, September 3, 2019b. **https://oko.press/sedzia-bator-ciesielska-nie-chce-sadzic-z-radzikiem.**

————— "Sędzia, który uniewinnił działaczy KOD, ma zarzuty dyscyplinarne. Bo rzekomo źle sądzi [The judge who acquitted KOD activists faces disciplinary charges]." *Oko Press*, April 20, 2018. **https://oko.press/sedzia-ktory-uniewinnil-dzialaczy-kod-ma-zarzuty-dyscyplinarne-bo-rzekomo-zle-sadzi/.**

—————— "Sędzia zwolniła z aresztu prokuratora, bo immunitet uchyliła mu nielegalna Izba Dyscyplinarna [The judge released the prosecutor from detention because his immunity was revoked by the illegal Disciplinary Chamber]." *Oko Press*, September 2, 2021c. **https://oko .press/sedzia-z-warszawy-zwolnila-z-aresztu -prokuratura/**.

—————— "Sędziowie wzywają do bojkotu naboru do nowego Sądu Najwyższego [Judges are calling for a boycott of the new Supreme Court]." *Oko Press*, July 24, 2018. **https://oko .press/sedziowie-wzywaja-do-bojkotu-naboru -do-nowego-sadu-najwyzszego/**.

—————— "Sędziowie wygrywają z Ziobrą. Mogą protestować i go krytykować. A sędzia Żurek zastosował prawo UE. [The judges win with Ziobro]." *Oko Press*, February 1, 2022. **https:// oko.press/sedziowie-wygrywaja-z-ziobra -moga-protestowac-i-go-krytykowac-a-sedzia -zurek-zastosowal-prawo-ue**.

—————— "Wielka akcja w obronie sędziego Igora Tulei w krakowskim sądzie [A great action in defense of judge Igor Tuleya in a Krakow court]." *Oko Press*, December 6, 2020. **https:// oko.press/wielka-akcja-w-obronie-sedziego -igora-tulei-w-krakowskim-sadzie**.

—————— "Wielki historyczny apel polskich sędziów w obronie prawa UE. Ostateczna lista 4219 nazwisk [Great historical appeal of Polish judges in defense of EU law. The final list of 4219 names]." *Oko Press*, July 31, 2021b. **https://oko.press/wielki-historyczny-apel -polskich-sedziow-w-obronie-prawa-ue -ostateczna-lista-4219-nazwisk/**.

—————— "Wolta Manowskiej z SN. Apeluje do ludzi Ziobry, by zaprzestali represji sędziów apelacyjnych [Manowska's Protest in the Supreme Court]." *Archiwum Osiatyńskiego*, August 16, 2022. **https://archiwumosiatynskiego .pl/wpis-w-debacie/wolta-manowskiej-z-sn -apeluje-do-ludzi-ziobry-by-zaprzestali-represji -sedziow-apelacyjnych/**.

—————— "Wygrana sędziego Żurka. Został przeproszony za „alimenciarza" i wyrodnego męża [Judge Żurek won. He apologized for the "alimony payer" and degenerate husband]." *Oko Press*, April 20, 2021a. **https://oko.press /wygrana-sedziego-zurka-zostal-przeproszony -za-alimenciarza-i-wyrodnego-meza**.

—————— "Ziobro breached the CJEU judgment and suspended Judge Synakiewicz for applying EU law." *Oko Press*, September 10, 2021d. **https://ruleoflaw.pl/ziobro-breached-the-cjeu -judgment-and-suspended-judge-synakiewicz -for-applying-eu-law/**.

—————— "Ziobro żąda dyscyplinarki dla sędziów z Krakowa za powieszenie plakatów w obronie wolnych sądów [Ziobro demands disciplinary action against judges from Krakow for hanging posters in defense of free courts]." *Oko Press*, June 16, 2020. **https://oko.press/ziobro-zada -dyscyplinarki-dla-sedziow-z-krakowa -za-powieszenie-plakatow-w-obronie -wolnych-sadow**.

**Jaskiernia,** A. "Standardy Rady Europy dotyczące wolności słowa w odniesieniu do relacji prasowych z działań wymiaru sprawiedliwości [Council of Europe standards on freedom of expression in relation to press coverage of judicial activities]." In *Transformacja systemów wymiaru sprawiedliwości, t. I, Pozycja ustrojowa władzy sądowniczej i uwarunkowania transformacji [Transformation of justice systems, vol. I, The systemic position of the judiciary and conditions of transformation]*, edited by J. Jaskiernia, 330–50. Toruń: Adam Marszałek, 2011.

**Judge** 2017 blog. "Brawo Kraków [Bravo Cracow]." *Judge 2017*, February 28, 2018a. **https://judge2017.home.blog/2018/02/28 /brawo-krakow/**.

—————— "Ci niedobrzy sędziowie [Those bad judges]." *Judge 2017*, April 4, 2019c. **https:// judge2017.home.blog/2019/06/04/ci-niedobrzy -sedziowie/**.

————— "Dziarskie chłopaki z WSW PK [Perky boys from WSW PK]." *Judge 2017*, December 30, 2020. **https://judge2017.home.blog /2020/12/30/dziarskie-chlopaki-z-wsw-pk/**.

————— „Nie teraz Pani Prezes ! (Not now Madam President!)." July 6, 2018; **https:// judge2017.home.blog/2018/07/06/nie-teraz -pani-prezes/**.

————— "Praca u podstaw [Basic work]." *Judge 2017*, April 13, 2018b. **https://judge2017.home .blog/2018/04/13/praca-u-podstaw/**.

————— "Trudny czas decyzji [Difficult decision time]." *Judge 2017*, July 22, 2018d. **https:// judge2017.home.blog/2018/07/22/trudny -czas-decyzji/**.

————— "Uparcie przypominać [Stubbornly remind]." *Judge 2017*, December 2, 2017b. **https://judge2017.home.blog/2017/12/02 /uparcie-przypominac/**.

————— "Wallenrodzi poszukiwani [Wallenrods Wanted]." *Judge 2017*, December 22, 2020. **https://judge2017.home.blog/2017/12/22 /wallenrodzi-poszukiwani/**.

————— "We shall fight, September 22, 2018." *Judge 2017*, February 8, 2019a. **https:// judge2017.home.blog/2019/02/08/we-shall -fight-original-text-published-on-september -22-2018/**.

————— "Żale sędziego Czajkowskiego [Regrets of Judge Czajkowski]." *Judge 2017*, February 28, 2019b. **https://judge2017.home .blog/2019/02/28/zale-sedziego -czajkowskiego/**.

————— "Znów kradzież [Theft again]." *Judge 2017*, June 25, 2017a. **https://judge2017.home .blog/2017/06/25/znow-kradziez/**.

"**Judiciary** Turns the Corner," *Dawn*, July 21, 2007. **http://dawn.com/2007/07/21/top1.htm**.

"**Judges** after hours: Warsaw legal cafe (2018)." *Fundacja Edukacji Prawnej*, November 21, 2018. **https://www.edukacja.iustitia.prawo .pl/wiadomosci/warszawska-kafejka-prawna-55/**.

"**Judges** Resume Work After 50-day Strike." *The New Humanitarian*, October 22, 2003. **https://www.thenewhumanitarian.org/fr /node/214742**.

**K-112. https://trybunal.gov.pl/sprawy-w-trybu nale/katalog/k-112M**.

**Kamiński,** I. C. "Swoboda wypowiedzi a zachowanie powagi i bezstronności wymiaru sprawiedliwości—uwagi na kanwie orzecznictwa Europejskiego Trybunału Praw Człowieka [Freedom of expression and maintaining the seriousness and impartiality of the judiciary]." *Krajowa Rada Sądownictwa* 1 (2017): 5–28.

**Khan,** A. "The Lawyers' Movement in Pakistan: Law Beyond Politics." *Social Science Research Network*, December 26, 2007. **http://papers .ssrn.com/sol3/papers.cfm?abstract_id =1078727**.

**Klimkiewicz,** B. "Media Pluralism Monitor 2016 Monitoring Risks for Media Pluralism in the EU and Beyond Country report: Poland." *Centre for Media Pluralism and Media Freedom*, 2016. **https://cadmus.eui.eu/bitstream/handle /1814/46807/Poland_EN.pdf?sequence =1&isAllowed=y**.

**Kmiec,** K.Z. "The Origin and Current Meanings of 'Judicial Activism'." *California Law Review* 92, no. 5 (October 2004): 1441–77.

**Kmieciak,** Z. "Ochrona tymczasowa w sprawie ze skargi Komisji przeciwko Polsce dotyczącej przepisów ustawy obniżającej wiek przejścia w stan spoczynku sędziów SN. Glosa do postanowienia TSUE z 19.10.2018 r., C-619/18 R [Interim Relief in the Case Concerning the Commission's Complaint against Poland for the Law Lowering Retirement Age for Supreme Court Judges]." *Państwo i Prawo* 1 (2019): 143–50.

**Kociołowicz-Wiśniewska,** G., Pilitowski B. *Bilans efektów reform polskiego wymiaru sprawiedliwości w latach 2017-2020 [The balance of the effects of the reforms of the Polish justice system in 2017-2020].* Toruń: Court Watch Polska Foundation, **2021. https://courtwatch.pl /wp-content/uploads/2021/10/Raport-FCWP -Ocena-polskiego-sadownictwa-w-swietle -badan-vol.-3-2021.pdf.**

**KOD.** "Search Engine for Judges Appointed by Neo-NCJ." https://ruchkod.pl/neokrs/.

**Koncewicz,** T.T. "Constitutional Capture in Poland 2016 and Beyond: What is Next?" *VerfBlog,* December 19, 2016. **https://verfassungsblog .de/constitutional-capture-in-poland-2016 -and-beyond-what-is-next/.**

**————** "'Emergency Constitutional Review': thinking the unthinkable? A Letter from America." *VerfBlog,* March 29, 2016. **https:// verfassungsblog.de/emergency-constitutional -review-thinking-the-unthinkable-a-letter -from-america/.**

**————** "Of institutions, democracy, constitutional self-defence and the rule of law: The judgments of the Polish Constitutional Tribunal in Cases K 34/15, K 35/15 and beyond." *Common Market Law Review* 53, no. 6 (2016): 1753–92. **https://kluwerlawonline.com /journalarticle/Common+Market+Law +Review/53.6/COLA2016149.**

**Kościerzyński,** J. "Sędziowie pod presją—raport o metodach szykanowania przez władzę niezależnych sędziów [Judges under pressure—a report on the methods of harassment of independent judges by the authorities]." *Iustitia Report,* 2019, updated January 24, 2024: **https://iustitia.pl/represje-jako -metoda-walki-o-przejecie-kontroli-nad-wladza -sadownicza-i-prokuratura-w-polsce-w-latach -2015-2023/.**

**Kowalski,** W. "Kolejna odsłona sporu kompetencyjnego pomiędzy SN a TK [The next stage of the dispute over powers between the Supreme Court and the Constitutional Tribunal]." *Prawo.pl,* September 7, 2010. **https://www .prawo.pl/prawnicy-sady/kolejna-odslona -sporu-kompetencyjnego-pomiedzy-sn-a -tk,32785.html.**

**Krajewska** A. "The judgment of the Polish Constitutional Tribunal on abortion: a dark day for Poland, for Europe, and for democracy." *U.K. Const. L. Blog.* **https://ukconstitutionallaw.org/.** Accessed February 3, 2021.

**Krajewski,** K., Ziółkowski. M. "Can an Unlawful Judge be the First President of the Supreme Court?" *VerfBlog,* May 26, 2020. **https:// verfassungsblog.de/can-an-unlawful-judge -be-the-first-president-of-the-supreme-court/.**

**Kryszkiewicz,** M. "Kiełbasa, Seneka i świeczki. Rzecz o reformie sądownictwa [Sausage, Seneca and candles]." *Dziennik Gazeta Prawna,* December 12, 2017. **https://prawo.gazetaprawna .pl/artykuly/1091299,kto-jest-winny-w -reformie-sadownictwa.html.**

**————** "Nowy sędzia Sądu Najwyższego żali się na kolegów [The new Supreme Court judge complains about his colleagues]." *Dziennik Gazeta Prawna,* October 19, 2019. **https:// prawo.gazetaprawna.pl/artykuly/1435152 ,antoni-bojanczyk-zali-sie-za-stanislawa -zablockiego.html.**

**————** "Ustawa kagańcowa zadziałała. Miała zapobiec chaosowi, ale to 'droga donikąd' [The 'Muzzle law' worked]." *Dziennik.pl,* July 20, 2020. **https://wiadomosci.dziennik.pl /wydarzenia/artykuly/7776144,ustawa -kagancowa-sad-najwyzszy-sn-sedzia.html.**

**Laskowski** M. *Uchybienie godności urzędu sędziego jako podstawa odpowiedzialności dyscyplinarnej [Violation of the dignity of the office of judge as the basis for disciplinary liability].* Warsaw: Wolter Kluwer Polska, 2019.

**Lasocki,** J. "Turning propaganda into public service broadcasting in Poland." *Notes From Poland*, November 12, 2021. **https://notesfrompoland.com/2021/11/12/turning-propaganda-into-public-service-broadcasting-in-poland/**.

**Laurence** Ross, H., Foley, J.P. "Judicial Disobedience of the Mandate to Imprison Drunk Drivers." *Law and Society Review* 2 (1987): 315–24.

**Lipski,** J.J. *KOR: A History of the Workers' Defense Committee in Poland, 1976-1981.* University of California Press, 1985.

**Łazarska,** A. *Niezawisłość sędziowska i jej gwarancje w procesie cywilnym [Judicial independence and its guarantees in a civil trial].* Warsaw: Wolters Kluwer Polska, 2018.

————— "Sędziowie muszą wyjść z wieży z kości słoniowej [The judges must come out of the ivory tower]." **https://www.prawo.pl/prawnicy-sady/sedziowie-powinni-byc-obecni-w-zyciu-publicznym-ocenia-sedzia,432800.html**.

«Les mesures d'austérité dans la Justice nuisent gravement aux droits de l'Homme.» *RTBF Actus*, June 7, 2016. **https://www.rtbf.be/article/les-mesures-d-austerite-dans-la-justice-nuisent-gravement-aux-droits-de-l-homme-9318527**.

**Łętowska,** E. «Dekalog dobrego sędziego [Judge's decalogue].» *Gazeta Wyborcza*, February 6–7, 1993.

————— «Dekalog sędziego. Dwadzieścia pięć lat później» [Judge's decalogue. Twenty-five years later].» *In Konstytucja, praworządność, władza sądownicza. Aktualne problemy trzeciej władzy w Polsce [Constitution, Rule of Law, Judiciary. Current Problems of the Third Power in Poland],* edited by Łukasz Bojarski, Krzysztof Grajewski, Janusz Kremer, Grzegorz Ott, and Włodzimierz Żurek. Warsaw: Wolters Kluwer, 2019.

**Łętowska,** E., Wiewiórowska-Domagalska, A. "A 'Good' Change in the Polish Constitutional Tribunal?" *Osteuropa-Recht* (2016).

**Levitsky,** S., and L. A. Way. *Competitive Authoritarianism: Hybrid Regimes After the Cold War (Problems of International Politics).* Cambridge University Press, 2010.

**Łukaszewicz,** A. «Teresa Romer: Bycie sędzią to nie przymus" [Teresa Romer: Being a Judge is not a Compulsion]. *Rzeczpospolita*, December 14, 2012. **https://www.rp.pl/sady-i-trybunaly/art13320141-teresa-romer-bycie-sedzia-to-nie-przymus**.

————— "Specwydział prokuratury: z wielkiej chmury mały deszcz" [Spec Prosecutor's Office: From a Big Cloud a Little Rain]. *Rzeczpospolita,* September 11, 2018. **https://www.rp.pl/Prokuratorzy/309109910-Specwydzial-prokuratury-z-wielkiej-chmury-maly-deszcz.html**.

**Łukaszewski,** J. «Prokuratura Krajowa żąda od prokuratorki 250 tys. zł za wywiad w „Wyborczej"» [The National Prosecutor's Office Demands 250,000 from the Prosecutor for an Interview in "Gazeta Wyborcza"]. *Gazeta Wyborcza*, May 5, 2021. **https://wyborcza.pl/7,75398,27053862,prokuratura-krajowa-zada-od-prokuratorki-250-tys-zl-za-wywiad.html**.

**Mahapatra,** D. "Can Judges Strike Work Over Woes?" *The Economic Times*, July 4, 2016. **https://economictimes.indiatimes.com//news/politics-and-nation/can-judges-strike-work-over-woes/articleshow/53042580.cms**.

**Mamoń,** M. "Rzecznik Radzik nie poradził, za to minister Ziobro odsunął od orzekania sędziego z Częstochowy. Za stosowanie się do wyroków TSUE" [Spokesman Radzik Did Not Advise, But Minister Ziobro Removed the Judge from Częstochowa from Adjudicating]. *Gazeta Wyborcza*, September 9, 2021. **https://czestochowa.wyborcza.pl/czestochowa/7,89625,27552679,rzecznik-radzik-nie-poradzil-za-to-minister-ziobro-odsunal.html**.

**Maniewska,** E. "Apoliticzność jako wyznacznik granic wolności wypowiedzi sędziego dotyczących ustawowych reform sądownictwa (ich krytyki)" [Apoliticality as a Determinant of the Judge's Freedom of Expression Regarding Statutory Reforms of the Judiciary]. *Państwo i Prawo* 7 (2019): 26–7.

**Map** of legal cafes organized by Iustitia (2020). **https://www.iustitia.pl/79-informacje /3733-mapka.**

**Marsi,** F. "Tunisian Judges on Strike as Fears Grow Over Authoritarian Rule." *Al Jazeera*, February 9, 2022. **https://www.aljazeera.com /news/2022/2/9/tunisian-judges-on-strike-as -fears-grow-over-authoritarian-rule.**

**Martin,** B. *Justice Ignited: The Dynamics of Backfire.* Lanham: Rowman & Littlefield, 2007.

**Matczak,** M. "The Clash of Powers in Poland's Rule of Law Crisis: Tools of Attack and Self-Defence." *Hague Journal on the Rule of Law* 12 (2020): 421–50. **https://doi.org/10.1007 /s40803-020-00144-0.**

**Matthes,** C. Y. "Judges as activists: how Polish judges mobilise to defend the rule of law", *East European Politics*, 38:3 (2022), 468-487, **https:// doi.org/10.1080/21599165.2022.2092843.**

**Mazur,** D. "From Bad to Worse—Polish Judiciary in the Shadow of the 'Muzzle Act'." *Themis*, November 20, 2020. **http://themis-sedziowie .eu/wp-content/uploads/2020/11/From-bad -to-worse-Polish-judiciary-in-the-shadow-of -the-muzzle-act-report-1.pdf**.

**—————** "Humiliate in Order to Subordinate— Judge Beata Morawiec Case Study." *Themis*, October 8, 2020; **http://themis-sedziowie .eu/materials-in-english/humiliate-in-order -to-subordinate-judge-beata-morawiec-case -study-prepared-by-judge-dariusz-mazur/.**

**—————** "In-Depth Report: Challenging the Principles of Primacy and Direct Applicability of EU Law by the Polish Authorities, 6 Months After the CJEU's Rulings of July 2021." *Themis*, January 25, 2022. **http://themis-sedziowie .eu/wp-content/uploads/2022/01/Challenging -the-principles-of-primacy-and-direct -applicability_extended_wer.pdf.**

**—————** "In-Depth Report: 'Internal Affairs Department of the State Prosecution Service as a Politicized Tool of Oppression of Polish Judges and Prosecutors." *Themis*, December 6, 2021. **http://themis-sedziowie.eu/wp-content/uploads /2021/12/Internal-Affairs-Department_as -oppression-tool_wer.pdf.**

**—————** "Judges Under Special Supervision, Namely 'The Great Reform' of the Polish Justice System." *Themis*, April 5, 2019. **http:// themis-sedziowie.eu/wp-content/uploads/2019 /04/Judges_under_special_supevision _second-publication.pdf.**

**—————** "The Real Objective and the Results of the So-Called 'Great Reform' of the Polish Justice System." *Netherlands Justenbland*, November 21, 2020. **https://www.njb.nl /media/4021/njb40_praktijk_2.pdf.**

**—————** "Ustawa kagańcowa jako przejaw ustawowego bezprawia" [The Muzzle Act as a Manifestation of Statutory Lawlessness]. *Rzeczpospolita*, January 11, 2020. **https://www .rp.pl/opinie-prawne/art9083321-dariusz -mazur-ustawa-kagancowa-jako-przejaw -ustawowego-bezprawia.**

**Mekki,** M., & Bastawisi, H. "When Judges Are Beaten." *The Guardian*, May 9, 2006. **https:// www.theguardian.com/commentisfree/2006 /may/10/comment.egypt.**

**Miecik,** I.T. "Akcja Demokracja: Jedno Kliknię- cie i Wybuchło. Jak Kilka Młodych i Nikomu Nieznanych Osób Pociągnęło Za Sobą Tłum Pod Sąd Najwyższy i Sejm" [Action Democ- racy: One Click and It Exploded. How a Few Young and Unknown People Led the Crowd to the Supreme Court and the Sejm]. *Gazeta Wyborcza*, July 21, 2017. **https://wyborcza.pl /magazyn/7,124059,22131208,akcja -demokracja-jedno-klikniecie-i-wybuchlo .html.**

**Morawski,** L. "Aktywizm Sędziowski a Sprawy Polskie" [Judicial Activism and Polish Case]. *Prawo i Więź* 2 (2016): 7–13.

**Müller,** I. *Furchtbare Juristen*, 2nd edition. Ber- lin: 2020.

**Najda,** M., and T. Romer, *Etyka dla Sędziów. Rozważania [Ethics for Judges. Consider- ations]*. Warsaw: Wolters Kluwer Polska 2007.

*Newsweek.* "To Nie Koniec Walki o Sąd Na- jwyższy. Protesty Pod Senatem i Pałacem Prezydenckim" [The Fight for the Supreme Court is Not Over. Protests in Front of the Sen- ate and the Presidential Palace]. July 24, 2018. **https://www.newsweek.pl/polska /spoleczenstwo/protesty-w-obronie-sadu -najwyzszego-lista-protestow/4nf7wgc.**

**Niezależna.pl.** „Iustitia murem za Tuleyą: Zapowiadają uliczne manifestacje i apelują o przerwanie rozpraw." Accessed May 24, 2024. **https://niezalezna.pl/polska/iustitia -murem-za-tuleya-zapowiadaja-uliczne -manifestacje-i-apeluja-o-przerwanie-rozpraw /333002**.

**Obywatele** RP. *ObyPomoc.* Report. April 11, 2017 – January 31, 2018. **https://obywatelerp .org/wp-content/uploads/2018/02/Raport -ObyPomoc-Zbiorczy-do-2018-01-31-ENG.pdf.**

–––––– "Żądamy Delegalizacji ONR!" [We De- mand the Delegalization of ONR!]. January 23, 2018. **https://obywatelerp.org/zadamy -delegalizacji-onr/.**

**Olszewski,** W. "Solidarność sędziów krakows- kich w latach 1980-1981" [Solidarity of Krakow's Courts in 1980-1981]. In *Obywatelskie Centrum Inicjatyw Obywatelskich Solidarności 1980- 1990*, 546–7, edited by K. Barczyk, S. Grodziski, S. Grzybowski. Warsaw: Wydawnictwo Sejmowe, 2001.

**Ombudsman's** Office. "Wyrok TSUE—i co dalej? Spotkanie Sędziów w Biurze Rzecznika Praw Obywatelskich" [Judgment of the CJEU—What Next? Meeting of Judges at the Office of the Commissioner for Human Rights]. **https://bip .brpo.gov.pl/pl/content/wyrok-tsue-%E2%80 %93-i-co-dalej-spotkanie-s%C4%99dzi%C3 %B3w-w-biurze-rzecznika-praw-obywatelskich.**

**Onken,** M., Shemia-Goeke, D., & Martin, B. "Learning from Criticisms of Civil Resistance." *Critical Sociology* 47, no. 7-8 (2021): 1191–203. **https://doi.org/10.1177/08969205211025819.**

**Opole** Legal Cafe. "Meeting with Judge Igor Tuleya." *Facebook*, September 8, 2018; **https://www.facebook.com/1445952262179507 /photos/gm.319687535276719/1852597631 514966.**

**Osiel,** M.J. "Dialogue with Dictators: Judicial Resistance in Argentina and Brazil." *Law and Social Inquiry* 19, no. 4 (1995).

**Pankowska,** M. "Smear Campaign Coordinat- ed by the Ministry of Justice, Aimed to Dis- credit Polish Judges, Discovered." *Oko Press*, August 27, 2019. **https://oko.press/why-did -the-polish-deputy-minister-of-justice-resign -everything-you-need-to-know-about-the -piebiak-scandal/.**

**Pankowska,** M., & Jałoszewski, M. "OKO.press Prześwietla Ustawę Kagańcową, Czyli Wszyst- kie Powody, By Iść Na Marsz 1000 Tóg" [OKO. press X-rays the Muzzle Act]. *Oko Press*, Janu- ary 11, 2020. **https://oko.press/oko-press -przeswietla-ustawe-kagancowa-czyli-czyli -wszystkie-powody-by-isc-na-marsz-1000-tog/.**

**Pech,** L., and K. L. Scheppele. "Illiberalism Within: Rule of Law Backsliding in the EU." *Cambridge Yearbook of European Legal Studies* 19 (December 2017): 3–47.

**Pech,** L., P. Wachowiec, and D. Mazur. "Poland's Rule of Law Breakdown: A Five-Year Assessment of EU's (In)Action." *Hague J Rule Law* 13 (2021): 1–43. **https://doi.org/10.1007/s40803-021-00151-9.**

**Phelps,** J. "Pakistan's Lawyers Movement (2007-2009)." Washington: ICNC, 2009. **https://www.nonviolent-conflict.org/wp-content/uploads/2016/02/Pakistan-Lawyers-Movement-4.pdf.**

**Pietraszewski,** M. «Jarosław Gwizdak Już Nie Jest Sędzią: Dobrze Wam Radzię, Unikajcie Sądów!» [Jarosław Gwizdak Is No Longer a Judge: I Advise You Well, Avoid the Courts!]. *Gazeta Wyborcza*, June 16, 2019. **https://katowice.wyborcza.pl/katowice/7,35055,24867197,jaroslaw-gwizdak-juz-nie-jest-sedzia-dobrze-wam-radze-unikajcie.html.**

**Pilich,** M. "Disobedience of Judges as a Problem of Legal Philosophy and Comparative Constitutionalism: A Polish Case." *Res Publica* (2021). **https://doi.org/10.1007/s11158-021-09501-8.**

**Pilitowski,** B., Kociołowicz-Wiśniewska, B. "Obywatelski Monitoring Sądów 2021 [Civic Monitoring of Courts 2021]." *Court Watch Foundation*, 2021. **https://courtwatch.pl/wp-content/uploads/2021/09/FCWP_raport_Obywatelski_Monitoring_S%C4%85d%C3%B3w_2021.pdf.**

**President** of Poland. "President: I have decided to veto the law on the Supreme Court and the National Council of the Judiciary; July 24, 2017." Statement. **https://www.prezydent.pl/aktualnosci/wydarzenia/prezydent-zdecydowalem-o-zawetowaniu-ustawy-o-sadzie-najwyzszym-i-krs,669.**

**Puchalski,** R. Pierwszy w historii III RP protest sędziów [The first protest of judges in the history of the Third Republic of Poland]. Interview. *Iustitia,* April 7, 2008. **https://www.iustitia.pl/katowice/index.php/home/artykuly-publikacje-i-wywiady/91-pierwszy-w-historii-iii-rp-protest-sedziow.**

**Puleo** L., Coman R. "Explaining judges' opposition when judicial independence is undermined: insights from Poland, Romania, and Hungary", *Democratization,* 31:1 (2024), 47-69, **https://doi.org/10.1080/13510347.2023.2255833.**

**Radbruch,** G. "Gesetzliches Unrecht und übergesetzliches Recht." *Süddeutsche Juristenzeitung* (1946): 105–8.

**Radziewicz,** P., Tuleja, P., (editors). *Konstytucyjny spór o granice zmian organizacji i zasad działania Trybunału Konstytucyjnego czerwiec 2015—marzec 2016 [Constitutional dispute over the limits of changes in the organization and operation of the Constitutional Tribunal June 2015—March 2016].* Warsaw: Wolters Kluwer Polska, 2017.

**Rafiq,** A. "The Long March Ends: Islamabad Comes Alive." *The Pakistan Policy Blog*, June 13, 2008. **http://pakistanpolicy.com/2008/06/13/the-long-march-ends-islamabad-comes-alive/.**

**Rafto** Foundation for Human Rights. "Ombudsman Adam Bodnar." *The Rafto Prize*, 2018. **https://www.rafto.no/en/the-rafto-prize/ombudsman-adam-bodnar.**

**Reuters** in Cairo. "Egypt Police Suppress Protests Against Sisi Government." *The Guardian,* April 25, 2016. **https://www.theguardian.com/world/2016/apr/25/cairo-protests-egypt-red-sea-islands-saudi-arabia.**

**Rigamonti,** M. "Tuleya: Będą musieli wziąć mnie za mordę [Tuleya: They'll have to take me for a face]." *Dziennik Gazeta Prawna*, November 27, 2020. **https://prawo.gazetaprawna .pl/artykuly/1497394,sedzia-igor-tuleya -immunitet-zarzuty-polityka-izba-dyscyplinarna .html**.

**Rogowska,** B. "Łódzkiej sędzi grozi zwolnienie ze stanowiska za wspieranie wolnych sądów. Protest sędziów 18 stycznia [A judge from Łódź is threatened with dismissal for supporting free courts]." *Gazeta Wyborcza*, January 12, 2021. **https://lodz.wyborcza.pl/lodz/7,35136 ,26677668,lodzkiej-sedzi-grozi-zwolnienie -ze-stanowiska-za-wspieranie.html**.

**Rudnicki,** S. "NSZZ 'Solidarność' w Sądzie Najwyższym—refleksje z perspektywy lat [NSZZ 'Solidarity' in the Supreme Court—reflections from the perspective of years]." In *Ius et lex. Księga jubileuszowa ku czci prof. Adama Strzembosza*, edited by A. Dębiński, A. Grześkowiak, K. Wiak, 293–300. Lublin: KUL, 2002.

*Rzeczpospolita.* "Ruszyła Społeczna Komisja Kodyfikacyjna środowisk prawniczych [The Social Codification Commission of legal circles has been launched]." December 16, 2017. **https://www.rp.pl/zawody-prawnicze /art10031701-ruszyla-spoleczna-komisja -kodyfikacyjna-srodowisk-prawniczych**.

————— "Trzech znanych sędziów nie będzie ściganych. Żądał tego Ziobro.» February 14, 2022a. **https://www.rp.pl/sady-i-trybunaly /art35685271-trzech-znanych-sedziow-nie -bedzie-sciganych-zadal-tego-ziobro**.

————— "Tuleya odwieszony i zawieszony. Sędziowie: To jest ohydne i haniebne [Tuleya reinstated and suspended. Judges: This is disgusting and disgraceful]." August 8, 2022b. **https://www.rp.pl/sady-i-trybunaly /art36833191-tuleya-odwieszony-i-zawieszony -sedziowie-to-jest-ohydne-i-haniebne**.

**Sadurski,** W. *Poland's Constitutional Breakdown*. Oxford, 2019. **https://doi.org/10.1093 /oso/9780198840503.001.0001**.

————— "How Democracy Dies (in Poland): A Case Study of Anti-Constitutional Populist Backsliding." *Sydney Law School Research Paper No. 18/01* (2018): 1–72.

**"Sądy** są najważniejszym bastionem starego systemu [The courts are the most important bulwark of the old system]." *TVP Info,* 2020. **https://www.tvp.info/48903026/kaczynski -sady-sa-najwazniejszym-bastionem-starego -systemu-wieszwiecej**.

**Safjan,** M. "Polityka a Trybunał Konstytucyjny. Konstytucja—ostatni środek obrony przed polityką" [Politics And The Constitutional Tribunalthe Constitution—The Last Instrument Of Defence Against Politics]. *Ruch Prawniczy, Ekonomiczny i Socjologiczny* 1 (2016): 35–42.

————— "Prawo do skutecznej ochrony sądowej—refleksje dotyczące wyroku TSUE z 19.11.2019 r. w sprawach połączonych C-585/18, C-624/18, C-6J25/18" [Right to effective judicial protection—reflections on the judgment of the CJEU of 19/11/2019 in joined cases C-585/18, C-624/18, C-625/18]. *Palestra* 5 (2020): 5–29.

**Sajó,** A. "The Rule of Law as Legal Despotism: Concerned Remarks on the Use of 'Rule of Law' in Illiberal Democracies." *Hague Journal on the Rule of Law* 11 (2019): 371–376.

**Sanders,** A., von Danwitz, L. "Defamation of Justice—Propositions on how to evaluate public attacks against the Judiciary." VerfBlog, 2017/10/31. **https://verfassungsblog.de /defamation-of-justice-propositions-on -how-to-evaluate-public-attacks-against -the-judiciary/**.

**Scheppele,** K.L. "Autocratic legalism." *The University of Chicago Law Review* 85 (2018): 545–83.

**„Sędziowie** protestują przeciw ocenom okresowym" [The judges protest against periodic evaluations] (2010). *Dziennik Gazeta Prawana*, June 23, 2010. **https://prawo.gazetaprawna .pl/artykuly/431151,sedziowie-protestuja -przeciw-ocenom-okresowym.html**.

"**Sędziowie** warszawscy odmawiają opiniowania kandydatów na sędziów, krytyczni o działaniach rzeczników dyscyplinarnych, wspierają sędzię Annę Bator-Ciesielską i Pawła Juszczyszyna [Warsaw judges refuse to give opinions on candidates for judges]." *Iustitia*, December 13, 2019. **https://www.iustitia .pl/81-uchwaly/3489-sedziowie-warszawscy -odmawiaja-opiniowania-kandydatow-na -sedziow-krytyczni-o-dzialaniach-rzecznikow -dyscyplinarnych-wspieraja-sedzie-anne -bator-ciesielska-i-pawla-juszczyszyna**.

**Sękowski,** S. "Prawo i Praworządność" [Law and Rule of Law]. *Tygodnik Powszechny*, August 15, 2022. **https://www.tygodnikpowszechny .pl/prawo-i-praworzadnosc-177619**.

**Sharp,** G. "The Meanings of Non-Violence: A Typology (Revised)." *Journal of Conflict Resolution* 3, no. 1 (1959): 41–64.

—————— *The Politics of Nonviolent Action*. Boston: Porter Sargent, 1973.

**Siedlecka,** E. "55 zarzutów dyscyplinarnych dla sędziego. Pachnie PRL-em" [55 disciplinary charges against a judge. It smells like PRL]. *Polityka*, October 4, 2019. **https://www.polityka .pl/tygodnikpolityka/kraj/1934434,1,55-zarzutow -dyscyplinarnych-dla-sedziego-pachnie-prl-em .read**.

**Siedlecka,** E. "Dyscyplinowanie sędziego Stępnia" [Disciplining judge Stępień]. *Polityka*, May 15, 2018. **https://www.polityka.pl /tygodnikpolityka/kraj/1748534,1 ,dyscyplinowanie-sedziego-stepnia.read**.

—————— "Na straży praworządności. Odbył się II Kongres Prawników Polskich" [Upholding the rule of law. The 2nd Congress of Polish Lawyers was held]. *Polityka*, June 4, 2019. **https://www.polityka.pl/tygodnikpolityka /kraj/1795260,1,na-strazy-praworzadnosci -odbyl-sie-ii-kongres-prawnikow-polskich.read**.

—————— "Prof. Łętowska: Zmiany w Trybunale to demontaż państwa prawa" [Prof. Łętowska: Changes in the Tribunal mean the dismantling of the rule of law]. *Gazeta Wyborcza*, December 29, 2015. **https://wyborcza.pl/7,75398 ,19403189,prof-letowska-zmiany-w-trybunale -to-demontaz-panstwa-prawa.html**.

—————— "Sędziowie krytykują prezesa Trybunału Konstytucyjnego" [Judges criticize the president of the Constitutional Tribunal]. *Gazeta Wyborcza*, December 14, 2012. **https:// wyborcza.pl/7,75398,13047249,sedziowie -krytykuja-prezesa-trybunalu-konstytucyjnego .html**.

**Silesian** Legal Café—Bielska Edition. "Meeting with Judge Paweł Juszczyszyn." *Facebook*, 2022. **https://www.facebook.com/events /3135388126719314/?ref=newsfeed**.

**Sitnicka,** D. "Captured Constitutional Tribunal rules on the Supreme Court: Implementation of CJEU judgment inconsistent with EU law." *Rule of Law in Poland*, April 22, 2020: **https:// ruleoflaw.pl/captured-constitutional-tribunal -rules-on-the-supreme-court-implementation -of-cjeu-judgment-inconsistent-with-eu-law/**.

—————— "SN uchylił postanowienie sędziego Izby Karnej, powołanego przy udziale neo-KRS" [The Supreme Court annulled the decision of a judge of the Criminal Chamber]. *Oko Press*, September 16, 2021. **https://oko.press/sn-uchylil -postanowienie-sedziego-izby-karnej -powolanego-przy-udziale-neo-krs/**.

**Skuczyński,** P. "Aktywizm sędziowski a etyka sędziowska w Polsce" [Judicial activism and judicial ethics in Poland]. In *Między tradycją a nowoczesnością. Prawo polskie w 100-lecie odzyskania niepodległości [Between tradition and modernity. Polish law on the 100th anniversary of regaining independence]*, edited by Ł. Pisarczyk and K. Wolter, 359-382. Warsaw: Wolter Kluwer Polska, 2019.

————— "Postawy prawników wobec kryzysu konstytucyjnego a niezawisłość sędziowska" [Attitudes of lawyers towards the constitutional crisis and judicial independence]. In *Granice niezawisłości sędziów i niezależności sądów? [The limits of the independence of judges and the independence of the courts?]*, edited by G. Borkowski, 153–9. Warsaw: Toruń, 2016.

"Spanish Judges on strike." *Stuff*, February 19, 2009. **https://www.stuff.co.n/world/1750466 /Spanish-judges-on-strike**.

SSP Iustitia. "Photo." *Facebook Post*, March 10, 2022. **https://www.facebook.com/sedziowie /photos/a.260887620624303 /5212342798812069/**.

————— "SSP Iustitia." *Facebook Page*. Accessed May 24, 2024. **https://www.facebook .com/sedziowie**.

Stawecki, T. "Aktywizm i pasywizm sędziowski" [Judicial activism and passivism]. In *Leksykon etyki prawniczej. 100 podstawowych pojęć [Lexicon of legal ethics. 100 basic concepts]*, edited by P. Skuczyński and S. Sykuna, 5–17. Warsaw: C.H. Beck, 2013.

Stawecki, T., Winczorek, J. Wykładnia konstytucji. *Inspiracje, teorie, argumenty [Interpretation of the Constitution. Inspiration, Theories, Arguments]*. Warsaw: Wolter Kluwer Polska, 2014.

Strzembosz, A. "Sądownictwo polskie u początków „Solidarności", w stanie wojennym i w okresie poprzedzającym przełom w 1989 roku" [Polish judiciary at the beginning of "Solidarity", during martial law and in the period preceding the breakthrough in 1989]. In *Sędziowie warszawscy w czasie próby 1981- 1988 [Warsaw judges during the time of trial 1981-1988]*, edited by M. Stanowska and A. Strzembosz, 42–66. Warsaw: Wydawnictwo IPN, 2005.

Subbotko, D. "Sędzia Włodzimierz Wróbel: Najlepszym sposobem na kręgosłup bywa wstyd" [Judge Włodzimierz Wróbel: Shame is the best remedy for the spine]. *Gazeta Wyborcza*, June 11, 2021. **https://wyborcza.pl/magazyn /7,124059,27185454,sedzia-wlodzimierz -wrobel-najlepszym-sposobem-na-kregoslup .html**.

Świątkowski, A.M. «Materialnoprawne rozważania na temat nieusuwalności z powodu wieku sędziów Sądu Najwyższego w świetle orzecznictwa Trybunału Sprawiedliwości» [Substantive law reflections on the removability of the judges of the Supreme Court because of age in the light of EU case law]. *Przegląd Sądowy* 9 (2019): 7–22.

Szabó, D. G. "A Hungarian Judge Seeks Protection from the CJEU—Part I." *VerfBlog*, July 28, 2019. **https://verfassungsblog.de/a-hungarian -judge-seeks-protection-from-the-cjeu-part-i/**.

Szcześniak, A., D. Sitnicka, and M. Danielewski. "Imponujący pokaz odwagi sędziów i solidarności obywateli: 30 tysięcy osób w Marszu Tysiąca Tóg" [An impressive show of judges' courage and citizens' solidarity: 30,000 people in the Thousand Robes March]. *OkoPress*, January 11, 2020. **https://oko.press/idzie-marsz -tysiaca-tog-zobacz-relacje-live/**.

Szczygielska-Jakubowska (2020). "Bydgoski sędzia biega dla represjonowanego sędziego Igora Tulei: Nigdy nie będziesz szedł sam!" [Bydgoski judge runs for repressed judge Igor Tulei]. *Gazeta Wyborcza*, December 8, 2020. **https://bydgoszcz.wyborcza.pl/bydgo-szcz/7,48722,26584513,bydgoski-sedzia-bie-ga-dla-represjowanego-sedziego-igora-tuleyi. html**.

Szente, Z. "Stepping Into the Same River Twice? Judicial Independence in Old and New Authoritarianism." *German Law Journal* 22 (2021): 1316–26. doi:10.1017/glj.2021.69.

**Szuleka,** M., M. Wolny, and M. Kalisz. "The Time of Trial: How Do Changes in the Justice System Affect Polish Judges?" Warsaw, Helsinki Foundation for Human Rights, 2019. **https://www.hfhr.pl/wp-content/uploads/2019/07/Czas-proby-EN-web.pdf**.

**Szymaniak,** P. "Nadzwyczajny Kongres Sędziów: Ponad 1000 zainteresowanych spotka się w Warszawie" [Extraordinary Congress of Judges: Over 1,000 interested parties will meet in Warsaw]. *Dziennik Gazeta Prawna*, August 23, 2016. **https://prawo.gazetaprawna.pl/artykuly/969493,nadzwyczajny-kongres-sedziow-warszawa.html**.

**Szymaniak,** P., and M. Kryszkiewicz. "Sądy już badają powołania. Praktyczny skutek wyroku ETPC." *Dziennik Gazeta Prawna*, August 26, 2021. **https://serwisy.gazetaprawna.pl/orzeczenia/artykuly/8232071,sady-etpc-badanie-powolania-nowa-krs-uchylenie-wyroku.html**.

**Taborowski,** M. *Mechanizmy ochrony praworządności państw członkowskich w prawie Unii Europejskiej. Studium przebudzenia systemu ponadnarodowego [Mechanisms of protection of the rule of law of the member states in the law of the European Union]*. Warsaw: CH Beck, 2019.

*The 2020 Rule of Law Report.* **https://ec.europa.eu/info/sites/info/files/communication_2020_rule_of_law_report_en.pdf.** Accessed 3 February 2021.

**The** Justice Case in *3 TRIALS OF WAR CRIMINALS BEFORE THE NUREMBERG MILITARY TRIBUNALS 50*, 1951. **https://archive.org/details/TrialsOfWarCriminalsBeforeTheNurembergMilitaryTribunalsUnderControlCouncil/Trials%20of%20war%20criminals%20before%20the%20Nuremberg%20Military%20Tribunals%20under%20Control%20Council%20law%20no.%2010.%20-%20Nuremberg%2C%20October%201946-%20April%2C%201949%20Volume%201/**.

**Themis.** "Autodenunciation made by 73 judges in a gesture of solidarity with Judges wanted for hanging posters with the demands of the Associations of Judges." *Themis,* March 15, 2020. **http://themis-sedziowie.eu/materials-in-english/autodenunciation-made-by-73-judges-to-president-of-district-court-in-krakow-in-a-gesture-of-solidarity-with-judges-wanted-for-hanging-posters-with-the-demands-of-the-associations-of-judges/**.

————— "Position of the Board of the "Themis" Judges' Association of 28 May 2020 regarding the appointment of the First President of the Supreme Court." *Themis*, May 31, 2020. **http://themis-sedziowie.eu/materials-in-english/position-of-the-board-of-the-themis-judges-association-of-28-may-2020-regarding-the-appointment-of-the-first-president-of-the-supreme-court/**.

————— "Response of the Polish authorities to the CJEU judgment of 19 Nov 2019 (the report containing translations of source documents). *Themis*, May 28, 2020. **http://themis-sedziowie.eu/wp-content/uploads/2020/05/Response_Polish_Authorities_CJEU_Judgement_19.11.2019.pdf**.

**Tilles,** D. "EU withholding billions in cohesion funds from Poland over rule-of-law concerns." *Notes from Poland,* October 17, 2022. **https://notesfrompoland.com/2022/10/17/eu-withholding-billions-in-cohesion-funds-from-poland-over-rule-of-law-concerns**.

**TOK** FM. "Prokurator Kwiatkowska dostała pozew o ponad 2 mln złotych. „Ma na celu zastraszenie mnie i innych prokuratorów" [Prosecutor Kwiatkowska received a lawsuit for over PLN 2 million. "Aims to intimidate me and other prosecutors"]. *TOK FM*, August 18, 2021. **https://www.tokfm.pl/Tokfm/7,103085,27468951,prokurator-kwiatkowska-dostala-pozew-o-ponad-2-mln-zlotych.html**.

**Tokson,** M. "Judicial resistance and legal change." *The University of Chicago Law Review* 82 (2015): 901–73.

**Trochev,** A. and Ellett, R. "Judges and Their Allies: Rethinking Judicial Autonomy through the Prism of Off-Bench Resistance." *Journal of Law and Courts* 2, no. 1 (Spring 2014): 67–91.

**"Tunisia:** Judges strike in protest against Kais Saied." *Middle East Monitor*, February 18, 2022. **https://www.middleeastmonitor .com/20220218-tunisia-judges-strike-in -protest-against-kais-saied/**.

**Vadász,** V. "A Hungarian Judge Seeks Protection from the CJEU—Part II." *VerfBlog*, August 7, 2019. **https://verfassungsblog.de/a-hungarian -judge-seeks-protection-from-the-cjeu-part-ii/**.

**Vinthagen,** S. *A Theory of Nonviolent Action: How Civil Resistance Works*. London: Zed Books, 2015

**Von** Notz, A. "How to Abolish Democracy: Electoral System, Party Regulation and Opposition Rights in Hungary and Poland." *VerfBlog*, December 10, 2018. **https://verfassungsblog .de/how-to-abolish-democracy-electoral -system-party-regulation-and-opposition -rights-in-hungary-and-poland/**. DOI: 10.17176/20190116-210647-0.

**Wachowiec,** P. "Courts challenge legality of Poland's lockdown, encouraging businesses to reopen." *Notes From Poland*, February 2, 2021. **https://notesfrompoland.com/2021/02/02 /courts-challenge-legality-of-polands-lockdown -encouraging-businesses-to-reopen/**.

*Wirtualnemedia*. "Sprzeczne opinie Lecha i Jarosława Kaczyńskich o KRS na plakatach przeciw reformie sądownictwa [Contradictory opinions of Lech and Jarosław Kaczyński about the National Council of the Judiciary on posters against the reform of the judiciary]." March 22, 2017. **https://www.wirtualnemedia .pl/artykul/akcja-demokracja-z-reklama-ze -sprzecznymi-opiniami-lecha-i-jaroslawa -kaczynskich-o-krs**.

**Wójcik,** A. "CJEU President: European Union is not crushing the member states. They are the EU." Interview with Koen Lenaerts. *Rule of Law in Poland*, January 30, 2020. **https://ruleoflaw .pl/cjeu-president-european-union-is-not -crushing-the-member-states-they-are-the-eu/**.

**Wolne** Sądy. "Free Courts Initiative." Accessed May 24, 2024. https://wolnesady.org/en/.

**Woźnicki,** Ł. "1,200 judges under assault? The ruling camp wants to punish all judges who signed an open letter to the OSCE." *Gazeta Wyborcza*, August 25, 2020. **https://wyborcza .pl/7,173236,26238794,1-200-judges-under -assault-the-ruling-camp-wants-to-punish.html**.

————— "Koszulki z "Konstytucją" nie dla sędziów. Nowa KRS zakazuje symbolu, bo jest "nacechowany politycznie" [T-shirts with "Constitution" not for judges]." *Gazeta Wyborcza*, December 13, 2018. **https://wyborcza .pl/7,75398,24276226,koszulki-z-konstytucja -nie-dla-sedziow-nowa-krs-zakazuje.html**.

————— "Ujawniamy: tak rzecznik dyscyplinarny Radzik zatwierdził 'akcję medialną' hejterów [We reveal: this is how the disciplinary spokesman Radzik approved the 'media action' of the haters]." *Gazeta Wyborcza*, September 20, 2019. **https://wyborcza.pl/7,75398,25212906 ,jak-rzecznik-radzik-zatwierdzil-akcje-medialna -hejterow.html**.

**Wróbel,** W. "Izba dyscyplinarna jako sąd wyjątkowy w rozumieniu art. 175 ust. 2 konstytucji RP." *Palestra* 1-2 (2019).

**Wróblewski,** M. "Granice ekspresji i wypowiedzi sędziego—zarys problemu [The limits of the judge's expression and speech—an outline of the problem]." *Krajowa Rada Sądownictwa* 1 (2017): 29–34.

**Wyrzykowski,** M. "Bypassing the Constitution or charging the constitutional order outside the constitution." In *Transformation of law systems in Central, Eastern and Southwestern Europe in 1989–2015*, edited by A. Szmyt, B. Banaszak, W. Sadurski, 58–95. Gdańsk: Gdańsk University Press, 2019.

————— "Experiencing the Unimaginable: the Collapse of the Rule of Law in Poland." *Hague Journal on the Rule of Law* 11 (2019): 417–22.

**Zajadło,** J. *Formuła Radbrucha. Filozofia prawa na granicy pozytywizmu prawniczego i prawa natury [Radbruch formula. Philosophy of law on the verge of legal positivism and the law of nature].* Gdańsk: Arche, 2001.

————— "Nieposłuszeństwo sędziowskie [Judicial disobedience]." *Państwo i Prawo* 1 (2016): 18–39.

————— "Sumienie sędziego [Judicial Conscience]." *Ruch Prawniczy, Ekonomiczny i Socjologiczny* 4 (2017). **https://doi.org/10.14746 /rpeis.2017.79.4.3**.

**Zawiślak,** T. "Niektórzy mówią o nich kamikadze [Some call them kamikazes]." *Iustitia* 3 (2019). **https://www.kwartalnikiustitia.pl /niektorzy-mowia-o-nich-kamikadze,9559**.

# Acknowledgments

This book would not have been possible without Michał Rauszer, professor of anthropology at the University of Warsaw. After I defended my PhD thesis, he suggested doing something together to join our research interest: he was writing about the resistance of peasants in Poland, I was interested in the Rule of Law crisis in Poland. Why not write about the resistance of judges? So, it was his idea and although he resigned from researching together, he inspired me to continue working on the project.

This book would not have been possible also without help of two judges: Krystian Markiewicz from Iustitia and Waldemar Żurek from Themis. We spent a lot of time talking about resistance, all issues, ethics, problems, etc. Despite the fact they were two of the busiest judges in Poland at that time—dealing not only with the backlog of cases, defending themselves in bunch of disciplinary proceedings, traveling all over Poland and Europe to fight for independence for judges—they were always ready to help me understand the phenomenon of judicial resistance in Poland. They also contacted me with other judges. Therefore, thanks to them, I had a chance to interview so many judges, prosecutors, lawyers, and activists. Special thanks to Judge Dariusz Mazur, who provided me with a lot of documentation concerning judicial resistance.

I would also like to thank Maria Ejchart, who contacted me with many judges and supported the project. I had learned about the International Centre for Nonviolent Conflict from Prof. Adam Bodnar in one of his podcasts where he was talking about Maciej Bartkowski. I wrote to Maciej to consult the project, and this is how it started.

I wouldn't write this book without Maciej Bartkowski's support, vast knowledge, and experience in resistance movements. I've learned a lot from him and I am glad that he's a part of this book too.

I'd like to thank to the book editors that spent a lot of time asking important questions. It's not easy to explain to the Americans things that are so common for Poles. Thanks to Bruce Pearson this book has a more universal message and character, and is available for every reader all over the world.

This book would not have been written without the constant fight for the rule of law of such organizations like Iustitia, Themis, OSSSA, Lex Super Omnia, FreeCourts Initiative, Osiatynski Archive, KOD, KOS, Helsinki Foundation for Human Rights, Polish Commissioner for Human Rights' Office, Akcja Demokracja, and Amnesty International. Behind resistance there are judges and prosecutors' lives, dramas, dilemmas, and courageous stances, but foremost, citizens' support and constant protest.

I'd like to express my gratitude to Prof. Kamil Zajączkowski who invited me to joint the Centre for Europe at the University of Warsaw and supported this project and to Dr. Marek Łukaszuk from the Polish Commissioner for Human Rights' Office for all the good words.

Finally, I thank my family for their support and understanding during the long days and weekends I spent writing this book.

Marcin Mrowicki

## About the Author

**Marcin Mrowicki, PhD,** is Assistant Professor of EU Law and Human Rights at the University of Warsaw (Centre for Europe). He is an author of many academic and popular science publications. He worked as a lawyer at the European Court for Human Rights in Strasbourg (2012-2016), and at the Polish Commissioner for Human Rights' Office in Poland (2016-2024). Since February 2024, he is also a Secretary of the Inter-ministerial Committee for Restoring Rule of Law and Constitutional Order and a Deputy Head of the Criminal Law Department of the Ministry of Justice in Poland.

www.ingramcontent.com/pod-product-compliance
Lightning Source LLC
Chambersburg PA
CBHW061148030426

42335CB00002B/148